SOLIDARITIES BEYOND BORDERS

SOLIDARITIES BEYOND BORDERS
Transnationalizing Women's Movements

Edited by Pascale Dufour, Dominique Masson,
and Dominique Caouette

UBCPress · Vancouver · Toronto

21 20 19 18 17 16 15 14 13 12 11 10   5 4 3 2 1

Printed in Canada on FSC-certified ancient-forest-free paper (100% post-consumer recycled) that is processed chlorine- and acid-free.

Library and Archives Canada Cataloguing in Publication

   Solidarities beyond borders : transnationalizing women's movements / edited by Pascale Dufour, Dominique Masson and Dominique Caouette.

Includes bibliographical references and index.
ISBN 978-0-7748-1795-0

   1. Feminism – International cooperation – Case studies. 2. Women – Social networks. 3. Feminists – Social networks. 4. Globalization – Social aspects. 5. Transnationalism. I. Dufour, Pascale, 1971- II. Masson, Dominique III. Caouette, Dominique, 1962-

HQ1155.S65 2010   305.42   C2010-902166-5

Canadä

UBC Press gratefully acknowledges the financial support for our publishing program provided by the Government of Canada (through the Canada Book Fund), the Canada Council for the Arts, and the British Columbia Arts Council.

This book has been published with the help of a grant from the Canadian Federation for the Humanities and Social Sciences, through the Aid to Scholarly Publications Program, using funds provided by the Social Sciences and Humanities Research Council of Canada.

UBC Press
The University of British Columbia
2029 West Mall
Vancouver, BC V6T 1Z2
www.ubcpress.ca

Contents

Part 2: Deepening Solidarities among Women and Women's Issues

Part 3: Stretching the Scope of Solidarities

Preface

DIANE MATTE

When I heard about the seminar titled "Transnationalization of Solidarities and Women's Movements," which took place in April 2005 (and from which this book originated), I wanted to be there to explore with academics why so many women and groups were – and continue to be – attracted to our global action. Having been the coordinator of the International Secretariat of the World March of Women during its first nine years of existence gave me a multitude of opportunities to learn from other women and reinforced my belief that feminist and women's movements are both a tool and a process that we must renew and keep alive. The process of renewal is especially important when we consider the contemporary global reality of a delocalizing world and economy. Listening to and reading over the presentations given in that seminar sparked some thoughts that I wanted to share with you as we participate in a collective effort to understand the impact of global transformations and to articulate the kind of social change that we are striving for in our lives and in our communities.

The World March of Women is a global feminist movement that was conceived in 1995, when feminists in Quebec were organizing the Bread and Roses women's march against poverty. I had the privilege of coordinating this march and was also one of the women who thought that we should link our action with women's and feminist groups in other countries. Subsequently, we began spreading the idea of a global feminist march. Although we encountered various challenges on the road to making it a reality, the ongoing action/movement known as the World March of Women was, and still is, a remarkable feminist success story. Why?

Some of the answers are in this book.

The transnationalization of feminist movements can be understood as a transposition to another scale of the community outreach work inherent to social movements. To have a sustainable impact, movements for change must be controlled and managed by the people affected by systems of oppression, and they must keep learning from these groups. Movements must constantly stay in touch with the changes in people's lives. Social change is not a top-down process, nor can it be directed by experts.

The same is true of transnationalization. It will not be effective if it is a process that concerns and reaches only a few chosen experts. It is essential that we reach out to women in other nations and to other feminist and women's movements on the basis of women's common experiences and, in doing so, strengthen our movements transnationally. We need to think, act, and change not only from the local to the global scale, but also from the global to the local scale. It could be said that the transnationalization of solidarity is a response to postmodern and neoliberal attacks on social movements and their global analysis. It may also be seen as a global response to the "No alternative" refrains of global institutions. The case studies presented here eloquently demonstrate this. They also tackle the very important discussion of how and with whom radical social change can be achieved.

As one of the contributions in this book suggests, the word "transnationalization" may not be the most appropriate one to describe what we are doing, since we do not confine solidarity to the notion of geopolitical borders. Rather, for more and more of us, the concept of transnationalization gives political meaning to solidarity that not only extends across borders but attempts to overcome our tendency to compartmentalize struggles. It is a constant challenge to build and maintain solidarity when we are confronted with language barriers, different political cultures, and stark disparities in access to resources. Nonetheless, the contributors to this book demonstrate that these alliances are the best response to individualism and global indifference.

Solidarity, or transnationalization, in this context, necessitates recognizing our diversity and building on it or, if necessary, around it; it also means recognizing our privileges and identifying our common purposes. In other words, solidarity comes with an understanding of oppression and a commitment to act upon it with others and, when required, for others. It implies equality, not charity or uniformity.

As you will see from this book, working together creates new opportunities for fruitful cooperation and new analyses. We must constantly remind ourselves, however, of the importance of maintaining strong women's and feminist movements. Part of the challenge that confronts the women's and feminist movements today has to do with how "global feminism" has been defined and practised in the last few years. Changing the institutions is not sufficient. The women's and feminist movements at the global level do not, and should not, revolve solely around the United Nations. Large institutions and governments tend to occupy a preponderant place on our agendas; while we must monitor and ask more from them, it is a mistake to build our movements around them.

In order to change women's lives, we have to change the world. The opposite is also true: in order to change the world, we must change women's lives. The radicalism of feminism resides in its capacity to recognize the need to confront class and race at the same time as patriarchy. Clearly, feminism is about reclaiming our bodies and ourselves, but failing to consider the colour of those bodies and their economic role will result only in maintaining existing power relations and advancing women who are more privileged. It weakens our movements.

Like many other groups, organizations, and networks that you will read about in this book, the World March of Women works to bring solidarity to a new level and to increase the impact of feminism. This collection of case studies and analyses will help us discuss the challenges that we face and articulate the importance of building and sustaining global movements for social change.

Acknowledgments

Our most heartfelt thanks go to the contributors to this volume for all their hard work in the course of putting this book together. Tasks involved, for most of them, transforming a workshop paper into a full-fledged, well-thought-through chapter, responding to editorial suggestions by the three co-editors and by the anonymous reviewers at various stages of their writing, reading each other's chapters and finding further inspiration in each other's ideas, and diligently responding to our e-mails and supporting the project from start to finish.

We are happy to be able to say that this book has been published with the help of a grant from the Canadian Federation for the Humanities and Social Sciences, through the Aid to Scholarly Publications Program, using funds provided by the Social Sciences and Humanities Research Council of Canada. Our thanks for providing financial assistance in the course of this project also go to the Faculty of Social Sciences of the University of Ottawa and the Centre de recherche sur les politiques et le développement social (Research Centre on Social Policies and Social Development) and the Réseau d'études des dynamiques transnationales et de l'action collective (Research Network on Transnational Dynamics and Collective Action), both based at the Université de Montréal.

We would like to express our special thanks to Stephanie MacKay, PhD candidate at the University of Ottawa, who did a great job with the linguistic revisions of the chapters written by non-native English speakers, and to Carmen Díaz Alba and Patricia Garcia for their work in preparing the final version of this manuscript.

Finally, we are grateful to the two anonymous external reviewers for their evaluation and their suggestions, as well as to Emily Andrew, Senior Editor at UBC Press, for her unfailing support.

SOLIDARITIES BEYOND BORDERS

Introduction

PASCALE DUFOUR, DOMINIQUE MASSON,
AND DOMINIQUE CAOUETTE

Solidarities among the world's women are not new. Like labour movements, women's movements and feminist activism have been internationalized since the nineteenth century. Nevertheless, from the second half of the twentieth century on, quantitative and qualitative changes have occurred in the linkages that women have built at the supranational and global scales. Global networks have grown in numbers, especially in the wake of the increasing attention paid to women by international institutions. Beginning with the proclamation of International Women's Year in 1975 by the United Nations and the Women's Decade that followed (1975-85), women's historical struggles for their rights and the improvement of their living conditions have gained stronger institutional recognition on the world scene. The nature of cross-border linkages among women has also changed, becoming more and more diverse. Today, for example, international non-governmental networks, multinational networks of women's groups, and transnational feminist networks coexist with mixed coalitions of groups advocating for women's rights. Yet, in spite of their numbers and diversity, these sustained and widely recognized global ties are still considered, or so it seems, "women's affairs" by mainstream analysts, who have not granted them the attention bestowed upon other contemporary transnationalizations in the environmental, labour, anti-globalization, and global social justice movements. This relatively sudden realization formed the point of departure for this book. For instance, an abundance of social movements literature has addressed transnational collective action, especially since the mid-1990s, with large, worldwide protests and demonstrations increasingly taking centre stage; women's movements, however, have rarely been studied as an empirical case, much less as a basis for theorizing transnationalization. Yet, women's movements, like labour movements, have long experience with transnationalization and constitute an important part of the transnational social movement sector. They certainly deserve specific attention beyond the specialized feminist literature.

Our second realization was the strong geographical homogeneity of those who have researched and published on the topic of transnational social movements. Most social movement discourse is circulated in the English language, is produced by researchers living in the North (North America or Europe), and privileges Northern perspectives. Yet, we know that some of the most radical transformations are occurring in Southern countries – in Latin America, Africa, and Asia. Diversifying the geographical origin of both researchers and cases seemed essential in order to provide a platform for experts from the South to share their experiences and analyses of transnational movements.

Finally, the standard definition of transnational social movements as sustained protests involving activists from at least two countries and targeting international institutions (see the literature review below) appeared to us to be too limited to cover the full range of activists' and groups' lived experiences in the building of solidarities beyond national borders. Was it possible to open up the dominant conception of transnationalization?

In April 2005, these initial considerations crystallized in the organization of an international workshop, Transnationalization of Solidarities and Women's Movements, held at the Université de Montréal. Feminist researchers from diverse disciplines (political science, sociology, anthropology, and women's studies) and origins (Latin America, Europe, Southeast Asia, Australia, and Canada) were invited. The workshop, subsidized by the Social Sciences and Humanities Research Council of Canada, the Centre de recherche sur les politiques et le développement social, and the Faculty of Arts and Sciences of the Université de Montréal, had two main objectives: reflecting upon the available knowledge of transnationalization in feminist and women's movements, and initiating a collective search for approaches suited to making analytical linkages among the different transnationalization processes documented by the participants. After forty-eight hours of debate and exchange, we were able to agree on the following basic assumption: transnationalization demands daily convergence of interests and identities among activists who have multiple territorial and organizational affiliations. In this respect, it is a construction process that can take a variety of forms. Instead of defining it a priori, we chose to adopt a more inductive approach and see what kinds of transnationalization women and feminists create in their respective networks. Transnationalization is also a process of stretching and contracting the scope of collective action and the result of complex interactions between actors' strategies and their institutional and movement environments. In other words, transnationalization is always located somewhere – including inside national territories – and not "up there"; it sometimes happens in different places at the same time. Moreover, it cannot be reduced to a simple change in the institutional level targeted by movement activists, but involves a wider variety of movement processes.

Solidarities beyond Borders: Transnationalizing Women's Movements emerged from this preliminary reflection. Bringing together scholars and cases from various locations, this volume is intended to contribute to the advancement of feminist approaches on the topic, and to bring to a larger audience the richness and diversity of feminist research and of the experience of transnationalization in contemporary feminist and women's movements. Unfortunately, one continent is still missing from our sample of researchers and cases: Africa. This absence is not the result of choice, but of circumstances that have to do with the way structural inequalities affect collaboration among academics.

We have decided to write about what we call transnationalization of solidarities because this notion focuses on the processes by which transnationalization is produced daily in organizations, networks, events, and movements. As Chandra Talpade Mohanty (2003, 7) stresses, solidarities involve "mutuality, accountability, recognition of common interests as the basis for relationships among diverse communities." In this perspective, the political work necessary to build solidarities becomes the heart of the analysis, and the transnationalization of solidarities is always the result of a convergence, beyond national borders, of actors' differing interests and identities. Consequently, our analyses reveal how diverse are the paths to transnationalization and how complex – and creative – is the articulation of activists' interests and identities in such a context of extreme diversity.

Here, the term "transnational" refers to "a connection among several units (cells, sections, branches, delegations) that are spread over several national territories, all of which participate in the solidarity relationship as such" (Devin 2004, 20, our translation). The substance, or content, of solidarity is as important as how the various units are organized and how solidarity diffuses within networks. In other words, the building of solidarities by actors involved in transnationalization processes goes hand in hand with the decisions made, strategies formulated, and specific mechanisms established within their respective organizations, movements, or networks. In this volume, we call attention to both the meaning of solidarities and their deployment (or implementation). As we will see, the two combine in different ways.

Thus, the transnationalization of solidarities refers to the processes not only by which solidarities travel beyond established national borders, but also by which they are deepened among women or among feminists. The deepening of solidarities involves mutual recognition and the constitution of stronger ties among activists. It also opens up the possibility for the establishment and cultivation of shared understandings of situations, problems, and, sometimes, solutions. These processes are the focus of Part 2 of the book. Solidarities may also be "stretched" beyond feminists and women's constituencies and beyond women's issues to include "progressive" allies and their goals. Issues related to the stretching of solidarities are the subject of Part 3. Finally, we have chosen to draw together literature from various fields of study. One of the main purposes of this volume is to propose an original dialogue between feminist approaches to transnationalization and the mainstream literature on the topic in the fields of social movement studies and international relations (IR). This introductory chapter thus features a review of the literature from these three research fields, followed by a discussion. We begin with recent work addressing the transnationalization of collective action in social movement studies and in IR – bodies of literature that, while quite distinct, share a number of features. Second, we examine feminist contributions in IR. Contrary to mainstream IR scholars, feminists have addressed nontraditional issues and non-state actors, providing a rich and complex understanding of global dynamics. Third, we provide an overview of the ways in which a wider, interdisciplinary feminist scholarship has approached transnationalization in feminist and women's movements. Our objective is to present the main theoretical offerings currently available for apprehending and understanding transnationalization. How do current conceptions help or hinder us in addressing the issues raised by transnationalization? What are the preferred lines of questioning in the three fields of study, how are they useful, and what are their limitations?

Transnationalization in the Social Movements and International Relations Fields

As Janet Conway (2004) explains, cycles or waves of mobilization have often produced important "theoretical moments." The recent increase in transnational connections among collective actors is one of these. Key studies conducted in the social movement field in the last few years have focused mostly on the mobilizations of the 1990s and 2000s against neoliberal globalization (Bandy and Smith 2005; della Porta and Tarrow 2005; della Porta et al. 2006; Tarrow 2005). At the same time, IR research has revealed an increased presence of transnational movement actors in world governance processes, and underscored the necessity of considering these actors and their influence in decision-making processes at the international level (Risse-Kappen 1995; Risse, Ropp, and Sikkink 1999). With rare exceptions (for instance, Keck and Sikkink 1998; Macdonald 2005), transnational feminist and women's movements have not received sustained attention in the social movements and IR fields (except for the work of IR feminists, which will be discussed separately).

The Nature of the Object and the Preferred Unit(s) of Analysis

In 2005, Johanna Siméant, building on Sidney Tarrow's (2001) initial classification, identified different types of transnational collective action. She proposed to distinguish between simultaneous or coordinated actions in different states (for example, the huge demonstrations around the world against the war in Iraq); mechanisms of diffusion of activist practices (for example, during the fall of communist regimes in 1989 and 1990); mechanisms for the transfer of resources, know-how, and information among movements; mobilizations targeting international institutions and their politics; non-governmental organization (NGO) activism directed toward international institutions; counter-summit mobilizations; protests against multinational corporations; protests against one state by activists from another state (for example, the anti-apartheid movement outside South Africa); activism in favour of a cause located outside one's country (for example, Western activism against child labour); large movement gatherings such as the World Social Forum; and the building and consolidation of transnational organizations. The purpose of this classification was to put some order into actions and processes generally labelled "social movements' transnationalization." It was also indicative of the different facets of the phenomena that count as transnationalization for social movements and IR scholars.

In its bare form, transnational activism has been broadly defined as social movements, other civil society organizations, and individuals operating across national borders (Piper and Uhlin 2004, 4-5). This definition has been further refined by two social movements specialists, Donatella della Porta and Sidney Tarrow (2005, 7), who refer to *transnational collective action* as "the coordinated international campaigns on the part of networks of activists against international actors, other states, or international institutions." There are two main components to della Porta and Tarrow's definition. First, the transnational aspect of collective action is defined by the presence of activists or groups belonging to more than one nation-state; the focus is therefore on the *international* or *multinational* character of the coalitions. Second, the target of the actions must also be *international* or *multinational,* and it must possess institutional features (governmental or non-governmental). Margaret E. Keck and Kathryn Sikkink (1998) use *transnational networks* as their unit of analysis. In their view, these networks have become a concrete expression of transnational social movements. Jeffrey Ayres and Sidney Tarrow (2003) distinguish *transnational social movements* from other categories of analysis. According to these authors, social movements are characterized by protests and contentious politics, while NGOs and networks use more routine and accepted methods in working with international institutions. Joe Bandy and Jackie Smith (2005, 4) recommend considering the various forms of *transnational alliances* in which collective actors are involved. Transnational networks lie at one end of the spectrum, with the most informal types of cooperation, and transnational social movement organizations lie at the other end, with the most formal types. Transnational coalitions fall between these two poles. The issue is not so much what kind of action is transnationalized, but the degree of formalization of transnational connections.

Understanding the Emergence of Transnationalization

The majority of scholars in the social movements and IR fields relate the expansion of the transnationalization of solidarities to globalization and its impacts on social institutions and relationships. Initially, structural changes at the macro level favoured transnationalization through technological developments (with the Internet assuming a key function in the speed of world-scale mobilizations and the long-distance coordination of multinational networks) (Tarrow and della Porta 2005, 228), the rise in international exchanges (the increase in international business going hand in hand with increased travel and contact among activists from multiple national territories), and consideration of the fundamental role of certain international institutions such as the UN (della Porta, Kriesi, and Rucht 1999; Tarrow 2001). Tarrow (2005) and della Porta and Tarrow (2005) use the expression "complex internationalism" to describe the last phenomenon – that is, "the expansion of international institutions, international regimes, and the transfer of the resources of local and national actors to the international stage, producing threats, opportunities and resources for international NGOs, transnational social movements, and indirectly, grassroots social movements" (Tarrow and della Porta 2005, 234).

Tarrow (2005, 3), however, emphasizes that transnational activism is much more than a mechanical response to globalization. Not only must the institutional context be ripe for transnationalization, offering a "multilevel opportunity structure," but the actors must also seize these new political opportunities. It is a matter of ascertaining both how international political contexts have allowed for the emergence of transnational collective action (Keck and Sikkink 1998; Smith, Chatfield, and Pagnucco 1997), and how these broader conditions articulate with the specificities of national political contexts (della Porta and Tarrow 2005; Tarrow 2005). For instance, Kathryn Sikkink (cited in Tarrow 2005, 171) suggests that international institutional arenas should be viewed as an ensemble of constraints on, as well as opportunities for, the action of transnational movements. She proposes an analytical grid outlining the interactions of domestic and international political institutions to explain the emergence (and success) of transnational actions by using two concepts, the boomerang effect and the spiral model. These concepts, which have become very influential in the literature, describe patterns of action that develop when activists operating within a domestic opportunity structure that is closed off to their pressures – due either to exclusion from the system of national representation or to political repression – search for allies in international political opportunity structures that offer more openings to their claims in order to "import" pressure "from above" to bring to bear on their own national government.

Tarrow (2005, 32) further complicates such an understanding of the relations between national and international contexts by considering another series of political processes. Global framing (the mobilization of international symbols for the purpose of framing domestic conflicts) and internationalization (a response to foreign or international pressures from within domestic politics) establish connections between national actors and international issues on national territory. Conversely, diffusion (the transfer of forms of protest from one country to another) and scale shift (the coordination of collective action at a level other than the one at which it began) establish a connection between domestic conflicts and international conflicts and institutions. Lastly, externalization (the vertical projection of domestic demands toward international institutions or foreign actors) and transnational coalition formation (the horizontal formation of networks among activists from different countries sharing similar claims) occur at the international level. According to Tarrow's analysis, these last two processes have the greatest likelihood of giving rise to transnational social movements.

In their search for explanations for the emergence of transnational practices, these authors have tended to ignore the "daily activist work" that is required for transnationalization to occur. Similarly, the accent on macro-level conditions (globalization) and institutional contexts means that the relative autonomy of movement activists and organizations in the construction of transnational solidarities, as well as in shaping the form that they take and their (varied) political content, is not sufficiently considered in these analyses.

Evaluating the Impacts of Transnationalization

Another important issue, which has been dealt with at length in recent studies, relates to the impact of transnational collective action, generally measured through the degree of influence achieved on decisions made at various institutional levels, and in particular by international institutions. For the majority of authors, transnationalization is seldom viewed as having a direct impact; rather, it is usually understood as mediated through relays such as public opinion or political and administrative instruments. Therefore, collective actions that have successfully affected institutions have not "revolutionized" the existing political order. Instead, they have allowed for change involving the incremental pluralization of existing structures of governance (O'Brien et al. 2000). Tarrow (2005) uses the metaphor of the coral reef to describe these incremental changes. Transnational protests occur in waves: national organizations leave the national scene to take part in transnational coalitions and protest activities that form around new "coral reefs" created by international institutions. They then return to their national level of action, having been transformed by their transnational experience. Incremental changes can be perceived within institutions (international or national) each time that national organizations participate in successful transnational action and each time that they return to have an impact on their national targets.

Jackie Smith, Charles Chatfield, and Ron Pagnucco (1997, 73-74) argue that while transnational collective actions may not have a direct effect on policies, they do play a role in the politicization of global issues and their appearance on the international agenda. Organizations involved in transnational collective actions also contribute to the learning processes of governments by gathering information and making it available through transnational communication networks. Lastly, they are involved in modelling political processes that are responsible for generating global policies.

The nature and scope of these impacts may vary as a result of several factors. According to Thomas Risse-Kappen (1995, 25), "under similar international conditions, differences in domestic structures determine the variation in the political impacts of transnational actors." Smith, Chatfield, and Pagnucco (1997, 60) maintain that the impact varies as a function of the structure of the mobilizations, the political opportunities offered by the various contexts in which they evolve, and how participants go about mobilizing their resources to take action.

The Difficult Task of Building Transnational Solidarities
Transnational mobilizations are forced to deal with difficulties that limit their potential, frequency, and success. As early as 1992, Dennis Young identified four major obstacles to the building of cross-border coalitions: political, cultural, and linguistic *diversity,* which jeopardizes the very notion of coalition since it makes agreeing on common interests arduous; the *physical distance* separating activists, who then require significant resources in terms of travel; *economic barriers* to the movement of people, goods, and information that restrict opportunities to form coalitions; and the specificities of *local political contexts* that determine, in part, the opportunities for local groups to act at a global level. Young (1992, 14; also cited by Bandy and Smith 2005, 8) suggested that these elements, which played against the emergence of transnational coalitions, could be expected to disappear or diminish over time because structural developments (technological, economic, and political) would eventually facilitate the formation of such coalitions and cause the interdependency among both issues and actors to become increasingly obvious.

Today, many scholars instead highlight the restrictive effects of structural economic transformations on the building of solidarities beyond national borders. In the field of work and labour relations, for instance, the liberalization of trade and business exchanges places workers in competition with each other, thereby limiting perspectives for cross-border solidarities (Azouvi 2000; Gobin 2002; Gobin, Hilal, and Decoene 2007). As well, it has been noted that problems related to the multinational nature of trans-national solidarities prevail (Bandy and Smith 2005). John D. McCarthy (1997, 245) underscores the inherent weaknesses in social movements' transnational networks and, specifically, the difficulty in building a common cognitive frame that allows for large-scale mobilizations.

The social movements and mainstream IR bodies of literature that have addressed transnational collective action have attempted to define trans-nationalization in relation to international political arenas. Researchers have examined the factors favouring the emergence and/or continuity of these mobilizations and attempted to measure their impacts. They have also reflected upon the conditions facilitating or preventing the formation of transnational solidarities. Surprisingly, however, research in this field, while very abundant, does not feature many studies addressing transnationaliza-tion and the building of cross-border solidarities in feminist and women's movements. It is feminist scholars, in IR or operating outside mainstream literature, who have made these issues central.

Contributions from Feminist IR

From within the IR field, a sustained current of feminist criticism has chal-lenged the masculine assumptions embedded in the "malestream" paradigm (Tickner 1992, 2001). Feminist IR scholars note that such a paradigm reifies and legitimizes the status quo in IR by normalizing existing power relations and suggesting that the patriarchal order is natural. Cynthia Enloe (1989), in particular, questioned the apparent absence of women in IR theory very early, arguing that transnational issues such as prostitution, sex tourism, and the sex trade were relevant to the field and required a rethinking of its analytical lens. Besides making women visible, Enloe's pioneering work (1983, 1989) also highlighted the contribution of feminist and women's movements in international processes and political change.

Much of the feminist IR literature focuses on transnational dynamics in relation to women and how they organize. At one end of the spectrum are numerous studies that emphasize the role of international processes and institutions in the formation of transnational women's organizations (Fried-man 2003; Joachim 2003; Valk, Van Dam, and Cummings 1999). With the growing emphasis on the role of women in development and the large international conferences organized by the United Nations (Bunch 1993; Chen 1995; Hilkka and Vickers 1994), global women's networks and caucuses are seen emerging. This is the case, for instance, for the International Women's Tribune Centre, created in 1976, Development Alternatives with Women for a New Era, established in preparation for the Third World Conference held in 1985, and, more recently, the Women's Environment and Development Organization, founded in 1991 (Antrobus 2004; Bunch and Reilly 1994). Writing about the 1985 conference, Peggy Antrobus (2004, 18-19) suggests, "It was there that a conscious attempt was made to bring together local and regional experiences as the beginning of a process for the preparation of a platform document for a global event." According to this view, the large gatherings and conferences of the 1980s and 1990s, sponsored by the UN, created momentum for the transnationalization of women's solidarities. Scholars also highlight the important contribution of women's NGOs in "gendering the agenda" (Friedman 2003; Jaquette 1995) of these conferences and in lobbying for and monitoring the agreements reached during these multilateral gatherings (Meyer and Prügl 1999; Stephenson 1995).

At the other end of the spectrum are studies that trace the transnationalization of women's solidarities and action back to larger global processes with a much longer history. Feminist IR scholars who carry out these studies also tend to emphasize the endogenous dimension of women's transnational organizing – the building of feminist solidarities in the struggles against gender regimes and patriarchal rule that are embedded in national and international institutions.

Transnationalization is thus viewed as responding both to exogenous opportunities and to more specific logics internal to women's mobilizations (Estrada-Claudio, this volume; Antrobus and Sen 2005; Stienstra 1994, 2000). Within these twin dynamics, gendered issues such as women's rights (Peters and Wolper 1995), abortion (Ferree and Gamson 1999), female workers' migrations (Parrenas 2001), violence against women (Piper 2001), sexual harassment (Zippel 2004), sexual equality (Cichowski 2002), and women's work, carework, and globalization (Moghadam 2005; Zimmerman and Litt 2006) have increasingly been framed as transnational and have spurred women's cross-border organizing.

Within IR theory, the area of international norms is probably where feminist scholars have made their most important and recognized contribution.

With the work of Martha Finnemore (1996) and Sikkink (1998), "norms" have acquired accepted status as an explanatory variable influencing policy-making in both state and international institutions. As defined by Peter J. Katzenstein (1996), norms are standards of behaviours considered appropriate for specific actors with given identities. Some of the significant work on women's rights (Thompson 2000) and violence against women (Keck and Sikkink 1998), for instance, has been conducted within such an international norms approach. In addition, explanatory models that underline the impact of norms and norm entrepreneurs have been devised to explain how women's transnational advocacy networks might be able to influence state policies through the boomerang effect (Keck and Sikkink 1998), cascading patterns of norms and norms life cycles (Finnemore and Sikkink 1998), and norm spiralling (Risse, Ropp, and Sikkink 1999).

It is in the reciprocal dynamics between the local/national and the global political processes in which women's movements are involved that one can understand the contribution of women's transnational organizing. Referring to the Convention on the Elimination of All Forms of Discrimination against Women, Mary Geske and Susan C. Bourque (2001, 262), for instance, suggest that regional middle-level organizations, such as International Women's Rights Action Watch Asia Pacific, act as "an effective mechanism linking local organizations to an international deliberative body."

Finally, feminist IR scholars also reveal how transnational social movement coalitions may be gender-blind and may end up reproducing exclusionary practices despite their progressive goals. Coalitions opposing free trade in the Americas, Laura Macdonald (2005, 21) notes, "are not free of exclusionary practices." Such a critical view is echoed by Catherine Eschle (2005, 1743; see also Eschle 2001, 2004), who argues that exclusionary hierarchies within transnational movements and organizations need to be exposed and that "received understandings of what constitutes the movement are being challenged" by feminists. Macdonald (2005, 23) further suggests that "interpretative frames, dominant within society at large, within states, and even within activist networks tend to be characterized by sexist assumptions, making infinitely more difficult feminist activists' struggles to challenge these assumptions and to bring their concerns within social movements' frames." The same applies within the field of expert knowledge produced by global coalitions and non-feminist movements, in which gendered assumptions help to delegitimize the "types of knowledge and skill typically dominated by women" (Macdonald 2005, 37), especially in the area of global economics and trade agreements (see also Caouette, this volume; Díaz Alba, this volume).

Feminist Scholarship on Transnationalization in Feminist and Women's Movements

Quite apart from the mainstream literature and separate from the work done in feminist IR, there exists a distinct feminist body of work that makes up the lion's share of current publications on women's movements, feminism, and transnationalization. This scholarship is distinctively feminist in the sense that it is grounded primarily in feminist theories and debates – that is, in feminism as an autonomous academic field of study. It is also interdisciplinary in that it draws, although much less visibly and oftentimes critically, on conceptual tools and approaches associated with other disciplines of the social sciences and humanities. Although this scholarship has some degree of affinity with feminist IR work on transnationalization, it does not share the latter's disciplinary orientations.

A Politics of Naming Around Basic Concepts

Approaching transnationalization through the lens of feminist scholarship is made arduous by the existence of a "politics of naming" around basic concepts (Naples 2002, 5). "When women mobilize" and transnationalize "to pursue a wide variety of interests," are all such mobilizations to be considered "women's movements"? Are all "automatically to be considered feminist" (Ferree 2006, 6)? If not, what counts as such? There is no general agreement in the literature on this issue, and responses range from the conflation of women's with feminist movements (and vice versa) to attempts (many of them viewed as exclusionary) at making sharp distinctions (see Hawkesworth 2006, 25-27). A useful way out of this conundrum is provided by Myra Marx Ferree (2006, 6), for whom these terms refer to distinct realities to be understood in a dynamic and relational way. "Naming 'women' as a constituency to be mobilized and building strategy, organization, and politics around issues defined as being particularly 'women's' concerns are the two factors that make a women's movement." Feminism, on the other hand, is to be seen as both theory and movement activism, oriented toward the specific goal of challenging the gender order while taking a plurality of forms and meanings. A dynamic and historically changing relationship between feminism(s) and women's movements thus exists that begs for closer investigation in an era of increased transnational connectivity (Ferree 2006, 8). The expression "feminist and women's movements," used here, is meant to acknowledge both the lack of a consensus in the literature and the interest of Ferree's proposition.

The meanings of "international," "global," and "transnational" in feminist scholarship are, similarly, plural and contested. Distinctions between international and transnational activism, for instance, often rest on an assumption of "newness" in the context of emergence of cross-border activism (that is, contemporary globalization), the logic of claims-making (transcending localisms and nationalisms), or organizational form (free-floating networks) that are disputed by other feminist scholars on historical, factual, or analytical grounds (see, for example, Hawkesworth 2006; Miller 1999; Rupp and Taylor 1999). Terminological disagreements around naming may be indicative of various ways of seeing the interconnectedness of nations (Mackie 2001) or, for the matter, of women. In fact, the labels "global feminism" and "transnational feminisms" are indexical of divergent positions in a debate concerned with the grounds, possibilities, and limitations for transnational solidarity among women who are differently located around the globe and within intersecting relations of power and difference.

This debate finds its starting point in Robin Morgan's (1984) notion of "global sisterhood," premised on the assumption of a worldwide, organic solidarity among women against patriarchal rule. Criticism of Morgan focused on her overly homogeneous conception of patriarchy and her erasure of differences and inequalities among women. Against presumptions of undifferentiated patriarchal oppressions, sameness, and automatic and unproblematic solidarity among women, the label "global feminism" emerged, as a feminist discourse and a politics, to acknowledge differences in power and privilege among women and the localized specificities of women's struggles against patriarchy and capitalism. Within global feminist perspectives, however, differences among women are not considered irreducible. They are to be reconciled, if not superseded, through the development of a common "global feminist agenda," fashioned around universalizable claims and associated with a human rights discourse. Anchored in a postmodern and postcolonial feminist critique of both "global sisterhood" and "global feminism," transnational feminism theorists (Alexander and Mohanty 1997; Grewal and Kaplan 1994; Kaplan 1994; Kaplan, Aleron, and Moallem 1999) are more sceptical about the possibilities for a truly universal and egalitarian feminist politics across "discrepant and distinct social conditions" (Mendoza 2002, 302). Rather, they advocate an analytical focus on the politics of location (Mohanty 1992) to unravel the tensions, contradictions, and power relations that necessarily affect attempts at alliances among differently situated women. Strategies based on practices of affiliation (Kaplan 1994) or dialogic transversal politics (Yuval-Davis 2006) are also presented as alternatives to the relativistic treatment of difference and unrecognized hegemonies that are perceived to mar the analysis of global feminism.

Outside of these terminological and strategic-theoretical debates, "transnational," "transnationalism," and even "global feminism" are terms widely used in feminist scholarship to refer to the myriad practices involved in networking and organization-building; mobilizing and transferring resources; framing claims, deploying discourses, and constructing collective identities; and collaborating and acting at the local, national, and supranational levels *in ways that involve feminists and/or women's movement actors working across or beyond national boundaries.* In this literature, transnational practices are both organizational and discursive. Its actors are variously identified as activists, groups, organizations and networks, and local and national women's movements, and they also include feminist NGOs and international NGOs that work "to alter gender power relations" (Alvarez 1999, 186).[1] Such work can be roughly divided into two strands: one concerned with the way in which feminist and women's movement activisms take shape and operate in the transnational public sphere, and the other with the encounter between domestic struggles and the new field of transnational feminist connectivity. A preoccupation with the tensions and power dynamics stemming from various axes of difference and inequality runs through both strands, harking back to issues of feminist theory and political strategy.

Transnational Actors in Transnational Settings

The first strand focuses on cross-boundary practices taking place in transnational settings and in the transnational public sphere. Valentine M. Moghadam's work (1996, 2000, 2005) is an important contribution to such an inquiry because it centres on exposing the origins, membership, organizational structure, goals, activities, and achievements of diverse transnational feminist networks. Other scholars document the nature and characteristics of a variety of transnational experiences, from attempts at bilateral collaboration between local women's organizations (Sampaio 2004; Weber 2002) to the organization of planetary gatherings such as the World March of Women (Conway 2008; Dufour and Giraud 2005; Giraud 2001). Although overlooked in analytical terms, a regional level of activism is prominent in numerous case studies featuring transnational organizations and networks, for instance in Africa (Adams 2006; Tripp 2005), Latin

America (Alvarez 2000; Mendez 2002), Europe (Helfferich and Kolb 2001), North America (Gabriel and Macdonald 1994; Liebowitz 2001), and Asia (Menon-Sen 2002). Strategies and pressures to expand women's rights in the transnational public sphere are also examined (see, in particular, Antrobus 2004; Cichowski 2002; Hawkesworth 2006). However, the extent of the influence of transnational campaigns on policymaking is disputed.[2] A recent addition to this strand is concerned with the intricacies of the relationship between transnational women's, alter-globalist, and social justice movements (see Alvarez, Faria, and Nobre 2004; Conway 2007; Latoures 2007; Vargas 2003; Wilson 2007).

Issues of Power, Voice, and Solidarities

Power relations and struggles underlying attempts at creating transnational solidarities are of particular interest to feminist scholars. Unearthing the politics of voice ("What gets said by whom about women's needs and interests" – Hawkesworth 2006, 131) and representation (what gets to be represented as the issues, priorities, and goals of feminist and women's movement organizing in the transnational public sphere) is central to understanding the conflictual nature of such attempts and the contingent and changing character of their outcomes. Chronicles of the construction of shared agendas for the world's women at UN conferences (Basu 2000, 2004; Desai 2005; Druelle 2004; Hawkesworth 2006; Snyder 2006; Stienstra 2000; Tripp 2006) and in other venues (Giraud 2001; Snyder 2005) exemplify such concerns. Together, these stories show that while transnational organizing does bring together the voices of diversely located women, these voices do not speak in unison, nor do they have equal weight in the crafting of common agendas. In the last three decades, tensions have arisen along the North-South divide. Issues deemed of major importance to women from the South – such as poverty, development, colonialism, racism, militarization and political repression, structural adjustment policies and debt, environmental degradation, and so forth – have been slow to find their place in common political platforms due to Northern reticence. The economic, political, and cultural hegemony exercised by Northern feminists in transnational organizing, the centrality of gender in defining women's issues, and major items on Northern feminists' agenda – lesbian rights and abortion rights, among others – have been the object of open contestation in transnational settings.

Categories such as "women from the South" or "Northern feminists," however, are overly homogenizing and should not be reified (Mackie 2001;

Mendoza 2002). Although they may be useful insofar as they indicate differing locations in global relations of power and dominance, these terms fail to acknowledge real differences in priorities and strategies among transnational movement actors from the same hemisphere, region, or country. As well, they preempt our understanding that politico-discursive positionings are not fixed, but, rather, are likely to evolve and change over time (Tripp 2005). Moreover, North-South tensions are crosscut and often compounded by the combined effects of other hegemonies and power struggles. Some scholars explicitly point to the class character of transnational activism. Access to the transnational sphere is contingent on monetary resources, while dominant strategies – international gatherings, reliance on knowledge experts and the Internet – favour participation by middle-class and educated (often white) women of the North and the South (Basu 2000; Desai 2005; Stienstra 2000). The way that the politics of class, race/ethnicity, sexuality, language, nationality (among others) intertwine and play out in contemporary transnational organizing needs more sustained attention (Hawkesworth 2006; Sampaio 2004; Snyder 2005).

While it is argued that the balance is shifting in favour of the South in transnational agenda-setting, notably at the UN, and that various means are being developed for greater inclusion of previously marginalized women and their issues in transnational activism, continuing differences and divergences around priorities, discursive framings, political strategies, and terrains of action reveal that the construction of transnational solidarities remains a problematic endeavour. Despite claims of mutual learning, this process of iterative adjustments remains replete with tensions. Consensual or cohesive strategies masking crucial differences and power dynamics are questioned (Hawkesworth 2006; Snyder 2005; Stienstra 2000), while the "compromise language" of common political platforms is said to bear the "traces of Western feminist hegemony" (Hawkesworth 2006, 132).

Domestic Encounters with Transnationalization

A second strand in the literature focuses on the nature and outcomes of the encounter between domestic activism (grassroots, local, or national) and various processes, events, and actors in a broadly defined field of transnational feminist connectivity. This body of work encompasses very diverse realities, including domestic involvement with international or foreign feminist donor organizations and local or national engagement in transnational campaigns or events – such as the Wages for Housework Campaign, the NGO forums at the UN World Conferences on Women, the Latin American feminist Encuentros, and the World March of Women. It also includes contacts with and the subsequent deployment of transnational feminist frames, such as the Beijing Platform, and other feminist discourses and ideas whose travels are associated with transnational linkages. As transnationalism fast becomes a major dimension of feminist and women's movement activism, feminist scholars debate its benefits and drawbacks for domestic actors and struggles.

On the whole, encounters with transnational actors, processes, and travelling feminist discourses are riddled with contradictory effects for domestic groups and movements. Some impacts may be very positive. Involvement with international and foreign donor organizations and programs that are feminist or broadly supportive of feminist goals is often beneficial in bringing much-needed financial and political resources. Participation in transnational campaigns or events does enable domestic movements by facilitating knowledge-sharing and political learning among differently located women and networking among activists and organizations, enhancing the movements' visibility and legitimacy at home, and reinforcing mobilization more generally (Adams 2006; Alvarez 1998; Beaulieu 2007; Sandberg 1998; Snyder 2006). Moreover, agendas, discourses, and strategies developed elsewhere or in transnational settings can be profitably "'translated' and redeployed locally" (Alvarez 2000, 35; see also Thayer 2000; Wing 2002).

Encounters with the transnational may, however, be detrimental. Funding may have the effect of imposing bureaucratic procedures on recipient groups; of shaping orientations and agendas in ways that privilege Western-style priorities, discourses, and models of feminist organizing over domestic ones; and, on the whole, of colonizing, dividing, and fragmenting domestic movements (Alvarez 2000; Bagic 2006; Friedman 1999; Hrycak 2002; Mendoza 2002). Engagement with UN processes, Latin American feminist scholars have argued, has fuelled the growth of strategies oriented toward international and domestic policymaking, privileging lobbying, expert knowledge, and watered-down liberal feminist framings to the detriment of the awareness raising, direct democracy, and more radical politics anchored in the discourses and practices of community-based women's groups (Alvarez 1998, 2000; Alvarez, Faria, and Nobre 2004; Friedman 1999; Mendoza 2002). Such shifts have also produced new power imbalances among domestic women's movement actors (Alvarez 2000) and cleavages that "often [run] along divisions of class, race and sexuality" (Mendoza 2002, 309).

Yet again, some work suggests, analyses of outcomes for domestic struggles need to be refined. Impacts depend on various factors, such as the nature of the encounter – funding being particularly infused with power relations – or the specific "action logic" at work in transnational campaigns or events. Sonia E. Alvarez (2000), for example, contrasts the identity-solidarity logic of the Encuentros and similar types of gatherings with what she calls the IGO-advocacy logic of UN processes. The capacity of local and national women's groups to exert their agency productively in the power dynamics of these encounters also needs more attention. It is possible for local groups to defend their autonomy successfully against funders' exigencies (Thayer 2001). It is also possible for "imported ideas and practices" to "constructively interact" with the ideas and practices of local actors and to be altered to serve their objectives, even in situations of unequal exchange (Sperling, Ferree, and Risman 2001, 1159; see also Thayer 2000, 2001).

Discussion

With the exception of feminist IR scholars, who have critically and constructively engaged with the dominant assumptions and theoretical frameworks in international relations, feminist work on transnationalization has developed, on the whole, in relative isolation from mainstream perspectives. Proponents of social movement and IR approaches to transnationalization, for their part, have notoriously ignored gender in their conceptualizations and analyses, as well as in the choice of movements and issues they have privileged. Nevertheless, we believe that there is room for cross-fertilization, and laying out the groundwork for a more extended conversation is one of the aims of this book. The juxtaposition of the three perspectives highlighted in this Introduction sketches out a series of criss-crossing avenues of research, debate, and dialogue between feminist and mainstream approaches to transnationalization.

First, there is a general lack of consensus on the very nature of the phenomenon under study, as well as on what the privileged units of analysis should be. More restrictive definitions dominate the social movements and IR literature (including feminist IR), associating transnationalization with organizations, campaigns, events, and normative discourses understood in relation to international institutions and multinational actors. By contrast, the interdisciplinary feminist literature proposes a broader understanding of the phenomenon encompassing a much wider variety of processes, levels, sites, and actors. Thus, a first series of questions concerns the object of study itself. Should we consider transnationalization to be simply a higher-level form of organizing and mobilizing, or the succession of actions, events, and campaigns organized by transnational coalitions? Should we attempt to apprehend transnationalization as a process (or processes) involving a wider range of actors? What, exactly, is transnationalized?

Second, there are diverging views around the issue of the dynamics presiding over contemporary transnationalizations. Mainstream literature emphasizes either the role of globalization (especially economic and technological) or of a new, complex institutional internationalism. Similar assumptions regarding the conditions of emergence of transnationalization in feminist and women's movements are shared by many feminist scholars across disciplines. Others, however, insist that the field of transnational connectivity has a longer history and that endogenous factors are important in accounting for the cross-border activity of feminist and women's movements. Another series of questions, thus, concerns our analytical approach to the dynamics of transnationalization. Is transnationalization to be analyzed as the product of abstract-structural causes, or of external political factors? Should we adopt the point of view of the actors themselves and try to understand how they construct transnationalization? Can these different levels of analysis be usefully reconciled? Is it possible to capture the interplay of external and endogenous factors?

Third, scholars from all three fields of study concur that the construction and maintenance of solidarity networks across and beyond borders presents a challenge for movement actors. In this perspective, mainstream work in social movements and IR highlights the constraints posed by global economic restructuring, as well as by the specificities of national political and cultural contexts. Feminist scholars focus most of their theory-building and analytical interest on the tensions and conflicts stemming from the co-presence of collective actors who are differently positioned in intersecting webs of structural relations of power and privilege. How can these different explanations be productively integrated for a better understanding not only of the obstacles posed to the construction of transnational solidarities, but also of the strategies developed, or in need of development, by movement actors? Can a focus on the ways that global and structural relations of power "touch ground" and materialize in the specificities of places (national and local) be helpful in this endeavour?

Finally, there are sharp differences among approaches regarding the terrains on which the impacts of transnationalization are considered. Mainstream research, including feminist IR, evaluates the consequences of transnationalization in relation to international (and sometimes national) institutions. The accent, thus, is on institutional change. Interdisciplinary feminist scholars, on the other hand, have tended to focus on the ways in which transnationalization in feminist and women's movement activism affects the movement sector, be it from the point of view of domestic actors and their struggles or of the constitution of a new, struggle-ridden field of alliances with other transnationalizing movements. Research on impacts is still in its early stages and clearly calls for more attention. In addition, as Elsa Beaulieu (this volume) and Manisha Desai (2005) remark, the way that transnationalization in feminist, women's, and other movements impacts the everyday lives and experiences of women and men in different locales – how it contributes to social change in specific settings – is remarkably absent from current reflections in both feminist research and more mainstream work.

Pursuing theoretical conversations on these issues among feminists, but also through critical engagement with mainstream perspectives, would, we contend, be useful in inspiring and expanding feminist scholarship. Conversely, integrating feminist approaches would be beneficial to mainstream scholars, helping them to refine their analyses regarding the effects of gender and intersectional power relations on transnational action, discourses, and coalitions and broadening their general outlook on transnationalization. We will continue this discussion in the book's conclusion.

Outline of the Book

Because feminist research is by definition interdisciplinary, contributions from less-well-known perspectives, we argue, deserve more attention. The first part of this book thus aims to add to our theoretical toolkit. Conceptual frameworks from geography and anthropology, we contend, bring a fresh outlook on transnationalization, raising new questions for our research agendas and showing strong heuristic potential for feminist analysis. Introducing them from the start sets the stage for further developments in the other sections of the book. Geographical concepts of space, scale, and place, for instance, elaborated on in Dominique Masson's chapter, also feature prominently in the various contributions to this volume. Anthropological approaches and methodologies presented by Beaulieu allow for an understanding of transnationalization processes as involving day-to-day practices – a theme that is also taken up, in various ways, in other chapters. Both conceptual offerings hold much promise for better capturing the situated experiences of women and feminist activists involved in transnationalization processes. Masson's chapter presents the theoretical questions and empirical contributions arising from recent work that develops a geographical perspective on transnational movements and scale. It aims to highlight the

potential that a focus on geographical scale presents for studying transnationalization in women's movements. Laying out the research agenda that
this new literature suggests to feminist scholars, she advocates for greater
attention to issues of spatiality, relations between scales of movement activity, and the role of place in analyses of transnationalization in feminist and
women's movements. Beaulieu proposes a feminist anthropological framework for conceptualizing social movement practices as products and producers of social change processes. She explores anthropological redefinitions
of the political as political culture and cultural politics, as well as contributions to practice theory aimed at giving analytic visibility to a wide range of
feminist and women's movement practices, including mundane and routine
ones. She then stages a dialectical encounter between her theoretical, epistemological, and methodological propositions and empirical data drawn
from the case study of the World March of Women in Brazil. Her methodological preoccupations prefigure further discussion of this topic in the conclusion of the book.

The second part of the book focuses on the deepening of solidarities
among feminist and women's organizations and activists – that is, on issues
of mutual recognition of identities and interests, the reinforcement of social ties, and the elaboration of shared understandings. This dynamic is
complex. Using case studies of three NGOs in Singapore, Lenore Lyons
examines the multiple ways in which NGOs working to address the rights
of female migrant workers understand and articulate their activism in light
of transnational feminist discourses. Widening our understanding of transnational feminist activism to include how the transnational is constructed
within the activist practices of feminist organizations and how transnational feminisms are framed at the local level allows for an exploration of the
ways in which ideas circulate among different scales and are translated into
concrete practices within specific organizational contexts. Sylvia Estrada-
Claudio provides us with an insider's look into the work involved in attempts
to deepen solidarities at the International Women and Health Meeting
(IWHM). Focusing on organizational practices at the IWHM, she argues
that the key to its successes resides in its continually renewed capacity for
recognition of the multiple identities that shape the category "women."
Estrada-Claudio identifies the internal mechanisms and strategies that have
contributed to the negotiated inclusion and deployment of various identities at the IWHM over the course of three decades. She also addresses the
limitations and tensions inherent to such efforts at inclusiveness and reflects upon the consequence of such complexity for transnational feminist

politics. Débora Lopreite's chapter explores the linkages between, on the one hand, transnational women's discourses and strategies in the United Nations and regional (Latin American) arenas, and, on the other hand, women's organizing in Argentina. She argues that a global gender regime has emerged in the international public sphere, and provides discourses, strategies, and sites of activism that have become increasingly significant for Argentine women's struggles, especially in the area of reproductive rights. The transnational character of Latin American women's organizing has also provided an intermediate scale of activism, in which women from the region have been able to build shared understandings and common goals.

In the third part of the book, Janet Conway, Dominique Caouette, and Carmen Díaz Alba explore questions related to the stretching of solidarities – that is, to practices and strategies of transnational solidarity building that involve establishing linkages between, on the one hand, feminist and women's movement organizing and politics and, on the other hand, progressive movements, organizations, activists, and issues. Extending the scope of solidarities in this way and attempting to work with other progressive allies is not without tensions; yet, it could be a major future source of transformation for transnational feminist and women's movements and their politics. Conway's chapter presents a comparative study of transnational feminisms at the World Social Forum (WSF). She demonstrates that plural and competing transnational feminist projects coexist at the WSF and argues that this plurality and the complexity of the relationships among projects and with the WSF all complicate general theories of transnationalism and transnationalization. Conway concludes by arguing for the importance of empirically investigating, comparing, and specifying the highly variable practices of transnational feminism. Caouette examines the formation of three regional activist organizations rooted in Southeast Asia and involved in research and advocacy against mainstream economic globalization. He shows how women and their issues, while being the objects of advocacy by these organizations, remain excluded as agents of critical reflection, and feminism remains alien to theoretical engagement within the malestream movement for global social justice. On a more optimistic note, Díaz Alba shows how the Latin American Network of Women Transforming the Economy (REMTE), a feminist network with national chapters in eleven countries whose participants are rural and urban women, academics, NGOs, and grassroots organizations, has been able to build cross-movement transnational solidarities as a space for analysis and action. Díaz Alba presents REMTE's strategy of framing gender and feminist perspectives in relation to broader social movements' critical analysis of free trade, providing oppositional knowledge for collective action, common platforms, and research.

In our conclusion, we return to some of the main theoretical questions raised in this Introduction by our staged encounter between mainstream and feminist bodies of literature. The questions of how to conceptualize transnationalization, understand its underlying dynamics, and approach the issue of the constitution of solidarities are at the centre of a discussion that underlines the specific contribution of both feminist work and our contributors' chapters. The additional insights to be gained by the integration of geographically sensitive approaches are then highlighted. Finally, methodological orientations are offered with the objective of furthering feminist research on transnationalization.

NOTES

1 For a further discussion of the specificity of feminist NGOs as hybrids in the women's movement field, see Alvarez (1999).
2 Contrast Moghadam (2005) and Adams (2006), for instance, with Basu (2000), Hawkesworth (2006), Desai (2005), and Tripp (2006).

REFERENCES

Adams, Melinda. 2006. Regional Women's Activism: African Women's Networks and the African Union. In *Global Feminism: Transnational Women's Activism, Organizing, and Human Rights,* ed. Myra Marx Ferree and Aili Mari Tripp, 187-218. New York: New York University Press.

Alexander, M. Jacqui, and Chandra Talpade Mohanty, eds. 1997. *Feminist Genealogies, Colonial Legacies, Democratic Futures.* New York: Routledge.

Alvarez, Sonia E. 1998. Latin America Feminisms "Go Global": Trends of the 1990s and Challenges for the New Millennium. In *Cultures of Politics, Politics of Cultures: Re-Envisioning Latin America Social Movements,* ed. Sonia Alvarez, Evelina Dagnigno, and Alberto Escobar, 293-324. Boulder: Westview.

–. 1999. Advocating Feminism: The Latin American Feminist NGO "boom." *International Feminist Journal of Politics* 1 (2): 181-209.

–. 2000. Translating the Global: Effects of Transnational Organizing on Local Feminist Discourses and Practices and Latin America. *Meridians: Feminism, Race, Transnationalism* 1 (1): 29-67.

Alvarez, Sonia E., Nalu Faria, and Miriam Nobre. 2004. Another (also Feminist) World Is Possible: Constructing Transnational Spaces and Global Alternatives from the Movements. In *World Social Forum: Challenging Empires,* ed. Jai Sen, Anita Anand, Arturo Escobar, and Peter Waterman, 199-206. New Delhi: Viveka Foundation.

Antrobus, Peggy. 2004. *The Global Women's Movement: Issues and Strategies for the New Century*. London: Zed Books.

Antrobus, Peggy, and Gita Sen. 2005. The Personal Is Global: The Project and Politics of the Transnational Women's Movement. In *Claiming Global Power: Transnational Civil Society and Global Governance*, ed. Srilatha Baltiwala and David Brown, 142-58. Bloomfield: Kumarian.

Ayres, Jeffrey, and Sidney Tarrow. 2003. The Shifting Grounds for Transnational Civic Activity. *Social Science Research Council*. http://www.ssrc.org/sept11/essays/ayres.htm.

Azouvi, Alain. 2000. Introduction. In *Le syndicalisme dans la mondialisation*, ed. Annie Fouquet, Udo Rehfeldt, and Serge Le Roux, 1-23. Paris: Les Éditions de l'Atelier/Les Éditions Ouvrières.

Bagic, Aida. 2006. Women's Organizing in Post-Yugoslav Countries: Talking about "Donors." In *Global Feminism: Transnational Women's Activism, Organizing, and Human Rights*, ed. Myra Marx Ferree and Aili Mari Tripp, 141-65. New York: New York University Press.

Bandy, Joe, and Jackie Smith. 2005. *Coalitions across Borders: Transnational Protest and the Neoliberal Order*. Oxford: Rowman and Littlefield.

Basu, Amrita. 2000. Globalization of the Local/Globalization of the Global: Mapping Transnational Women's Movements. *Meridians: Feminism, Race, Transnationalism* 1 (1): 68-84.

–. 2004. Women's Movements and the Challenge of Transnationalism. In *Encyclopedia of Women's Studies*, vol. 1, *Women's Movements*, ed. Subhadra Channa, 259-66. New Delhi: Cosmo Publications.

Beaulieu, Elsa. 2007. Échelles et lieux de l'action collective dans la Marche mondiale des femmes au Brésil. *Lien social et politiques* 58: 119-32.

Bunch, Charlotte. 1993. Organizing for Women's Human Rights Globally. In *Ours By Right: Women's Rights as Human Rights*, ed. Joanna Kerr, 141-49. London and Ottawa: Zed Books and North-South Institute.

Bunch, Charlotte, and Niamh Reilly. 1994. *Demanding Accountability: The Global Campaign and Vienna Tribunal for Women's Human Rights*. New Brunswick, NJ/New York: Rutgers University Center for Women's Global Leadership/United Nations Development Fund for Women.

Chen, Martha Alter. 1995. Engendering World Conferences: The International Women's Movement and the United Nations. *Third World Quarterly* 16 (3): 477-93.

Cichowski, Rachel A. 2002. No Discrimination Whatsoever: Women's Transnational Activism and the Evolution of EU Sex Equality Policy. In *Women's Activism and Globalization: Linking Local Struggles and Transnational Politics*, ed. Nancy A. Naples and Manisha Desai, 220-38. New York: Routledge.

Conway, Janet M. 2004. *Identity, Place, Knowledge: Social Movements Contesting Globalization*. Halifax: Fernwood Publishing.

–. 2007. Transnational Feminisms and the World Social Forum: Encounters and Transformations in Anti-Globalization Spaces. *Journal of International Women's Studies* 8 (3): 49-70.

–. 2008. Geographies of Transnational Feminism: The Politics of Place and Scale in the World March of Women. *Social Politics* 15 (2): 207-31.

Della Porta, Donatella, Massimiliano Andretta, Lorenzo Mosca, and Herbert Reiter. 2006. *Globalization From Below: Transnational Activists and Protest Networks.* Minneapolis: University of Minnesota Press.

Della Porta, Donatella, Hanspeter Kriesi, and Dieter Rucht, eds. 1999. *Social Movements in a Globalizing World.* New York: Macmillan.

Della Porta, Donatella, and Sidney Tarrow, eds. 2005. *Transnational Protest and Global Activism.* Lanham: Rowman and Littlefield.

Desai, Manisha. 2005. Transnationalism: The Face of Feminist Politics post-Beijing. *International Social Science Journal* 57 (184): 319-30.

Devin, Guillaume, ed. 2004. *Les solidarités transnationales.* Paris: L'Harmattan.

Druelle, Anick. 2004. Que célébrer 30 ans après l'Année internationale de la femme: une autre crise au sein des mouvements internationaux de femmes? *Recherches féministes* 17 (2): 115-69.

Dufour, Pascale, and Isabelle Giraud. 2005. Altermondialisme et féminisme: pourquoi faire? Le cas de la Marche mondiale des femmes. *Chroniques féministes* 93 (August/December): 9-16.

Enloe, Cynthia. 1983. *Does Khaki Become You? The Militarization of Women's Lives.* Boston: South End Press.

–. 1989. *Bananas, Beaches and Bases.* Berkeley: California University Press.

Eschle, Catherine. 2001. *Global Democracy, Social Movements, and Feminism.* Boulder: Westview.

–. 2004. Feminist Studies of Globalisation: Beyond Gender, Beyond Economism? *Global Studies* 18 (2): 97-125.

–. 2005. "Skeleton Women": Feminism and the Antiglobalization Movement. *Signs: Journal of Women in Culture and Society* 30 (3): 1741-69.

Ferree, Myra Marx. 2006. Globalization and Feminism: Opportunities and Obstacles for Activism in the Global Arena. In *Global Feminism: Transnational Women's Activism, Organizing, and Human Rights,* ed. Myra Marx Ferree and Aili Mari Tripp, 3-23. New York: New York University Press.

Ferree, Myra Marx, and William A. Gamson. 1999. The Gendering of Abortion Discourse: Assessing Global Feminist Influence in the United States and Germany. In *Social Movements in a Globalizing World,* ed. Donatella della Porta, Hanspeter Kriesi, and Dieter Rucht, 40-56. New York: Macmillan.

Finnemore, Martha. 1996. *National Interests in International Society.* Ithaca: Cornell University Press.

Finnemore, Martha, and Kathryn Sikkink. 1998. International Norm Dynamics and Political Change. *International Organization* 52 (4): 887-917.

Friedman, Elisabeth J. 1999. The Effects of "Transnationalism Reversed" in Venezuela: Assessing the Impact of U.N. Global Conferences on the Women's Movement. *International Feminist Journal of Politics* 1 (3): 357-81.

–. 2003. Gendering the Agenda: The Impact of the Transnational Women's Rights Movement at the U.N. Conferences of the 1990s. *Women's Studies International Forum* 26 (4): 313-31.

Gabriel, Christina, and Laura Macdonald. 1994. NAFTA, Women and Organizing in Canada and Mexico: Forging a "Feminist Internationality." *Millennium: Journal of International Studies* 23 (3): 535-62.

Geske, Mary, and Susan C. Bourque. 2001. Grassroots Organizations and Women's Human Rights: Meeting the Challenge of the Local-Global Link. In *Women, Gender, and Human Rights: A Global Perspective*, ed. Marjorie Agosin, 246-63. New Brunswick, NJ: Rutgers University Press.

Giraud, Isabelle. 2001. La transnationalisation des solidarités: l'exemple de la Marche mondiale des femmes. *Lien social et politiques* 45: 145-60.

Gobin, Corinne. 2002. De l'Union européenne à l'européanisation des mouvements sociaux? *Revue Internationale de politique comparée* 9 (1): 119-39.

Gobin, Corinne, Nadia Hilal, and Aurélie Decoene. 2007. Mobilisations transfrontières et Union européenne: difficultés et réalités de la contestation syndicale – L'exemple du syndicalisme du transport. *Lien social et politiques* 58: 73-86.

Grewal, Inderpal, and Caren Kaplan. 1994. Introduction: Transnational Feminist Practices and Questions of Postmodernity. In *Scattered Hegemonies: Postmodernity and Transnational Feminist Practices*, ed. Inderpal Grewal and Caren Kaplan, 1-33. Minneapolis: University of Minnesota Press.

Hawkesworth, Mary E. 2006. *Globalization and Feminist Activism*. Lanham: Rowman and Littlefield.

Helfferich, Barbara, and Felix Kolb. 2001. Multilevel Action Coordination in European Contentious Politics: The Case of the European Women's Lobby. In *Contentious Europeans: Protest and Politics in an Integrating Europe*, ed. Doug Imig and Sidney Tarrow, 163-86. Lanham: Rowman and Littlefield.

Hilkka, Pietila, and Jeanne Vickers. 1994. *Making Women Matter: The Role of the United Nations*. London: Zed Books.

Hrycak, Alexandra. 2002. From Mothers' Rights to Equal Rights: Post-Soviet Grassroots Women's Associations. In *Women's Activism and Globalization: Linking Local Struggles and Transnational Politics*, ed. Nancy A. Naples and Manisha Desai, 64-82. New York: Routledge.

Jaquette, Jane. 1995. Losing the Battle/Winning the War: International Politics, Women's Issues, and the 1980 Mid-Decade Conference. In *Women, Politics, and the United Nations*, ed. Ann Winslow, 45-60. Westport: Greenwood.

Joachim, Jutta. 2003. Framing Issues and Seizing Opportunities: The U.N., NGOs and Women's Rights. *International Studies Quarterly* 47: 247-74.

Kaplan, Caren. 1994. The Politics of Location as Transnational Feminist Critical Practice. In *Scattered Hegemonies: Postmodernity and Transnational Feminist Practices*, ed. Inderpal Grewal and Caren Kaplan, 137-52. Minneapolis: University of Minnesota Press.

Kaplan, Caren, Norma Aleron, and Minoo Moallem, eds. 1999. *Between Woman and Nation: Nationalisms, Transnational Feminism and the State*. Durham: Duke University Press.

Katzenstein, Peter J. 1996. Alternative Perspectives on National Security 1996. In *The Culture of National Security: Norms and Identity in World Politics*, ed. Peter J. Katzenstein, 1-32. New York: Columbia University Press.

Keck, Margaret E., and Kathryn Sikkink. 1998. *Activists Beyond Borders: Advocacy Networks in International Politics*. Ithaca: Cornell University Press.

Latoures, Aurelie. 2007. Gender in the Bamako Polycentric World Social Forum (2006): Is Another World Possible? *Journal of International Women's Studies* 8 (3): 164-83.

Liebowitz, Debra J. 2001. Constructing Cooperation: Feminist Activism and NAF-TA. In *Feminist Locations: Global and Local, Theory and Practice*, ed. Marianne DeKoven, 168-90. New Brunswick, NJ: Rutgers University Press.

Macdonald, Laura. 2005. Gendering Transnational Social Movement Analysis: Women's Groups Contest Free Trade in the Americas. In *Coalitions Across Borders*, ed. Joe Bandy and Jackie Smith, 21-41. Lanham: Rowman and Littlefield.

Mackie, Vera. 2001. The Language of Globalization, Transnationality and Feminism. *International Feminist Journal of Politics* 3 (2): 180-206.

McCarthy, John D. 1997. The Globalization of Social Movement Theory. In *Transnational Social Movements and Global Politics: Solidarity Beyond the State*, ed. Jackie Smith, Charles Chatfield, and Ron Pagnucco, 243-59. New York: Syracuse University Press.

Mendez, Jennifer Bickham. 2002. Creating Alternatives from a Gender Perspective: Transnational Organizing for Maquila Workers' Rights in Central America. In *Women's Activism and Globalization: Linking Local Struggles and Transnational Politics*, ed. Nancy Naples and Manisha Desai, 121-41. New York: Routledge.

Mendoza, Breny. 2002. Transnational Feminisms in Question. *Feminist Theory* 3 (3): 295-314.

Menon-Sen, Kalyani. 2002. Bridges Over Troubled Waters: South Asian Women's Movements Confronting Globalization. *Development* 45 (1): 132-36.

Meyer, Mary K., and Elizabeth Prügl, eds. 1999. *Gender Politics in Global Governance*. Lanham: Rowman and Littlefield.

Miller, Francesca. 1999. Feminisms and Transnationalism. In *Feminisms and Internationalism*, ed. Mrinalini Sinha, Donna Guy, and Angela Woolacott, 225-36. Oxford: Blackwell.

Moghadam, Valentine M. 1996. Feminist Networks North and South: DAWN, WIDE and WLUML. *Journal of International Communication* 3 (1): 111-26.

–. 2000. Transnational Feminist Networks: Collective Action in an Era of Globalization. *International Sociology* 15 (1): 57-86.

–. 2005. *Globalizing Women. Transnational Feminist Networks*. Baltimore: Johns Hopkins University Press.

Mohanty, Chandra Talpade. 1992. Feminist Encounters: Locating the Politics of Experience. In *Destabilizing Theory: Contemporary Feminist Debates*, ed. Michèle Barrett and Anne Philips, 74-92. Stanford: Stanford University Press.

–. 2003. *Feminism without Borders: Decolonizing Theory, Practicing Solidarity*. Durham and London: Duke University Press.

Morgan, Robin. 1984. *Sisterhood Is Global: The International Women's Movement Anthology*. New York: Anchor Press/Doubleday.

Naples, Nancy A. 2002. Changing the Terms: Community Activism, Globalization, and the Dilemmas of Transnational Feminist Praxis. In *Women's Activism and*

Globalization. Linking Local Struggles and Transnational Politics, ed. Nancy A. Naples and Manisha Desai, 3-14. New York: Routledge.

O'Brien, Robert, Anne Marie Goetz, Jan Aart Scholte, and Marc Williams. 2000. *Contesting Global Governance: Multilateral Economic Institutions and Global Social Movements.* Cambridge: Cambridge University Press.

Parreñas, Rhacel Salazar. 2001. *Servants of Globalization: Women, Migration and Domestic Work.* Stanford: Stanford University Press.

Peters, Julie, and Andrea Wolper, eds. 1995. *Women's Rights, Human Rights: International Feminist Perspectives.* New York: Routledge.

Piper, Nicola. 2001. Transnational Women's Activism in Japan and Korea: The Unresolved Issue of Military Sexual Slavery. *Global Networks* 1 (2): 171-95.

Piper, Nicola, and Anders Uhlin, eds. 2004. *Transnational Activism in Asia: Problems of Power and Democracy.* London: Routledge.

Risse, Thomas, Stephen Ropp, and Kathryn Sikkink, eds. 1999. *The Power of Principles: Human Rights Norms and Domestic Political Change.* Cambridge: Cambridge University Press.

Risse-Kappen, Thomas. 1995. Bringing Transnational Relations Back In: Introduction. In *Bringing Transnational Relations Back In: Non-State Actors, Domestic Structures and International Institutions,* ed. Thomas Risse-Kappen, 3-33. Cambridge: Cambridge University Press.

Rupp, Leila J., and Verta Taylor. 1999. Forging Feminist Identity in an International Movement: A Collective Identity Approach to Twentieth-Century Feminism. *Signs: Journal of Women in Culture and Society* 24 (21): 363-86.

Sampaio, Anna. 2004. Transnational Feminisms in a New Global Matrix. *International Feminist Journal of Politics* 6 (2): 181-206.

Sandberg, Eve. 1998. Multilateral Women's Conferences: The Domestic Political Organization of Zambian Women. *Contemporary Politics* 4 (3): 271-83.

Sikkink, Kathryn. 1998. Transnational Politics, IR Theory and HR. *PS Online* 31 (3): 517-21.

Siméant, Johanna. 2005. What Is Going Global? The Internationalization of French NGOs without Borders. *Review of International Political Economy* 12 (5): 851-83.

Smith, Jackie, Charles Chatfield, and Ron Pagnucco, eds. 1997. *Transnational Social Movements and Global Politics: Solidarity Beyond the State.* New York: Syracuse University Press.

Snyder, Anna. 2005. Transnational Dialogue: Building the Social Infrastructure for Transnational Feminist Networks. *International Journal of Peace Studies* 10 (2): 69-88.

Snyder, Margaret. 2006. Unlikely Godmother: The U.N. and the Global Women's Movement. In *Global Feminism: Transnational Women's Activism, Organizing, and Human Rights,* ed. Myra Marx Ferree and Aili Mari Tripp, 24-50. New York: New York University Press.

Sperling, Valerie, Myra Marx Ferree, and Barbara Risman. 2001. Constructing Global Feminism: Transnational Advocacy Networks and Russian Women's Activism. *Signs* 26 (4): 1155-86.

Stephenson, Carolyn. 1995. Women's International Non-Governmental Organizations at the United Nations. In *Women, Politics, and the United Nations*, ed. Ann Winslow, 135-53. Westport: Greenwood.

Stienstra, Deborah. 1994. *Women's Movements and International Organizations.* New York: St. Martin's Press.

—. 2000. Dancing Resistance from Rio to Beijing: Transnational Women's Organizing and United Nations Conferences, 1992-6. In *Gender and Global Restructuring: Sightings, Sites and Resistances*, ed. Anne Sisson Runyan and Marianne Marchand, 209-24. London: Routledge.

Tarrow, Sidney. 2001. Transnational Politics: Contention and Institutions in International Politics. *Annual Review of Political Science* 4: 1-20.

—. 2005. *The New Transnational Activism.* Cambridge: Cambridge University Press.

Tarrow, Sidney, and Donnatella della Porta. 2005. Conclusion: "Globalization," Complex Internationalism, and Transnational Contention. In *Transnational Protest and Global Activism*, ed. Donatella della Porta and Sidney Tarrow, 227-46. Lanham: Rowman and Littlefield.

Thayer, Millie. 2000. Traveling Feminisms: From Embodied Women to Gendered Citizenship. In *Global Ethnography: Forces, Connections and Imaginations in a Postmodern World*, ed. Michael Burawoy, Joseph A. Blum, Sheba George, Zsuzsa Gille, Teresa Gowan, Lynne Haney, Maren Klawiter, Steven H. Lopez, Seán Ó Riain and Millie Thayer, 203-33. Berkeley: University of California Press.

—. 2001. Transnational Feminism: Reading Joan Scott in the Brazilian Sertao. *Ethnography* 2 (2): 243-71.

Thompson, Karen Brown. 2000. Women's Rights are Human Rights: Institutionalizing Global Norms about Women's Rights. In *Restructuring World Politics: Transnational Social Movements, Networks and Norms*, ed. Sanjeev Khagram, Jame V. Riker, and Kathryn Sikkink, 96-122. Minneapolis and St. Paul: University of Minnesota Press.

Tickner, J. Ann. 1992. *Gender in International Relations: Feminist Perspectives on Achieving Global Security.* New York: Columbia University Press.

—. 2001. *Gendering World Politics: Issues and Approaches in the Cold War Era.* New York: Columbia University Press.

Tripp, Aili Mari. 2005. Regional Networking as Transnational Feminism: African Experiences. *Feminist Africa*, April. http://www.feministafrica.org/.

—. 2006. Challenges in Transnational Feminist Mobilization. In *Global Feminism: Transnational Women's Activism, Organizing, and Human Rights*, ed. Myra Marx Ferree and Aili Mari Tripp, 296-312. New York: New York University Press.

Valk, Minke, Henk Van Dam, and Sarah Cummings. 1999. Women's Information Centers and Networks: A Global Perspective. In *Women's Information Services and Networks: A Global Sourcebook*, ed. Sarah Cummings, Henk Van Dam, and Minke Valk, 21-29. Amsterdam: Royal Tropical Institute.

Vargas, Virginia. 2003. Feminism, Globalization and the Global Justice and Solidarity Movement. *Cultural Studies* 17 (6): 905-20.

Weber, Clare. 2002. Women to Women: Dissident Citizen Diplomacy in Nicaragua. In *Women's Activism and Globalization: Linking Local Struggles and Transnational Politics,* ed. Nancy A. Naples and Manisha Desai, 45-63. New York: Routledge.

Wilson, Ara. 2007. Feminism in the Space of the World Social Forum. *Journal of International Women's Studies* 8 (3): 10-27.

Wing, Susanna D. 2002. Women Activists in Mali: The Global Discourse on Human Rights. In *Women's Activism and Globalization: Linking Local Struggles and Transnational Politics,* ed. Nancy A. Naples and Manisha Desai, 172-85. New York: Routledge.

Young, Dennis R. 1992. Organising Principles for International Advocacy Associations. *Voluntas* 3 (1): 1-28.

Yuval-Davis, Nira. 2006. Human/Women's Rights and Feminist Transversal Politics. In *Global Feminism: Transnational Women's Activism, Organizing, and Human Rights,* ed. Myra Marx Ferree and Aili Mari Tripp, 235-95. New York: New York University Press.

Zimmerman, Mary K., and Jacqueline S. Litt, eds. 2006. *Global Dimensions of Gender and Carework.* Stanford: Stanford University Press.

Zippel, Kathryn. 2004. Transnational Advocacy Networks and Policy Cycles in the European Union: The Case of Sexual Harassment. *Social Politics* 11 (1): 57-85.

PART 1

UNDERSTANDING COMPLEX TRANSNATIONALIZATION

1

Transnationalizing Feminist and Women's Movements
Toward a Scalar Approach

DOMINIQUE MASSON

"Scale" has recently surfaced in the theoretical vocabulary of social movement and feminist scholars as one of the possible ways to foster new understandings of the changes related to the increase in transnational movement connectivity and activity.[1] Such attempts to use scale as an analytical tool, however, show very little engagement with the existing and quite sophisticated interdisciplinary literature on transnationalization in social movements informed by theoretical developments and debates in geography over scale and rescaling, space, and place. Although this last body of literature seldom addresses women's movement organizing (but see Beaulieu 2007; Conway 2007), it does offer interesting ways to think about the transnationalization of movement activity that may benefit feminist research.

Literature reviews of social movement studies (Miller 2000; Sewell 2001) show that the field has remained largely blind to the spatial dimensions of collective action. Despite allusions to a wide variety of spaces and scales of movement activity – the local and the regional, the city and the neighbourhood, the transnational and the grassroots, and so on – scholars predominantly tie their analyses of movement politics to the spatial boundaries of the nation-state; geographical references function at best as indicators of sociopolitical contextualization. Theorizing is largely a-spatial, as space itself is treated as an unproblematized container for processes in which it plays merely a descriptive role as a site, scene, or background (Sewell 2001). "There is no recognition," Byron Miller (2000, 6) writes, "that the spatial

constitution" and spatial grounding of processes of collective action profoundly "affect ... their operation." The current displacement of state-centric
assumptions by an equally problematic "methodological globalism" (Conway 2005, 2) in which an undifferentiated "global" becomes the geographical unit of reference for transnational collective action only further obscures
issues related to the spatial dimensions of movement politics.

Within feminist work, with the multiplication of transnational organizations and networks, campaigns and events, practices and discourses, feminist analysts are, as Janet Conway (2006, 2) notes, "indeed, observing the
creation of new regionalizations" or more broadly, as will be argued in this
chapter, of new spatialities of transnationalization, but "all without a language of scale." Theoretical understandings of these developments, Conway
states, are limited by such absence. In addition, although place-based
specificity does shine through many case studies of feminist and women's
trans-local and transnational processes, practices, and discourses, it is in a
mostly descriptive and untheorized manner. The analytic import of such
specificity is too often subsumed into the "local" component of a global-
local binary or erased by globalocentric (Escobar and Harcourt 2005) narratives of transnationalization. Yet, feminist scholarship as a whole does
feature a theoretical vocabulary encompassing the use of concepts such as
location, situatedness, and positionality, which assume meanings that,
sometimes very explicitly, link women's positionings in social relations and
processes with places on the ground, in the specific instantiations of these
processes (see Grewal and Kaplan 1994; Kaplan 1994; Mohanty 2003). A
closer look at place and scale, as conceptualized in geography, could help
feminists inquire deeper, as Susan Stanford Friedman (2001, 17) suggests,
into "the meanings of spatiality" for feminist theory, practice, and analysis
of transnationalization.

In this chapter, I aim to show how feminist analyses of transnational activism could be furthered through the conceptual framework and research
agenda suggested by the geographically sensitive literature on scale and
transnational movement politics. This literature, I argue, offers new theoretical and empirical insights for studying transnational activity undertaken
by feminist and women's movements. In the first section, I briefly present
the main conceptual elements that underlie current scalar approaches to
transnationalization – space, scale, and place. In the remainder of the chapter, I further explore and flesh out the theoretical questions and research
avenues arising from these conceptualizations with the help of selected examples that highlight the usefulness of such contributions, as well as the

gaps in current feminist scholarship that they can help to address. This exploration is organized around the ways in which thinking in terms of scale (and place) sheds new light on crucial collective action processes – organizing, action, mobilization, and frame construction – as these processes get stretched beyond national boundaries and over ever-wider expanses of space. Variations in the spatialities of transnational organizing, the multiscalar character of movement action, the twin roles of scale and place in transnational mobilizations, and how both scale and place play out in the constitution of transnational framings are underscored as potential focal points for future feminist research.

Conceptual Elements: Space, Scale, and Place

Current conceptions of scale in the geographically sensitive literature on transnational movement politics stem from an understanding of space as a product of social relations. According to this perspective, social processes and the social relations that constitute them occur in space, are deployed through space, and thus shape space in ways that involve variations in the spatial distribution of people and activities, distances, geographical differentiation, and the production of various meanings attached to space(s). All social relations are thus necessarily space-forming; they are also spatialized in ways that are space-contingent (Feldman 2002, 32). "Spatial distributions and geographical differentiation may be the result of social processes, but they also affect how these processes work" (Massey quoted in Miller 2000, 10). Succinctly put, if the social relations and processes that constitute social movement activity are not only deployed in space but also contingent on it, then the spatial dimensions of movement organizing, action, and claims-making do matter for the study of movement politics: they are "part of the explanation" (10).

Although there are different ways of conceptualizing and operationalizing *scale* in the geographical debates on scale and rescaling, the most useful way of understanding scale is to see it, first and foremost, as a spatial property of social relations.[2] Social relations are not solely deployed *in* space; the different economic, political, and cultural processes that organize social relations and social life *extend and stretch over different (and variable) expanses of space*. The extent of such stretching is their scale. The main theoretical point here is that scale should be thought of not in a void or in the abstract, but always as a dimension of social processes (Masson 2006, 480; Swyngedouw 1997b, 141). Scale can further be defined, following John Agnew (1997, 100), as "the focal setting at which spatial boundaries are defined for a specific social claim, activity, or behavior," thus indicating that scalar deployments are actively organized by the social agents doing the acting and the defining. In short, scales are socially constructed.

Much of the geographical inquiry into scale construction has focused on processes of capitalist production and political regulation. Consequently, the role of major social actors, such as capital and states, in the making and remaking of scales has been privileged. Capital and states are seen, from this perspective, as responsible for the "fixation" of preferred scales of economic relations and political regulation (Brenner 1999), as well as for moments, such as the current one, of rescaling – that is, the profound reconfiguring of existing scalar deployments and hierarchies.[3] Although social movements have been the object of less attention in this literature, it has been argued that they, too, actively make and remake the scales of collective action (Conway 2005; Herod 1997; Masson 2006; Miller 1997). In this process, they often engage with the existing "scalar fixes" or attempts at rescaling initiated by dominant economic and state actors. However, they may organize their spatial deployments according to other rationales or logics (internal or external), creating new or aligning with variously defined scales of belonging and identification, environmental damage, or social justice, for instance (see Kurtz 2003; Silvern 1999; Towers 2000).

Developing an analytical understanding of the role and importance of scale in feminist and women's movement transnational politics is complicated by the fact that we are already provided with a scalar vocabulary from the smallest to the largest scales – from the local to the national, the regional, and the transnational or global. In this prevalent conception, scales are like Russian dolls: pre-given, fixed, nested, and empty containers for social processes in which they play no real part. Yet, from the constructionist point of view put forward by geography scholars, the transnational scale is not just there for the taking. Like any other scale of collective action (see Masson 2006), the transnational scale has to be constructed in order for women's movements to act. If scale is always to be associated with the deployment of specific social processes, then a transnational scale of movement activity cannot pre-exist this activity. For such a scale to emerge, crucial processes of collective action, such as movement organizing, action, mobilization, and the framing of claims, have to be deployed in ways that cross national borders. To construct "the transnational" as a full-fledged scale of movement activity, all of the types of social relations that constitute collective action have to be stretched beyond national boundaries and concretely established in more or less institutionalized ways in order to connect participants (individuals and/or organizations), issues, and claims across wider-than-before expanses of space.

Finally, place is often of central importance in the geographically sensitive literature on transnational movements and scale. Such focus expresses a deep, conceptual reluctance to detach transnational networks, events, and participants from their territorial moorings. Despite all the "globe talk," transnational social movement actors and actions seldom behave as free-floating cosmopolitans. As in any other production of globalities, the formation of transnational collective action should, to extend an argument made by Steven Flusty (2004, 7), "be seen as embedded both in space and in the lives of emplaced persons." A networks approach to transnationalization yields a somewhat similar line of reasoning: networks extend in various directions over more or less vast expanses of space; yet, each point in the network sits in a particular place (Bruno Latour, quoted in Miller 2005). Place, it is imperative to note, is not equivalent to "the local." Places are units of analysis, and thus may be set by the analyst at various scales. A useful way of understanding place is provided by Doreen Massey. In her view, a place should be theorized as a locus and a moment at which "economic, political and cultural relations, each full of power and with internal structures of domination" (Massey 1994, 154) and constructed at various scales intersect "in a distinct *mixture* of wider and more local social relations" (Massey 1994, 156, emphasis in original). Place can thus be seen as geographers' way of reintroducing space, spatialities, and their uneven development into what others grasp under more limited indications of the spatial situatedness inherent to lived experience and sociopolitical struggles. Because of the sophistication of its theorizing, especially in Massey's version, place should be an interesting addition to feminist scholars' existing concerns with the spatial grounding of social locations and positionalities.

Human and political geography's theorizing of scale suggests that we direct our attention to the processes of scaling and rescaling of collective action and to the scalar construction of the transnational in and through the activity of feminist and women's movements. More precisely, such theoretical observations beg the question of *exactly how, and according to what kind of logics, the transnational scale – in the diversity of its instantiations – is materially and discursively constructed by feminist and women's movement actors.* Moreover, sets of interrogations are fostered about *what happens to the relations and processes that constitute feminist and women's movements, as such processes are expanded and hyperextended transnationally, over ever-wider expanses of space.* What, for instance, are the difficulties and dilemmas "of political organizing across vast geographic expanses" (Johnston 2003, 93)? What about "the very complex tradeoffs, constraints and contradictions" (Feldman 2002, 42) associated with the rescaling of movement organizing and strategies to include the supranational scale? How are the relationships among the different scales of collective action being reorganized by transnationalization, and what are the related "problems of effecting politics between different geographical scales" (Routledge 2003, 333)? What happens to issues and claims when movements "scale up" to the transnational (Arts 2004; Conway 2005; Featherstone 2003; Routledge 2003; Soyez 2000)? And how do scale and place intertwine in attempts to construct solidarity across and beyond borders (Johnston 2003)?

Spatialities in Transnational Movement Organizing: Unpacking Varieties of Transnationalism

Leaving aside the complex theoretical and political debates about the term "transnational feminism" highlighted in Janet Conway's chapter and the Introduction to this book, it is possible to say that what minimally defines the transnational in movement activity is the cross-border nature of the forms of connectivity established among movement actors, practices, and discourses. The generic use of the scalar term "transnational" for all forms of cross-border connections, in this sense, has its theoretical justifications. From a geographically sensitive point of view, however, such generic use tends to obfuscate the rich variety of the ways in which collective actors construct the transnational scale of movement organizing. While the World March of Women is truly planetary in scope (Beaulieu, this volume), some forms of cross-border organizing, such as the Latin American Encuentros (Alvarez 2000), span world regions (see also Adams 2006; Menon-Sen 2002; Tripp 2005). Other examples reflect an even wider variety of spatial deployments that potentially indicate the existence of very different logics and rationales for transnational association.

For instance, among the transnational feminist networks studied by Valentine M. Moghadam (2005, 174), the Association of Women of the Mediterranean Region (AWMR) "unites women of Albania, Algeria, Cyprus, Egypt, France, Gibraltar, Greece, Israel, Lebanon, Libya, Malta, Morocco, Palestine, Spain, Syria, Tunisia, Turkey" around a variety of issues. Its spatial deployment is bounded by the discursive construction of the Mediterranean as a supra-national scale of movement identification that finds no direct counterpart in existing scales of political regulation. The European Women's Lobby (EWL) (Helfferich and Kolb 2001) and Women in Development in

Europe (WIDE) (Moghadam 2005), in contrast, recruit affiliates in the member states of the European Union as they attempt to influence policy-making in its institutions. The scalar deployment of EWL and WIDE is thus intimately entwined with the scalar reach of the supra-national state space that is its main political target, and it is fated to expand as the EU expands to new member states. Finally, Women Living Under Muslim Laws (WLUML) includes individuals and women's groups from "Muslim countries and communities" and maintains "three coordination offices – an international coordination office in Europe, one in Pakistan (Shirkat Gah) for Asia, and one in Nigeria (Baobob) for Africa" (Moghadam 2005, 162-63). WLUML's membership and action span three continents and aim at linking a diversity of noncontiguous places defined by the presence of institutionalized Islamic rule.

These examples, and those of other transnational feminist networks, such as the Asia-Pacific Research and Resource Organization for Women, the Latin American and Caribbean Women's Health Network (Moghadam 2005, 8, 11), and the Central American Network of Women in Solidarity with Maquila Workers (Mendez 2002), demonstrate that what we generically call the transnational scale of feminist and women's movement organizing exists, in fact, through a diversity of spatial expressions, each of which has its own supranational "stretch" or scale. Transboundary collective actors vary greatly in the geographic origin of the participants they bring together, the expanses of space they span, the spatial reach of their objectives, and the kinds of places they link together. As the above-mentioned examples also make clear, although transnational feminist networks may choose to organize on a scale coterminous with that of their targets, they do not always mimic the planetary scale of global capital or the scales of supranational regulatory institutions (such as the EU and the UN). Adopting a scalar approach thus suggests not only that we take stock of such varieties of transnationalism, but also that we further unpack the transnational by inquiring into the diverse rationales and logics of association that shape the concrete spatialities of feminist and women's transnational organizing. Thus, a scalar approach would stress the importance of bringing into view the historical dynamics of the constitution of these new spatialities – and the way these eventually shift and change (see Dufour and Giraud 2007).

The Multiscalar Character of Transnational Organizing and Action
Scales, human and political geographers tell us, are not discrete entities that can be studied in isolation. As Neil Brenner (2001, 605) notes in a

much-quoted passage, "The meaning, function, history and dynamic of any geographical scale can only be grasped relationally, in terms of its upwards, downwards, and sidewards links to other geographical scales situated within tangled scalar hierarchies and dispersed interscalar networks." In short, scales are relational. Processes being deployed at one scale may be influenced by, and have a direct relationship with, similar or different processes occurring at other scales. Feminist and women's movements, as we know, organize and act at a variety of scales, of which the growth in transnational organizing is only the most recent instantiation. "What is important," Virginie Mamadouh, Olivier Kramsch, and Martin Van Der Velde (2004, 457) argue, "is to understand the coexistence of multiple scales." Examining transnational organizing and action through a multiscalar, rather than a uniscalar, lens directs our attention toward exploring the linkages between the transnational and other scales of feminist and women's movement activity. How do transnational organizing and activity involve relationships with other scales? What kind of interscalar arrangements and dynamics are at play in these relations?

The multiscalar character of transnational organizing, it is important to note, may be difficult to appreciate from some current feminist work, such as Moghadam's (2005), that focuses almost solely on the supra-, trans-, or international dimension of organizing. Surely, such focus enables us to see how feminist and women's movement actors come together to create cross-border organizations and networks, mobilize the resources necessary for their functioning, produce diagnostic analyses and plans of action, and disseminate information and coordinate campaigns at the transnational scale. Yet, Moghadam's rendition of transnational feminist organizing is a very "flat" one: organizational dynamics seem to occur on a two-dimensional plane, internal processes and relations within these networks extending mostly, if not exclusively, horizontally. Although Moghadam (2005, 13) alludes to the fact that some of the transnational feminist networks that she studied have regional offices (WLULM, Development Alternatives with Women for a New Era [DAWN]) or member groups in different countries (AWMR, WIDE), and connections with what she calls "local partners," she says very little about this more vertical dimension of organizing. Most importantly, the linkages and dynamics existing between the parent organization and the constituent parts of the network remain obscure and untheorized. Transnational women's movement organizations and networks, I argue here, need to be analyzed as three-dimensional phenomena.

For Paul Routledge (2003, 336), for instance, transnational networks are "embedded in different places at a variety of spatial scales" through their member organizations, which become "links of various length in the network." Further, the "different geographic scales" of the constituent parts of a network, and the network itself, he suggests, "are mutually constitutive." Jennifer Bickham Mendez's (2002) study of the Central American Network of Women in Solidarity with Maquila Workers, although it does not adopt the theoretical vocabulary of scale, provides an empirical basis for demonstrating how transnational women's movement networks can be seen as instances of mutually constitutive, multiscalar organizing. Composed of autonomous women's organizations from Guatemala, Honduras, Nicaragua, and El Salvador, the network engages in information politics, disseminating data on "what happens behind the closed doors of the Maquila factories" (Mendez 2002, 130). It can do such work only through the involvement of its local member groups, which monitor labour conditions, human rights violations, and work processes within the *maquiladoras*. Member groups also run local programs for Maquila workers, educating them about their labour, human, and civil rights and about violence and sexual abuse. All of this material is circulated at network meetings and is shared and made available across borders to other member groups. The activities of the network and its member groups are thus closely imbricated and, furthermore, feed into one another and are dependent on one another. This illustrates what is meant by the relational and "mutually constitutive" character of scales in multiscalar organizing.

Although it may certainly involve professional social movement organizations, which exist and act solely in supranational contexts, transnational movement organizing, especially in its networked form, typically involves more than one scale. Some of the questions that should arise at this point for feminist scholars have to do with the scalar morphology of these forms of cross-border organizing. Do these organizational structures involve international and continental platforms, as DAWN does? Or do they bring together European and national organizations, as WIDE and EWL do? Or are they, rather, "trans-local" cross-border linkages, as can be seen in the collaboration between the (Madison) Wisconsin Coordinating Council on Nicaragua and the (Managua-based) Nicaraguan March 8 Intercollective documented by Claire Weber (2002)? Perhaps more important, how are the constituent parts of these transnational organizations and networks involved in doing transnational work – from their locally, nationally, or continentally embedded positions? What kinds of linkages, divisions of labour, and sorts of interscalar arrangements organize their life and activities? What internal tensions exist, if any, and what kinds of movement politics arise from such interscalar dynamics?

As the above examples indicate, we cannot assume that the internal operations of transnational feminist and women's organizations and networks are bound to the transnational scale. The existence and strength of these bonds is a subject for empirical research. Furthermore, transnational organizations and networks often engage in lobbying, protest, and collaboration at a variety of scales. Bas Arts (2004, 499), for instance, argues that transnational NGOs "such as Greenpeace, World Wide Fund for Nature, Pax Christi, Oxfam and Amnesty International have become effective political players at different governance levels: local, regional, national and international." In fact, transnational feminist networks, Moghadam (2005, 20) indicates, simultaneously target "local structures, national governments and global institutions." An interesting avenue for feminist research is, thus, the extent to which and the ways in which transnational feminist and women's organizations and networks are engaged in multiscalar action. What kinds of organizational structure and resources support or hinder their multiscalar activity? How are member groups and other women's movement organizations at other scales enrolled and within what kinds of interscalar arrangements? What kinds of difficulties does the enactment of such multiscalar activism encounter? And how effective is it?

Finally, carrying out and sustaining cross-border, multiscalar politics – be it in the form of social movement organization, network, coalition, or event – is not without intrinsic problems, due largely to bringing together and coordinating social movement actors anchored in different scales of organizing. "Geographical dilemmas arise in the attempt to prosecute multiscalar politics," Routledge (2003, 343) writes, "because activists tend to be more closely linked to the local, national or regional movements in which their struggles are embedded than to international networks." As Routledge shows in the case of People's Global Action, in a context of limited resources (time, energy, finances), the immediate imperatives of everyday, place-based struggles may jostle uneasily with parallel commitments to transnational engagement. Similarly, Pascale Dufour and Isabelle Giraud (2005) highlight the tension that arose for feminist grassroots activists in Quebec between the demands of their local and national struggles and the call for their participation in the transnational actions organized by the World March of Women.

Sociospatial Inequalities in Transnational Mobilizations

Another central issue raised by a scalar approach is that of unequal access to and participation in the (generically understood) transnational scale of activism for differently emplaced people. One of the salient characteristics of transnational networks, Flusty (2004, 10) suggests, may reside in the irregular spatial dispersion of their participants. In her study of the Indymedia network, Virginie Mamadouh (2004, 493) remarks, "Despite its truly global reach, the network is rooted in some places more than others. All continents are represented, but the distribution is skewed ... [with] three-quarters of the sites (96 sites) for the global North." Since transnationalization involves organizing over vast geographical expanses, it requires that movement organizers and network participants solve the problems posed by distance through the capacity for time-space compression – the contraction of time (through increased speed) and space (through increased mobility) made possible by recent economic, political, and technological developments. Yet, as Massey (1994, 148) aptly notes, "Time-space compression has not been happening for everyone in all spheres of activity." There is a "power-geometry of time-space compression," she argues: it needs to be differentiated socially and spatially (Massey 1994, 149).

The means of time-space compression are unequally distributed among people and places. Regarding the capacity to use the Internet for information-age transnational activism, Mamadouh (2004, 489) points to the existence of a "technological divide" between techies and ordinary participants, a (well-documented) "gendered digital divide," and a sociospatial divide "between a wired North and a poorly wired South." The last aspect evidently plays out in the above-mentioned geographical unevenness of the Indymedia network. It also does so in the Zapatismo transnational network studied by Josée Johnston (2003, 96), shaping power differentials between a privileged elite's "easy access to electronic information network and *Chiapaneco* struggles where participants are primarily indigenous and do not have access to computers." In addition, differences exist in terms of the means of physical mobility between a cosmopolitan group of mobile global activists, who enjoy the privileges of financial resources and the ability and freedom to travel internationally, and more place-bound actual or potential participants (Conway 2005; Johnston 2003; Routledge 2003). Such differences have occasionally been noted in feminist and women's movement transnational organizing, especially regarding attendance at UN women's conferences and NGO forums (Basu 2000; Desai 2002, 2005).

Thus, places – and positionality in those places, since there exist elites in the South and underprivileged "others" in the North – play a role in shaping a variety of power differentials that have real consequences for transnational organizing in terms of the density and spatial dispersion of participants in organizations, networks, or events, as well as their scalar reach and the kinds of places that they link together. Mapping and comparing these various spatialities would enable feminist scholars to mark overlaps, gaps, irregularities, and unevenness in transnational organizing in ways that would help to disaggregate further the apparent homogeneity of the transnational as a scale of feminist and women's movement activity. It would also illuminate, in different ways, the issues of access to transnational organizing and of the strategies developed by feminist and women's movement actors to circumvent the constraints posed by place and positionality on time-space compression.

Transnationalizing Frames of Collective Action

In social movement theory, collective action frames are discursive matrixes constructed by movement actors to make sense of social relations and endow them with meaning with the purpose of guiding action. "Collective action frames ... (a) construct a social grievance by defining an existing condition as unjust *(name)*, (b) attribute blame for the grievance, identifying a target of collective response *(blame)*, and (c) suggest responses or solutions to the grievance *(claim)*" (Kurtz 2003, 894, emphasis in original). When collective actors upscale and go transnational, it is argued, they produce qualitatively different discursive framings by attempting to mutualize resistant place-based identities and claims while setting these at a higher scale – supranational, international, global, planetary. Through transnational practices and discourses, organizations, networks, events, and meetings, feminist and women's movement actors do attempt to upscale issues, mutualize grievances and claims, and represent a broad constituency of women spanning a wide variety of place-based collectivities. Yet, transnational framing processes are not without tensions: there are intrinsic difficulties associated with going transnational and trying to "represent the needs, interests, and visions of such a diverse array of peoples" (Feldman 2002, 36).

Here, the geographically sensitive literature on transnational movement politics shares with feminist literature an interest in the impact of social inequalities on representation. Power differentials regarding the means of time-space compression are seen as having a direct bearing on the framing of claims in transnational movement politics: they determine whose voices are, in practice, in a position to contribute to the processes of transnational frame construction. In addition to affecting participation, sociospatial inequalities may locate actual participants "in distinct (more or less powerful) ways in relation to the flows and interconnections involved in the functioning of [transnational] resistance networks" (Routledge 2003, 337). These remarks speak directly to the issues of voice, discursive dominance and marginalization, and inclusion and exclusion, which are among the main concerns of the feminist literature on transnationalization in feminist and women's movements (see the Introduction to this book). Both bodies of literature thus follow similar lines of questioning: Whose voices are represented, and whose voices are heard? Whose are ignored or silenced? Whose claims are included or excluded? What exactly is mutualized in the production of transnational discourses, frames, agendas, and strategies, and on whose terms? And with what kind of consequences for the pursuit of movement politics? Geographically sensitive analyses of transnational framing processes differ from feminist ones, however, in granting a stronger role to place in the dynamics of transnational frame construction.

One of the main arguments of the geographically sensitive literature on transnational movement politics is the embeddedness of framings in the specificities of place. As social relations of gender, class, ethnicity, and so on are deployed in time and space, they shape places through distinct articulations, layers, and mixtures of "wider and more local social relations," as we have seen earlier with Massey (1994, 156). In doing so, they produce material realities that are both similar, in the sense that they are related to similar processes, and different, in the specificity of their historical and geographical instantiations. Place matters for framing processes, on the one hand, because of the differing realities that collective actors are embedded in, speaking from, and speaking about, and, on the other hand, as Dietrich Soyez (2000, 12) contends, because the discourses in which issues are framed are produced within "geographically differentiated assignments of meaning." To capture these variations, Soyez (2000, 13) offers the notion of "regional discourse formations" anchored in the material and cultural specificities of place (as a spatial unit of analysis that is not confined to "the local"). A similar point is made by Byron Miller (2000, 60), who argues that "place-specific circumstances" lead to the construction of collective action frames – of identity construction, problem identification, diagnostic analyses, and claims-making processes – that "vary from place to place." From a geographically sensitive perspective, the analytical questions that arise when feminist and women's movement actors upscale and engage in transnational alliance formation include: "What actually occurs when distant partners, who grew up in regions with totally different discourse formations, come into contact with each other?" (Soyez 2000, 13). How do transnational organizations and networks negotiate the constitution of increasingly spatially stretched, higher-scale discursive frames with the place-based movement actors that are their constituents, or participate in transnational events? And with regard to more strategic concerns, the questions are how to find a common ground among emplaced actors and how to "effectively create alternative imagined communities of solidarity ... when the scale is broadened to this extent" (Johnston 2003, 94).

Works by Conway and David Featherstone highlight some of the important ways in which "place matters" in transnational frame construction. The travels of the World Social Forum (WSF) and the multiplication of social forums at a variety of scales illustrate, according to Conway (2005, 4), the "significance of the territoriality of the ... event in determining who participated in what numbers, the themes, issues and alternatives under discussion, and the horizon of possible futures." Moving the WSF from Porto Alegre to Mumbai in 2004, for instance, considerably transformed the nature of participation in it – previously a "primarily light-skinned affair of the middle-class and non-poor" (Conway 2007, 10). The notable presence of Indian Adivasi (indigenous) peoples in Mumbai foregrounded issues of subsistence rights and "force[d] ecological questions at the center of the WSF's agenda" (Conway 2004, 358). The mobilization of Dalit (Untouchable) movements in Mumbai brought new issues, such as casteism and religious communalism, into the WSF's Charter of Principles. The holding of the 2005 Social Forum of the Americas in Quito enabled strong involvement by South American indigenous networks, and the representation of self-governance issues, the defence of indigenous identities and ancestral lands, and cultural diversity and biodiversity (Conway 2005). Social forums, Conway (2007, 52) further argues, "assume ... specificities that flow from space and scale, the historical-geographical conjuncture in which the process/event occurs, and the discourses, practices, preoccupations and strategies of the social movements and organizations that constitute any particular iteration of the forum." The implication of Conway's work is that transnational feminist and women's movement encounters, especially those of a participatory nature, are not placeless events and that the specificity of such "culturally-specific, geographically rooted social movement processes" (Conway 2005, 14) is certainly worth investigating by feminist scholars.

Conway provides very little indication of the political dynamics that have accompanied the transformations of the WSF transnational frame. However, the existence of potentially complex political dynamics between differently emplaced actors is highlighted in Featherstone's (2003) analysis of the 1999 London meeting of the Inter-Continental Caravan for Solidarity and Resistance. The Caravan's process of constructing a common frame of action against neoliberalism and biotechnologies was highly contentious on this occasion, and "was decisively shaped by the Karnataka State Farmer's Union" (KSFU) of India (Featherstone 2003, 406). With a contingent of four hundred representatives, the KSFU articulated Indian nationalist identities and understandings of globalization that "did not allow positive identifications to be constructed with others struggling against similar power geometries" (Featherstone 2003, 415) – in particular, Nepal. Yet, the emplacement of Indian activists allowed for more productive framings to be shared, for instance, around the issue of genetically modified seeds. Adoption of the KSFU slogan "No patents on life" enabled the Caravan as a whole to move away from prior European-based concerns with "'the threat of mixing' and other disruptions of the imagined 'purity' of the plants," marred by an undercurrent of eugenics (Featherstone 2003, 416). Bringing together a constellation of geographically emplaced actors, grievances, and visions of the world, Featherstone concludes, is "both a condition of possibility for these transnational alliances" and at the same time "exert[s] pressure on the formation of solidarities" (Featherstone 2003, 404).

These two examples advocate strongly for feminist analyses that integrate more specific geographical understandings of "place" into accounts of transnational framing processes and related power dynamics. There is a need for feminist scholars to go beyond loose geographical references to "North/South" or "First/Third World" divides and toward more in-depth analyses foregrounding the difference that place – the emplacement of events as well as the emplaced character of collective actors – makes in the construction of transnational framings in feminist and women's movements. Such an analysis, it is important to note, should rely neither on deterministic visions of place nor on essentializing or overly homogenizing accounts of place-based politics. Rather, it should highlight the ways in which feminist and women's movement actors draw on the – historical, cultural, and political; material and discursive – resources and circumstances of place to position themselves, along with and in tension with other actors, in their attempts to negotiate the mutualization of issues, grievances, and claims in transnational settings.

In addition, "successful international alliances have to negotiate between action that is deeply embedded in place, i.e., local experiences, social relations and power conditions, and action that facilitates broad transnational coalitions" (Routledge 2003, 336). Such negotiations may unfold in a variety of ways. Existing transnational frames may be the result of "voluntary or imposed adoption," "conflict," or marginalization or exclusion, as well as of "unhindered diffusion," "blending," or "hybridization" (Soyez 2000, 14). Accordingly, feminist scholars could probe more deeply the politics of transnational frame construction by attending not only, as they currently do, to conflict and to the (re)production of various hegemonies, but also to dynamics of cross-fertilization and innovation. Furthermore, conscious strategies may be developed by movement actors in their efforts to create common ground at the transnational scale. Transnational frames, suggest Routledge (2003) and Conway (2005), work better in terms of fostering inclusiveness and solidarity when they respect place-based difference. Such inclusiveness seems to be facilitated when unifying frames are explicitly open to interpretation "by participant movements in the context of their differing local realities" (Routledge 2003, 338) -- as occurred with the platform of the 2000 World March of Women, as analyzed by Isabelle Giraud (2001). Unity-creating strategies, as well as the historical dynamic of interaction, respect, and mutual learning among differently emplaced movement actors, must therefore also be taken into account in analyses of continuity and change in feminist and women's movement transnational framings. The extent to which the difficulties and dilemmas of transnational bridge-building across spaces, places, and scales of movement organizing are productively tackled through a feminist politics of difference and recognition or other forms of feminist transversal politics (Yuval-Davis 2006) is an empirical question that needs more attention from feminist scholars.

Finally, from the remarks made so far about the role of place, we cannot readily assume that existing feminist transnational framings are fully able to transcend place-based particularisms, as Moghadam (2005), for instance, would like us to believe. That such transcendence exists is, again, an empirical question that can be avoided neither by invocations of "global feminism" nor by other seemingly placeless framings of women's issues. That such transcendence or that truly universal framings are effectively possible at the transnational scale should not be taken for granted. Rather, it should remain an open and debated issue.

Conclusion

In this chapter, I have explored and attempted to clarify how thinking in terms of scale, with input from recent developments in human and political geography, may contribute to building a new research agenda for feminist scholars interested in transnationalization in feminist and women's movements. Specific questions arise when scholars look at movements and transnationalization through the lens of scale (and place). I have tried to sketch out the lines of inquiry that this literature suggests for feminist scholars and to demonstrate both their interest and relevance.

Developing a scalar approach to studying transnationalization in feminist and women's movements, I have suggested, means turning our attention to the different processes that constitute collective action – organizing, action, mobilization, framing – as these processes get extended across borders and over ever-wider expanses of space, and to the difficulties and dilemmas that arise in such endeavours. Adopting the constructionist view of scale offered by human and political geography implies that such research cannot rely on a conception of the transnational scale as fixed or pre-given to movement action. Because scale exists not in itself but only as a property of process, our analysis must attend to the ways in which feminist and women's movement actors construct themselves at the transnational scale and, in turn, construct "the transnational" as a scale of women's movement activity. To borrow from Erik Swyngedouw (1997b, 14), our "[analytical] priority ... never resides in a particular geographic scale, but rather in the process[es] through which particular scales become [constituted and] reconstituted." In this regard, I have suggested that our analysis should shed light on the various histories, rationales, and logics of association that account for the wide spatial and scalar variations noted in feminist and women's movement transnationalism, as well as on the material and discursive construction of such a transnational scale of activity. The role of place (and positionality) in shaping the density, dispersion, reach, and limits of transnational women's movement organizing also needs to be assessed and more fully documented. Furthermore, transnationalization does not occur in a void but as part of a multiscalar world of movement organizing and politics. An important part of our research agenda is thus, certainly, to explore the interscalar arrangements, interactions, dynamics, and difficulties that are involved in the organizational life and activities of transnational feminist organizations and networks. Linkages between the transnational and other scales of feminist and women's movement activity need to be elucidated and the dynamic and changing character of relations between such scales illuminated. Finally, how do feminist and women's movement framings change as collective actors not only upscale but attempt to mutualize an increasingly wide array of place-based constituencies, identities, grievances, and claims? What is the role of place in these encounters? How are place-based differences negotiated? And with what kinds of outcomes and/or consequences for feminist and women's movement politics at various scales? These are the kind of questions that, a scalar approach suggests, could contribute to guiding future feminist inquiries.

NOTES

1 See, in particular, Dufour and Giraud (2007), Tarrow and McAdam (2005).
2 For a brief review and bibliographical indications see Mamadouh, Kramsch, and Van Der Velde (2004, 455-57).
3 See, for instance, Brenner (1999, 2004), MacLeod and Goodwin (1999), Swyngedouw (1997a).

REFERENCES

Adams, Melinda. 2006. Regional Women's Activism: African Women's Networks and the African Union. In *Global Feminism: Transnational Women's Activism, Organizing, and Human Rights,* ed. Myra Marx Ferree and Aili Mari Tripp, 187-218. New York: New York University Press.

Agnew, John. 1997. The Dramaturgy of Horizons: Geographical Scale in the Reconstruction of Italy by the New Italian Political Parties, 1992-95. *Political Geography* 16 (2): 99-121.

Alvarez, Sonia E. 2000. Translating the Global: Effects of Transnational Organizing on Local Feminist Discourses and Practices and Latin America. *Meridians: Feminism, Race, Transnationalism* 1 (1): 29-67.

Arts, Bas. 2004. The Global-Local Nexus: NGOs and the Articulation of Scale. *Tijdschrift voor economische en sociale geografie* 95 (5): 498-510.

Basu, Amrita. 2000. Globalization of the Local/Localization of the Global: Mapping Transnational Women's Movements. *Meridians: Feminism, Race, Transnationalism* 1 (1): 68-84.

Beaulieu, Elsa. 2007. Échelles et lieux de l'action collective dans la Marche mondiale des femmes au Brésil. *Lien social et politiques* 58: 119-32.

Brenner, Neil. 1999. Globalization as Reterritorialisation: The Rescaling of Urban Governance in the European Union. *Urban Studies* 36 (3): 431-51.

–. 2001. The Limit to Scale? Methodological Reflections on Scalar Structuration. *Progress in Human Geography* 25 (4): 591-614.

–. 2004. *New State Spaces: Urban Governance and the Rescaling of Statehood.* Oxford: Oxford University Press.

Conway, Janet. 2004. Place Matters: India's Challenge to Brazil at the World Social Forum. *Antipode* 36 (3): 357-60.

—. 2005. The Empire, the Movement, and the Politics of Scale: Considering the World Social Forum. Paper presented at the conference *Towards a Political Economy of Scale*, 3-5 February, York University, Toronto.

—. 2006. Alternative Globalizations and the Politics of Scale: Considering the World Social Forum and the World March of Women. Unpublished paper, April.

—. 2007. Transnational Feminisms and the World Social Forum: Encounters and Transformations in Anti-Globalization Spaces. *Journal of International Women's Studies* 8 (3): 49-70.

Desai, Manisha. 2002. Transnational Solidarity: Women's Agency, Structural Adjustment, and Globalization. In *Women's Activism and Globalization: Linking Local Struggles and Transnational Politics*, ed. Nancy A. Naples and Manisha Desai, 15-33. New York: Routledge.

—. 2005. Transnationalism: The Face of Feminist Politics post-Beijing. *International Social Science Journal* 57 (184): 319-30.

Dufour, Pascale, and Isabelle Giraud. 2005. Altermondialisme et féminisme: pourquoi faire? Le cas de la Marche mondiale des femmes. *Chroniques féministes* 93 (August/December): 9-16.

—. 2007. Globalization and Political Change in the Women's Movement: The Politics of Scale and Political Empowerment in the World March of Women. *Social Science Quarterly* 88 (5): 1152-73.

Escobar, Arturo, and Wendy Harcourt. 2005. Introduction: Practices of Difference: Introducing *Women and the Politics of Place*. In *Women and the Politics of Place*, ed. Wendy Harcourt and Arturo Escobar, 1-17. Bloomfield: Kumarian Press.

Featherstone, David. 2003. Spatialities of Transnational Resistance to Globalization: The Maps of Grievance of the Inter-Continental Caravan. *Transactions of the Institute of British Geographers* 28: 404-21.

Feldman, Alice. 2002. Making Space at the Nations' Table: Mapping the Transformative Geographies of the International Indigenous Peoples' Movement. *Social Movement Studies* 1 (1): 31-46.

Flusty, Steven. 2004. *De-coca-colonization: Making the Globe from the Inside Out.* New York and London: Routledge.

Friedman, Susan Stanford. 2001. Locational Feminism: Gender, Cultural Geographies and Geopolitical Literacy. In *Feminist Locations: Global and Local, Theory and Practice*, ed. Marianne DeKoven, 13-36. New Brunswick, NJ: Rutgers University Press.

Giraud, Isabelle. 2001. La transnationalisation des solidarités: l'exemple de la marche mondiale des femmes. *Lien social et politiques* 45: 145-60.

Grewal, Inderpal, and Caren Kaplan. 1994. Introduction: Transnational Feminist Practices and Questions of Postmodernity. In *Scattered Hegemonies: Postmodernity and Transnational Feminist Practices*, ed. Inderpal Grewal and Caren Kaplan, 1-33. Minneapolis: University of Minnesota Press.

Helfferich, Barbara, and Felix Kolb. 2001. Multilevel Action Coordination in European Contentious Politics: The Case of the European Women's Lobby. In *Contentious Europeans: Protest and Politics in an Integrating Europe*, ed. Doug Imig and Sidney Tarrow, 163-86. Lanham: Rowman and Littlefield.

Herod, Andrew. 1997. Labor's Spatial Praxis and the Geography of Contract Bargaining in the U.S. East Coast Longshore Industry, 1953-1989. *Political Geography* 16 (2): 145-69.

Johnston, Josée. 2003. "We Are All Marcos"? Zapatismo, Solidarity and the Politics of Scale. In *The Global Civil Society and Its Limits*, ed. Gordon Laxer and Sandra Halperin, 85-104. New York: Palgrave MacMillan.

Kaplan, Caren. 1994. The Politics of Location as Transnational Feminist Critical Practice. In *Scattered Hegemonies: Postmodernity and Transnational Feminist Practices*, ed. Inderpal Grewal and Caren Kaplan, 137-52. Minneapolis: University of Minnesota Press.

Kurtz, Hilda. 2003. Scale Frames and Counter-scale Frames: Constructing the Problem of Environmental Injustice. *Political Geography* 22: 887-916.

MacLeod, Gordon, and Mark Goodwin. 1999. Space, Scale and State Strategy: Rethinking Urban and Regional Governance. *Progress in Human Geography* 23 (4): 503-27.

Mamadouh, Virginie. 2004. Internet, Scale and the Global Grassroots: Geographies of the Indymedia Network of Independent Media Centers. *Tijdschrift voor economische en sociale geografie* 95 (5): 482-97.

Mamadouh, Virginie, Olivier Kramsch, and Martin Van Der Velde. 2004. Articulating Local and Global Scales. *Tijdschrift voor economische en sociale geografie* 95 (5): 455-66.

Massey, Doreen. 1994. A Global Sense of Place. In *Space, Place, and Gender*, 146-56. Minneapolis: University of Minnesota Press.

Masson, Dominique. 2006. Constructing Scale/Contesting Scale: Women's Movement and Rescaling Politics in Québec. *Social Politics – International Studies in Gender, State and Society* 13 (4): 462-86.

Mendez, Jennifer Bickham. 2002. Creating Alternatives from a Gender Perspective: Transnational Organizing for Maquila Worker's Rights in Central America. In *Women's Activism and Globalization: Linking Local Struggles and Transnational Politics*, ed. Nancy A. Naples and Manisha Desai, 121-41. New York: Routledge.

Menon-Sen, Kalyani. 2002. Bridges Over Troubled Waters: South Asian Women's Movements Confronting Globalization. *Development* 45 (1): 132-36.

Miller, Byron. 1997. Political Action and the Geography of Defense Investment: Geographical Scale and the Representation of the Massachusetts Miracle. *Political Geography* 16 (2): 171-85.

–. 2000. *Geography and Social Movements: Comparing Antinuclear Activism in the Boston Area*. Minneapolis: University of Minnesota Press.

–. 2005. Is Scale a Chaotic Concept? Network and Scalar Dynamics of Social Struggle. Paper presented at the *Annual Studies in Political Economy Conference: Towards a Political Economy of Scale*, 3-5 February, York University, Toronto.

Moghadam, Valentine M. 2005. *Globalizing Women: Transnational Feminist Networks*. Baltimore: Johns Hopkins University Press.

Mohanty, Chandra Talpade. 2003. *Feminism without Borders: Decolonizing Theory, Practicing Solidarity*. Durham: Duke University Press.

Routledge, Paul. 2003. Convergence Space: Process Geographies of Grassroots Globalization Networks. *Transactions of the Institute of British Geographers* 28: 333-49.

Sewell, William H. Jr. 2001. Space in Contentious Politics. In *Silence and Voice in the Study of Contentious Politics,* ed. Ronald R. Aminzade, Jack A. Goldstone, Doug McAdam, Elizabeth J. Perry, William H. Sewell, Sidney Tarrow, and Charles Tilly, 51-88. Cambridge: Cambridge University Press.

Silvern, Steven E. 1999. Scales of Justice: Law, American Indian Treaty Rights and the Political Construction of Scale. *Political Geography* 18: 639-68.

Soyez, Dietrich. 2000. Anchored Locally – Linked Globally: Transnational Social Movement Organizations in a (Seemingly) Borderless World. *GeoJournal* 52: 7-16.

Swyngedouw, Erik. 1997a. Excluding the Other: The Production of Scale and Scaled Politics. In *Geographies of Economies,* ed. Roger Lee and Jane Wills, 167-76. London: Arnold.

–. 1997b. Neither Global Nor Local: "Glocalization" and the Politics of Scale. In *Spaces of Globalization: Reasserting the Power of the Local,* ed. Kevin R. Cox, 137-66. New York and London: Guilford Press.

Tarrow, Sidney, and Doug McAdam. 2005. Scale Shift in Transnational Contention. In *Transnational Protest and Global Activism,* ed. Donatella della Porta and Sidney Tarrow, 121-47. Lanham: Rowman and Littlefield.

Towers, George. 2000. Applying the Political Geography of Scale: Grassroots Strategies and Environmental Justice. *Professional Geographer* 52 (1): 23-36.

Tripp, Aili Mari. 2005. Regional Networking as Transnational Feminism: African Experiences, Feminist Africa, April. http://www.feministafrica.org/.

Weber, Clare. 2002. Women to Women: Dissident Citizen Diplomacy in Nicaragua. In *Women's Activism and Globalization: Linking Local Struggles and Transnational Politics,* ed. Nancy A. Naples and Manisha Desai, 45-63. New York: Routledge.

Yuval-Davis, Nira. 2006. Human/Women's Rights and Feminist Transversal Politics. In *Global Feminism: Transnational Women's Activism, Organizing, and Human Rights,* ed. Myra Marx Ferree and Aili Mari Tripp, 187-218. New York: New York University Press.

2

Theorizing Feminist and Social Movement Practice in Space

ELSA BEAULIEU

In an influential critique, Richard Flacks (2004) argued that the currently hegemonic paradigms in social movement studies – the "resource mobilization" perspective elaborated in the 1970s and the "political contention" framework derived from it – fall short of providing useful knowledge for those seeking social change and, I would add, for those trying to understand social change brought about by social movements. Flacks attributes this to the failure to adequately address the cultural and psychological dimensions of social movements and the fundamental structural issues of power inequalities. Other critiques of these paradigms have pointed in similar directions (see, for example, Buechler 2000; Guidry, Kennedy, and Zald 2000).[1] In my view, these critiques apply equally well to research on transnational social movements. Moreover, if the dominant frameworks fail to provide useful understandings of social change in general, they are likely to be of little use for feminism and the transformation of gender relations. Numerous feminists have advocated for the inclusion of gender as an analytical category in these frameworks (see, for example, Ferree and Roth 1998; Reger and Taylor 2002; Taylor and Whittier 1998, 1999). In my view, however, merely integrating gender as a peripheral analytical category in existing frameworks cannot be sufficient to gain an understanding of the dynamics of change in gender relations, because these frameworks are not designed to answer such research questions. Yet, for all the space in feminist literature dedicated to debating specific strategies for change and their outcomes, and despite the close relationship between feminist thought and feminist organizing, there is still no explicitly constituted body of feminist theory that views social movements as a means of transforming gender relations. One of the most extensively studied aspects of social movements is the demands that they make on the state, and the results and impacts of these in terms of laws and public policies. This is, indeed, one of the most important social movement strategies, and one that is widely used by feminist movements. I wish to focus on another aspect that has received less scholarly attention: the transformative potential of the building of ties of political solidarity among women across geographical space as a central aspect of feminist strategies for effecting changes in gender relations.

This chapter thus aims to elaborate on conceptual tools that are useful for understanding social movements in general, and transnational feminist movements in particular, as loci of social change. In the first part, I propose a general framework for expanding the definition of what is to be considered political, and for conceptualizing movement practices in terms that can help connect them to the production of new embodied experiences and political subjectivities, concrete struggles, and transformation of the prevailing gender orders. This will be done in two steps. The first step consists of an argument calling for expansion of the definition of what is considered political and of which social movement practices are worthy of study in relation to social change, drawing on contributions dealing with the cultural politics of social movements (Alvarez, Dagnino, and Escobar 1998). However, if we are to truly expand the range of practices considered relevant to the study of social movements as loci of social change, we need a more general theorization that can connect concrete and varied social practices to the reproduction and transformation of social orders. The second step thus explores reinterpretations of practice theory aimed at theorizing social transformation (Connell 1987; Crossley 2002, 2003, 2005; Ortner 1996, 2006), which I will relate to the study of social movements by suggesting relevant lines of inquiry. The second part of the chapter applies this framework to some of the spatial dimensions of transnational feminist organizing. More specifically, I look at the multiplication of scales of collective action through the lens of some feminist practices, particularly women-only meetings. I draw on conceptualizations of space, place, and scale proposed by Doreen Massey (1994, 2006) and Dominique Masson (this volume) in my analysis of the multiplication of scales of collective actions anchored in specific places and of the impact that this can have on gender relations.

By bringing together, in a new way, a relatively eclectic set of authors, I hope to contribute to the general project of understanding the various ways in which social movements contribute to social change. My purpose is to use theoretical discussions to elaborate hypotheses on the basis of which to formulate new research questions, or find fresh ways to ask old ones. I will not try to empirically answer all of these questions here, but I will use examples in the second part of the chapter to illustrate more concretely some of my arguments. My examples are drawn from the World March of Women (WMW) in Brazil, the subject of my doctoral research project for which I conducted multi-sited ethnographic fieldwork and interviews from 2004 to 2007. However, these examples do not constitute a complete case study, nor are they the result of an exhaustive analysis of my data.

Conceptualizing Social Movement Practice

My point of departure is the commitment to conceptualize social movements as producers and bearers of world visions and projects of change, and as producers of "oppositional culture" (Taylor and Whittier 1995), and not merely as predictable players in taken-for-granted political games, lobbies, or sectors of liberal democracies. I suggest drawing inspiration from anthropologists and ethnographers studying social movements (see, for example, Nash 2005). As I understand it, they start from the *situation* that is the object of the project of change, a dimension that has been utterly evacuated from resource mobilization and political contention frameworks (Buechler 2000; Crossley 2002). Then, the idea is to examine the complex mediations whereby actors are subjected to and comply with (or resist) structural constraints and produce understandings of the means (symbolic, material, relational, and institutional) by which they can seize or create opportunities for collective action and seek to produce or orient processes of change – including through the production of alternative subjectivities and social relations within the process of collective organization. It is thus necessary to investigate the relationship between the projects of change and the actual practices of social movements, including the organizational practices and social relations enacted within and around these projects and practices.

In order to give analytical visibility to social movements' practices in relation to the subversion of social hierarchies and power relations, two conceptual steps must be taken. The first is to expand the conventional definition of what is to be considered political and overcome the radical division between the cultural and the political on which political sociology and political science, and the theories on social movements issued from these disciplines, were originally built. Unlike some eminent students of contentious politics, feminist scholars studying feminist and women's movements have long argued in favour of this shift (see Reger and Taylor 2002; Staggenborg and Taylor 2005; West and Blumberg 1990).[2] According to these scholars, the narrow conception of the political used in social movement studies has rendered invisible important dimensions of practices in feminist and women's movements. The second step is to work out a conceptualization of practice that gives adequate analytical visibility to the socially productive dimensions of social and political practices, thereby bringing into view some of the less-studied mechanisms with which social movements and collective action might produce social and political change. I believe that bringing together the various solutions to these conceptual problems, which were put forth by Sonia E. Alvarez, Evelina Dagnino, and Arturo Escobar (1998), Sherry B. Ortner (1996, 2006), and Nick Crossley (2002, 2003, 2005), may be of significant assistance for the present purposes.

Expanding the Conceptualization of the Political

In the 1990s, an expansion of the conceptualization of the political was attempted through exploration of the relationship between politics and cultures in social movements. One of the most interesting contributions to this project is that of Alvarez, Dagnino, and Escobar (1998), who draw on two main concepts: *cultural politics* and *political cultures*. Rather than seeing "culture" as a separate sphere or secondary variable, as do most mainstream social movement studies in the United States (Buechler 2000), these authors stress the importance of understanding the inseparability and mutual constitution of power, meanings, material practices, and material conditions. They see the "conceptualization and investigation of the cultural politics of social movements" as a promising way to understand "the tension between the textual and that which underlies it, between representation and its grounding, between meanings and practices, between narratives and social actors, between discourse and power" and see how the "vital entanglement of the cultural and the political occurs in practice" (Alvarez, Dagnino, and Escobar 1998, 5).

Alvarez, Dagnino, and Escobar (1998, 8) define *political culture* as "the particular social construction in every society of what counts as 'political.'" This concept highlights the social constructedness of how what is actually open to political debate is defined, and how these political struggles are to be conducted. It can also serve to challenge what is studied as political practice within social movement studies, while providing analytical (and empirical) visibility to some important practices emerging from women's and feminist movements. *Cultural politics,* in turn, are enacted by social movements to challenge the dominant social and political orders, including political cultures. Alvarez, Dagnino, and Escobar concur with Jordan and Weedon's definition of cultural politics:

> The legitimation of social relations of inequality, and the struggle to transform them, are central to cultural politics. Cultural politics fundamentally determine the meanings of social practices and, moreover, which groups and individuals have the power to define these meanings. Cultural politics are also concerned with subjectivity and identity, since culture plays a central role in constituting our sense of ourselves ... The forms of subjectivity that we inhabit play a crucial part in determining whether we accept or contest existing power relations. Moreover, for marginalized and oppressed groups, the construction of new and resistant identities is a key dimension of a wider political struggle to transform society. (Jordan and Weedon cited in Alvarez, Dagnino, and Escobar 1998, 5-6)

However, Alvarez, Dagnino, and Escobar (1998, 3) are critical of how the concept of cultural politics is applied by Jordan and Weedon (1995) and in cultural studies in general, which tends to (over)emphasize "disembodied struggles over meanings and representation" and the abstract construction of subject positions in public discourse and the arts. In contrast, Alvarez, Dagnino, and Escobar (1998, 6-7) anthropologize the concept of cultural politics by bringing us back to "the actual or potential stakes and political strategies of particular social actors," and to concrete struggles to redefine social power waged by embodied actors through a wide range of practices that "must be accepted as political."

In a way, the project and contribution of Alvarez, Dagnino, and Escobar is akin to that of Alberto Melucci (1989, 1996), who is also concerned with the subversion of social and cultural orders, giving visibility to phenomena that are "hidden" and "cannot be reduced to politics" (in the conventional sense), and understanding the relationships between "collective social and political processes and the subjective personal experience of everyday life" (Melucci 1989, 11). Like Melucci (1989), Alvarez, Dagnino, and Escobar (1998) attempt to bridge the two main theoretical currents in social movement studies – the new social movement and resource mobilization approaches. Alvarez and Escobar (1992) also attempt to bridge "objectivist" and "subjectivist" approaches of social phenomena. All of these endeavours are crucial to my argument.

Yet, like Melucci (1989), Alvarez, Dagnino, and Escobar (1998) concentrate their conceptual efforts on practices of resignification of "dominant cultural meanings." They stop short of providing a more general theorization of a wider range of practices and life conditions; of other dimensions of practices and life conditions that cannot all be reduced to meaning (although meaning is always a crucial dimension); and of how they could be thought to relate to reproduction or transformation of a given social order. This brings us back to our second problem: that of the conceptualization of practice, in general, and social movement practices, in particular.

Theories of Practice and the Study of Social Movements

Cultures (in the very broad sense of social formations) "construct people as particular kinds of social actors, but social actors, through their living, on-the-ground, variable practices, reproduce or transform – and usually some of each – the culture that made them" (Ortner 2006, 129). I wish to further illustrate this central idea of practice theory and its importance in understanding the potential consequences of women's movements by using the definition of practice elaborated by R.W. Connell (1987, 95, emphasis in original), which reveals social structures in the process of being constituted and reconstituted through social practices:

> The crucial point is that practice ... is always responding to a *situation.* Practice is the transformation of a situation in a particular direction. To describe structure is to specify what it is in the situation that constrains the play of practice. Since the consequence of practice is a transformed situation which is the object of a new practice, "structure" specifies the way practice (over time) constrains practice. Since human action involves free invention (if "invention within limits" to use Bourdieu's phrase) and human knowledge is reflexive, practice can be turned against what constrains it; so structure can be deliberately the object of practice ... But practice cannot escape structure, cannot float free from its circumstances ... it is always obliged to reckon with the constraints that are the precipitate of history.

Ortner, a feminist anthropologist, drawing on and reinterpreting the work of Bourdieu, Sahlins, and Giddens (as well as her own works written between 1972 and 2006), recently contributed a particularly interesting version of practice theory (Ortner 1996, 2006). She argues that "objectivist" (such as anthropological political economy) and "subjectivist" (such as interpretive anthropology) perspectives are not opposed ways of doing social sciences. She maintains that the anthropological project must always include both, and she considers practice theory to be the only framework that "theorizes a necessary dialectic between the two" (Ortner 1996, 4). Ortner's version of practice theory thus permits us to combine a materialist analysis of unequal social relations of power with a full account of the actor's logic, creativity, reflexivity, and agency – both of which are necessary to the feminist project.

Ortner's idea is to conceptualize acting subjects as actors who are endowed with intentions and projects, but without falling into the trap of voluntarism by presuming that subjects can "triumph over their context through sheer force of will" and that society is merely "an aggregate product of individual action and intention" (Comaroff and Comaroff 1992 quoted in Ortner 2006, 131). In other words, Ortner (1996, 8) works to "restore agency without reproducing the bourgeois subject" by offering "a model of practice that embodies agency but does not begin with, or pivot upon, the agent, actor or individual" (Ortner 1996, 12). The concept that she proposes is "serious games," which has nothing to do with what is commonly known as game theory but, rather, is "a way of getting past the free agency question, theorizing a picture of 'people-in-(power)-relationships-in-projects' as the relatively irreducible unit of 'practice'" (Ortner 1996, 12-13). This analytical "unit of practice" is thus a collectivity, a set of actors unequally endowed with power and with differentiated interests in the playing out of particular cultural, economic, and political configurations. In my interpretation of Ortner's works, social movements can thus be conceptualized as actors in the playing out and transformation of some of the serious games in a society.

The concept of serious games is meant to capture the following five dimensions simultaneously (Ortner 1996, 12-13):

1 social life is culturally organized and constructed, in terms of defining the categories of actors, rules, and goals of the game;
2 social life is in fact social, consisting of webs of relationships and interaction between multiple, shifting interrelated subject positions, none of which can be extracted as autonomous "agents";
3 yet, at the same time, there is agency – that is, actors play with skill, intention, wit, knowledge, and intelligence;

4 the idea that the game is serious expresses the idea that power and inequality pervade the games of life in multiple ways, and that the stakes of
these games are often very high;

5 there is never only one game: there are always multiple games in play,
both at any given moment and across time, preventing closure.

The idea that there is never solely one game in play is important for the
feminist study of change and social movements. First, it conveys the image
of actors involved in multiple, intersecting sets of social relations and subjected to multiple and co-substantial systems of oppression (gender, race,
class, and so on). On the one hand, this multiplicity may be seen as giving
more weight to the constraints on dominated groups. On the other hand,
however, there is the idea that with the multiplicity and heterogeneity
present in any social setting, there are also instability and incompleteness in
the dominant social orders. Gender orders, for example, are always "partial
hegemonies" that never exhaust what is going on in gender relations (Ortner
1996, 18), and have internal contradictions and crisis tendencies (Connell
1987, 96). Ortner's subaltern/feminist version of practice theory, then, em-
ploys a looser notion of social structure, avoids looking exclusively at the
loop of reproduction, and provides analytical visibility to "slippages in reproduction, the erosion of long-standing patterns, the moments of disorder
and of outright 'resistances' ... with everything slightly – but not completely
– tilted toward incompleteness, instability, and change" (Ortner 1996, 18).
Players are defined and constructed by the game (the game defines their subject positions), but are never wholly contained by it. Moreover, "There are
always sites, and sometimes large sites, of alternative practices and perspectives available, and these may become the bases of resistance and transformation" (18). This specifies further a certain conceptualization of the possibilities
for historical change by way of the transformation of the prevalent political
and gender games, or even the introduction of new ones, through destabil-
ization of power relations and hierarchies, which can be provoked, among
other things, by collective actors such as social movements.

Another important element for the feminist study of how social movements relate to the social systems in which they operate is to conceptualize
further the relationship of social movement practices with the production
and transformation of embodied subjectivities. Crossley (2002, 2003, 2005)
provides an interesting practice-theory-based contribution that is useful
in this endeavour. He proposes a reinterpretation of Bourdieu's theory of

practice and concept of *habitus* to account for some of the ways in which social movements effect change in the lives of activists and sustain mobilization over time. As his detailed discussion and reinterpretation of Bourdieu's theory is beyond the scope of this essay, I will briefly sketch out the main points that are most useful here. Crossley (2005) argues, as do Ortner (1996, 2006) and Connell (1987; as well as other authors, such as Sewell [1992] and Lovell [2000]), that practice theory, originally more geared to account for reproduction, can be reworked as a tool for thought about change and social transformation. Crossley accomplishes this through his concept of *radical habitus* (2003) or *movement habitus* (2005). Starting with empirical findings showing that participation in protest generates sustained politicization and continued participation in protest actions over time, he goes on to propose a conceptualization of activism in terms of a sustained disposition toward a particular type of practice that is acquired through participation in that practice (Crossley 2003, 51):

> The generative schemas of movement practice, the movement *habitus,* moves through the social body, crossing generations, through the force of the very practices it generates and the learning situations they effect. Political activity generates a *habitus* which generates political activity, drawing in and socializing new recruits, and so on in a circuit of reproduction. However, this does not preclude change. To the contrary. The movement *habitus* constantly evolves as the contexts of activism demand innovation, improvisation and intelligent adaptation. (Crossley 2005, 22)

Ortner's subaltern practice theory and Crossley's concept of movement *habitus* can be put to work in two distinct but complementary threads of analysis.

The first thread consists of describing a process that not only creates a new *activist habitus,* but also has the potential to profoundly transform the different forms of *feminine habitus* (rooted in gender relations but also in class, race, sexuality, and other systems of hierarchical differentiation) of the women who come together in feminist movements. Thus, through the introduction of new practices into the lives of their participants, feminist movements' processes are, at least potentially, spaces of profound transformation of self and embodied patterns of experience. These transformations are effected (or at least initiated) within movements and are thus both collective and intersubjective. They do not pertain merely to a discursive level, but unfold on the bodily level of interactions that take place through physical presence and are directly related to the social structures that the movement intends to transform. This move gives analytical visibility to the reflexive dialogue between the project of change and the movement's organizing practices, which become in and of themselves means to embody or bring about change. Some use the term "prefiguration" or "building of alternatives" to describe the attempt to enact in the present, on a small scale (usually organizational), the egalitarian social relations that the movement envisions for the wider society. Students of the recent mobilizations of the Global Social Justice Movement have noted the prevalence of this temporality of the present (Bertho 2005) and the (at least rhetorical) importance given to horizontal networks – that is, "flexible, multicentric organizational structures" (della Porta et al. 2006, 237).[3] This perspective, which is familiar to many social justice activists, feminists, anarchists, and popular education practitioners and which resonates with the work of scholars interested in social movements as producers of knowledge (see, for example, Conway 2004; Frampton et al. 2006) and the organization of activist labour (see, for example, Dunezat 1998; Galerand 2007), remains markedly under-theorized in social movement studies.

To become coherent and operational, the perspective I propose in this chapter requires further specification regarding the theoretical approach to the formation of subjects and subjectivities. I wish to situate it partially within the tradition of political economy in anthropology, which is concerned with "the study of the formation of anthropological subjects within complex fields of social, economic, and political power" (Roseberry 2001, 61). The feminist variation of this approach strives to understand the multiple dimensions of social inequalities produced by multiple and intersecting systems of domination and exploitation, such as capitalism, colonialism, and patriarchy (Labrecque 2001). The anthropological subjects produced within these complex fields of power are not merely abstract subject positions, and not only collective subjects, but also individual, gendered subjects who embody in their daily lives the larger historical processes, the workings of their societies, and their position within its power structure (Labrecque 2001). Anthropological subjects are usually granted sufficient reflexivity and agency to actively insert themselves into the social structure in which they must take part, sometimes with varying degrees of resistance to certain of its aspects.

Here, the contributions to practice theory that we have considered introduce a variant in the political economic theories of the formation of anthropological subjects, by allowing a conceptualization of a specific type of agency exercised by and within social movements. My proposition is that, *as actors, counter-hegemonic social movements such as feminist movements exercise a higher degree of agency, made possible by the production, within the movements themselves, of partially transformed anthropological subjects, by the way of the creation of alternative practices and fields of social power.* Anyone who has been involved in feminist movements knows that in a patriarchal gender order there are no ready-made feminists. Feminists have to be "made" or produced somehow – and they are not self-made. It is not an individual process but a collective one – a *social* process. Social movements can be conceptualized as social milieus and networks within which people interact and, in some cases, spend a major part of their lives. Movements must create alternative fields of power relations, however small and fragile, however imperfect, tentative, and temporary, in which individuals can be at least partially transformed, so that they can become the subjects of another kind of social existence – that is, struggle against the very social structures of power within which, and *for* which, they were socialized. The idea here is to theorize the collective nature of social movements as a social process that can produce transformed (or partially resocialized) social beings – what Chandra Talpade Mohanty (2003, 8) calls "critical, self-reflective, feminist selves" or "oppositional selves." In order to exist, counter-hegemonic movements must produce people with different embodied subjectivities, ideally capable of occupying new subject positions that would be materially, symbolically, and discursively produced by the social, collective nature of social movements, through their practices and struggles within societies. It follows that *social movements' internal processes are crucially related to their more visible historical actions* and that these two dimensions should be studied together. This production of new subject positions and subjectivities in social movements is, then, part of the anthropological significance of solidarities (across time and space), at least in a context of sustained and organized social interaction, such as that which social movements can provide. In other words, social movements may be viewed as the intentional creation of new games that transform the players that take part in them so that they, in turn, can try to transform the other structural/serious games in which they are involved as social beings, individually and collectively.[4] At stake are discourses and meanings, concrete material practices and social relations – in short, people's ways of life and life conditions. It should be clear, however, that these phenomena cannot be properly understood outside of a political-economy analysis that accounts for their marginal position and for the more powerful effects of the historically specific hegemonic social order in the context of which the movements operate.

The second thread of analysis consists of describing the degree and content of differentiation of these tentative counter-hegemonic "new/alternative games" from the hegemonic games of the prevailing social, economic, and political order. In the face of powerful systems of domination such as patriarchy, capitalism, racism, and colonialism, counter-hegemonic projects of change and processes of alternative subjectivity formation are necessarily tentative, partial, incomplete, hybridized, and precarious. Moreover, in order to be intelligible at all, they must stabilize a certain amount of legitimacy and credibility based on meanings and practices that already make sense within the prevailing cultural orders – the very orders that the projects of change seek to destabilize and transform. There is thus a dialectical tension between reproduction and transformation in any project of change. The intelligibility and legitimacy of protests and demands for change will necessarily tend to rest on a set of elements in the cultural order (what Bourdieu calls *doxa*[5]) that remains unchallenged, if not explicitly defended.

Within this thread, it would be interesting to investigate the variations in patterns of challenged/unchallenged elements in different movements, allied and opposed, as well as variations in time and space. We might find that what is apparently the same framing (wording) of issues involves a very different pattern of challenged/unchallenged elements in different societal, political, and cultural contexts. Or, the same words may have a thoroughly different meaning when employed in different contexts of practice, or even by different actors/positions within the same "serious game." A crude example could be that the words "fighting poverty" mean, in practice, radically different things when uttered by the World Bank and the WMW. The "unit of meaning" would not be merely certain discourses, but a complete "unit of practice" (a serious game) – a particular and dynamic assemblage of signifiers, specific actors, and concrete social practices, for the study of which ethnography should be a privileged method.

Yet another line of inquiry would be to examine the effects and patterns of "conflicting games" in the lives of concrete individuals. Since people tend to have multiple identities (or, in the term used by Anthias, "translocal positionalities"[6]) and are almost always involved in more than one game in more than one social milieu, the broader relationships among different games coexisting in society are likely to have personalized echoes in individuals' lives. For example, we could see how activists manage the personal contradictions that they are likely to experience between their feminist or oppositional selves and what is expected of them in dimensions of their lives that are outside their activist circles.

Methodologically, both threads of analysis imply that researchers should study the entire range of movement practices, and not merely those that are most visible in the public sphere and thus readily considered political in the conventional sense. That is why this theoretical section started with an argument to expand the definition of what is considered political, followed by a general theorization of the relationship between social practices and social change, which is then applied to the study of social movement practices. Thus, movement practices should be studied from the educational methods to the way that sociabilities, activist labour, power relations, and diversity are organized and worked on; from recruiting and networking practices to the ways that activists construct and reorganize their daily lives around meetings, activities, and movement goals; from the intersubjective practices internal to the movement to coalition building and framing of public discourses; from decision-making to the performance of public actions; and so forth. It is worth noting, however, that all movement practices and dynamics, and not solely the ones that are the object of explicit discourse, should be studied in relation to the project of change. In other words, the idea is to not limit the investigation to what the movement says about itself, or to what the actors say that they do. A search for contradictions between discourse and practice, or for innovative or transformative practices that have been taken for granted, is potentially among the most productive endeavours. This is why ethnography should be privileged and combined with discourse analysis.

Spatial Dimension of Feminist Practices

How does this relate to transnational and multiscalar social movements? The conceptualizations of social movement practices presented in the last section provide resources with which to think through the spatial dimension of social movement practices, in particular of multiscalar movements such as the WMW, in order to work toward a better understanding of the significance of the extension of counter-hegemonic, feminist solidarities in geographical space. Of course, the examples analyzed in this section far from exhaust the possibilities for analysis of the spatial dimensions of feminist practices, let alone feminist and social movement practices in general. The objective is, rather, to illustrate some of the possible ways to articulate the conceptual tools presented so far in the analysis of concrete practices, and to combine them with the concepts of space, place, and scale presented by Masson (this volume). For this purpose, I will use the example of a central feminist practice: the practice of meeting, of gathering women in particular places for the purpose of solidarity building and political organizing. The data used to substantiate this analysis were collected through multi-sited ethnography, a method that I view as indispensable for the study of mult-iscalar and transnational movements anchored in national and local networks, groups, and struggles. I will briefly come back to this subject in the conclusion, in which I will highlight specific methodological challenges.

Meetings and gatherings are "scaled" (actors from a determinate geographical range participate). This simple fact will enable me to show the usefulness of the metaphor of serious games to understanding the social production of space and scale. Using the case of the WMW in Brazil, we will see that the production and multiplication of scales of collective action can be understood as the production of a multiplicity of scalar games anchored in certain places and played by specific sets and networks of actors. Then, focusing on the WMW in a specific region of Brazil, the western part of the state of the Rio Grande do Norte, I will show that the spatial dimensions of practices are in themselves socially productive, and that the practice of meeting and the multiplication of scales of collective action may modify some aspects of "gender games" by producing new, embodied, oppositional subjectivities (or, to put it differently, a feminist *habitus*) and interfering with the spatial regimes of patriarchy. But before examining these specific examples, I will consider how the practice theory framework can be combined with a social constructivist conception of space in the study of transnational and multiscalar social movements, and how this provides a point of departure from which we can take into account the spatialization of gender regimes in the analysis of feminist practices.

The practice theory framework proposed in this chapter is compatible with – and calls for – an anti-essentialist, social constructionist view of space. Massey (2006, 9-15) advances three main propositions for such a conceptualization of space. First, space is socially constructed, the product of interrelations and social interactions, "from the immensity of the global to the intimately tiny" (Massey 2006, 9). There is no geographical space that is not yet already produced through social relations and culturally interpreted. Second, space is understood as the sphere of the possibility of multiplicity, of contemporaneous plurality, of coexisting heterogeneity. Thus, space is a particularly pertinent concept in which to anchor feminist anthropological (and philosophical/ontological) thinking about the heterogeneity of the category "women" and ethnographic study of the concrete movements and coalitions that *are* being built, to this day, by feminists and women activists under this banner. In this regard, the WMW, because of its spatial scope, could be seen as a quasi-paradigmatic case of politically articulated feminist diversity. Third, if space is a product of social relations embedded in material practices, it is always in the process of being made (as are social relations). Space is "never finished, never closed. Perhaps we could imagine space as a simultaneity of stories-so-far" (Massey 2006, 9).

To sketch out some of the ways in which such a conceptualization of space might help with visualizing social movements' spatialities, let us take the WMW as a particularly relevant example of a transnational social movement.[7] Because it was originally constituted of approximately six thousand primarily pre-existing groups, collectives, and organizations present on every continent and dispersed across 163 countries and territories, what appears to be the most obvious contribution of this vast effort of building concrete political convergences and common actions is the reconfiguration of solidarities in geographical space. The very use of expressions such as "every continent" and "163 countries and territories" by the WMW in its description of itself conveys an image of its scope and extension in space while indicating the (power-related) potency of certain interpretations of the organization of space. It also suggests that some of the more culturally and politically established understandings of space are used strategically to build political legitimacy (related to the numerical importance and spatial extension of the constituency). As such, one line of inquiry to investigate would be the actors' use of spatial vocabulary. One of the crucial questions for feminism, however, is: Are such legitimacy and geographical imaginaries used in processes that transform the relationship of women, or of certain women, with space as defined by patriarchal and capitalist serious games?

Much has been said about how capitalism produces specific spatial patterns of relationships, while much less has been said about the socially productive aspect of the spatialization of gender relations (Marston 2000). Nonetheless, the theme has been explored, and I think that the study of women's movements could have much to contribute in this regard. Massey (1994, 179-80) has suggested that

> the limitation of women's mobility, both in terms of identity and space, has been in some cultural contexts a crucial means of subordination. Moreover the two things – the limitation on mobility in space, the attempted consignment/confinement to particular places on the one hand, and the

limitation on identity in the other, have been crucially related ... What is clear is that spatial control, whether enforced through the power of convention or symbolism, or through the straightforward threat of violence, can be a fundamental element in the constitution of gender in its (highly varied) forms.

Returning, for now, to Massey's (2006) three propositions on space enunciated above, and to the spatial practices of movements, we can imagine the WMW producing its own globalness through the relationships established among its constituent groups, especially if we accept Alvarez's (2000, 30) definition of transnationalization of social movements as "local movement actors' deployment of discursive frames and organizational and political practices that are inspired, (re)affirmed, or reinforced – though not necessarily caused – by their engagement with other actors beyond national borders through a wide range of transnational contacts, discussions, transactions, and networks, both virtual and 'real.'" We can also imagine that this relational/geographical space is the condition of the WMW's radical diversity, and that this relational/spatial process, just like the movement itself, is never closed but always in the process of constituting itself.[8] This spatiality is thus organized, and the relationships are spatially structured, by the movement's practices.

As Masson (this volume) argues, there is growing interest in the role played in the production of scale by different types of processes and actors, including social movements. In this last category, most of the existing literature concentrates on social movements' creation of their own scales of collective action. Yet, there seems to be little literature on how the spatial practices of social movements influence the spatialization of other social processes. I have proposed elsewhere (Beaulieu 2007) that different scales of collective action may serve as political opportunity structures for one another, that the production of these different scales seems to be associated with processes anchored in particular places, and that the temporalities of these processes and anchorages are variable (they may be occasional, transitory, or more durable). It is this last point that I wish to explore further next, particularly in relation to a "more durable" temporality. I suggest that the production of multiple scales of collective action can be seen as a series of intersecting serious games. This could help with visualizing the anchoring of "scales as games" in (multiple but specific) places, the relationships among scales of collective action within movements, and the possible impact of movements' spatial practices on deeper, more hegemonic, or more powerful structural games (such as gender relations). To illustrate how we might think of scales of collective action as produced through culturally and politically organized social interactions, and how the metaphor of serious games provides a way of interpreting them, let us turn once more to examples drawn from the WMW, this time in Brazil.[9]

Places, Games, and the Multiplication of Scales of Collective Action

First, let us consider the example of the national coordinating body of the WMW in Brazil through a very brief sketch of the role that some of the central actors play in different scalar games. The WMW in Brazil is a broad coalition of women's groups and women's committees in mixed-gender progressive social movements and trade unions. The national executive committee, as of the beginning of 2007, was composed of representatives from four women's committees of national movements that were members of the WMW (three of which have their coordinating operations based in the city of São Paulo; the other one is in Brasilia, the national capital) and three feminist organizations that are based in different parts of the country (São Paulo, Rio de Janeiro, and Rio Grande do Norte). The committee generally meets in the city of São Paulo two to three times a year. Most of the day-to-day coordination and circulation of information is provided by a feminist organization, Sempreviva Organização Feminista (SOF), which has chosen to invest most of its time and resources in building the WMW in Brazil and is located in the city of São Paulo. To further ensure the national scope and grassroots base of the WMW, there is a wider national coordinating body composed of two representatives from every state committee (each of which is composed of activists from the local or regional groups in their respective state) and the members of the national executive committee. This body meets in a different Brazilian city approximately once a year. It is this body that delegates representatives to the international bodies of the WMW and, approximately every two years, to the general international meeting. The general international meeting then selects ten representatives from the five regions of the world to form an international committee that organizes the international meetings, among other things, and ensures that there is coordination in every region. From 1998 to 2006, Brazilian participation at international meetings and the international committee was fulfilled primarily by a representative from SOF. Recently, the international secretariat of the WMW was moved to Brazil, and its new coordinator is from SOF. SOF also coordinates the WMW committee for the state of São Paulo (which meets in various venues around the city of São Paulo), and SOF's office is a regular meeting place for local groups, such as the WMW committee for the University of São Paulo.

If we look at the WMW in Brazil from the point of view of one of its main actors, SOF, we can distinguish four scalar games in which it is involved. The first is construed, by the actors involved, as local and concerns relationships with WMW groups in the city of São Paulo. Another is construed as *estadual* and concerns the WMW groups in the state of São Paulo. The third is construed as national and concerns all of the WMW member groups and networks in Brazil. And the final one is construed as international or global (the term transnational is not much used by the WMW to describe itself) and concerns the overall dynamic of the WMW. Each of these scalar games has more than one set of relationships associated with it – for example, relationships among individual and group members of the WMW (one could call them internal); relationships between the WMW and allied movements (which, for the activists who might be members of two or more of these movements, may be both internal and external); and relationships with "targets," opponents, or the general public (more clearly external), which may be either mainly symbolically mediated or personalized in some specific situations (or both) – for example, relationships with governments, organizations, other social movements, and corporations; and relationships with the dominant order through games of patriarchy, capitalism, racism, and so on. Serious games are multiple and intersecting, and the definition of their boundaries is an analytical choice. My point here is that games and scales do have heuristic value for each other. One does not play the national coalition game the same way as one plays a local game of awareness-raising and mobilization, even if some activists may be good at and play in both games.

This example shows that particular places may serve as organizational anchors or locations for the production of scalar games in which many actors from a determinate geographical range participate. Conversely, people located in particular places may be involved in several scalar games at the same time. This could be thought of as a kind of intensification of the spatial dimension of relations in certain places, or as an intensified spatial extension of social/political networks, for sets of actors located in specific places. One might ask, then: What is the geographical distribution of these intensifications for a given movement? How are different places specific loci for the construction and operation of multiple scales, and where are they located? What are the consequences of these intensifications for the actors involved, and for the movement as a whole? And aside from these intensifications, what are the other modalities of relations among scales of collective actions? These questions may, in turn, be related in various ways to the lines of inquiry proposed in the first part of this chapter. For example, we could ask: What type of skills and concrete attitudes – and, on a broader level, what different subject positions and types of embodied subjectivities – does each scalar game foster for movement activists – both those with more power and responsibilities (organizers, leaders) and the others – and how do these different subject positions and embodied subjectivities intersect with the dominant order's prevailing social stratification?

Massey's (1994, 2006) remarks on spatial control as a means to subordinate women suggest a different (though related) perspective on the connection between spatiality and the subversion of gender relations. The above example conveyed an image of the anchoring of spatial games in place, and I wish now to bring to the forefront the question of what it might mean for women to move through geographical space in the enactment of these scalar games in the context of feminist organizing. Let us leave the mega-city of São Paulo for the rural areas of the western part of the state of Rio Grande do Norte (RN). In this region, the multiplication of scales of collective action seems to foster processes that transform the relationship of particular women with space as defined for women by patriarchal and capitalist regimes. In other words, RN is a place where simultaneous participation in the dynamics of several scales of the WMW seems to transform the spatiality of women's lives, which has effects on gender relations. Let us look at the spatial dimension of a central feminist practice, women-only meetings, and see what it might mean for women to move through geographical space in the production of these scales in the context of feminist organizing for the WMW.

Solidarities Across Space Against the Spatial Regimes of Patriarchy

In RN, one feminist organization, Centro Feminista 8 de Março (CF8) invests much of its time and resources in mobilizing women and helping them organize into groups under the banner of the WMW. These women's groups, in turn, become the basis for awareness-raising, popular education, and training sessions. They organize projects and collective actions in their respective immediate social milieus. Prior to its involvement in the WMW, CF8's activities were limited to the municipality of Mossoró. Since 1999-2000, when its activities came under the banner of the WMW, CF8 has drastically changed its understanding of the relationship between "the local" and wider scales of collective action, of its own role in fostering organization at wider scales, and of the articulation between groups in different places.

Following the lead of CF8, since 2000 many of the region's women's groups have started to participate in activities and processes that mobilize them and articulate them with larger scales of collective action: regional/sub-state (western RN), state (RN), regional/sub-national (northeastern Brazil), and national. A few activists from the region have even been involved in trans-national activities. The region contains both urban and rural groups partici-pating actively in the WMW, but for illustrative purposes I will focus on rural women's groups.

In the rural areas of western RN, where I conducted ethnographic field-work in 2006, I observed a strong and widespread pattern of what Massey (1994, 179-80) has termed "limitation of women's mobility, both in terms of identity and space," as a "crucial means of subordination." To put it succinct-ly, most women marry and bear their first child very young (under or around the age of twenty). Thereafter, they tend to be confined, in terms of both identity and occupation, to motherhood (many, but not all, also participate regularly in agricultural work), under the variably strict authority and con-trol of their husbands. Domestic violence seems to be widespread, even though it is somewhat taboo to talk about or act upon it. If a woman wishes to escape a violent situation in her home and does not have family members willing to take her in, she has virtually nowhere to go (there are no shelters for battered women in the region). There seem to be two main sets of con-straints on women's spatial mobility. The first is economic: peasants tend to be very poor, and, in general, women tend to not have money of their own. Affording transportation, even to the nearest town, is problematic for most rural women. The second is related to gender subordination and a rigid sex-ual division of labour: women tend to have to negotiate with men (father or husband) to get out of their houses. In the worst cases of control and vio-lence, they must ask permission to visit their neighbours, and it is some-times refused. More commonly, women have to negotiate if they want to leave the house for the entire day, and negotiate harder still to leave for one or more nights. In most of the cases that I observed, this takes the form of women experiencing difficulties in escaping their domestic responsibilities and finding other women to fill in during their absence. Who will watch and care for the children? Who will prepare meals? What if a child gets sick? What if a baby is still nursing? Although this description is superficial and looks somewhat like a caricature of patriarchy – and there are, of course, important nuances and individual variations – I am confident in saying that these general patterns do play a very significant role in the lives of most women in RN.

The relationship between patriarchal gender relations, sexual division of labour, domestic responsibilities, and constraints on geographic mobility, on the one hand, and use of women's time, on the other, is not limited to the region under consideration here but widespread throughout the world (although the concrete form may vary). These patterns are fairly well documented in the feminist literature and are often referred to as "obstacles to the participation of women" (in social movements, public and community life, development projects, or other endeavours). It is also revealing that, in Brazil as in other places, many of the insults used by men against women who transgress the boundaries of their confinement link this mobility with culturally disapproved-of sexual behaviour. For example, a woman with some freedom is regularly insulted with the term *vagabunda*, which connotes both geographical mobility and promiscuous behaviour or adultery.

The majority of the WMW's activities and actions (and probably those of social movements in general) take the form of, or at least involve, meetings and gatherings, small and large, in which people's physical presence is a central element – notwithstanding the usefulness of phone, fax, and Internet. In many feminist traditions, forming women's collectives and/or finding ways for women to get together and build shared social and political understanding of their situation is the centrepiece and foundation of all other strategies. Therefore, if any feminist or women's movement is to be built, women must, at the outset of their participation, find ways to free themselves to attend meetings and gatherings. For some women, it may be years after they join a local group before they are able to participate in activities farther away from their home that entail an overnight stay (especially if they have young children). For example, at a regional training session in RN, an organizer, obviously quite moved, pointed at a woman from a rural group that was part of my study and exclaimed to me, "Look who came! Oh, but this is a great victory! We've been trying to get her to come [to a training session away from her village] for years!" In contexts such as this, the very act of attending a meeting may mean putting into question the prevailing spatialization of gender relations. Such a challenge can be seen as both a condition and an outcome of feminist movements. My hypothesis is that the collective character of feminist organizing, and thus the building of new solidarities between women and specific spatialization of movement practices, plays a key role both in creating the conditions that make movement building possible and in subverting, by the very practice of collective action and organization across space, some crucial aspects of women's subordination that fall within the serious games of gender relations.

In western RN, feminist mobilization under the banner of the WMW has succeeded in creating regional political networks of women that foster regular meetings and gatherings.[10] It is fairly clear that in this particular case, mobilization at the regional scale plays a key role in creating conditions under which women in the groups are able to negotiate with men (and other women) for geographical mobility and temporal availability. Owing to the success of mobilization and political solidarities at the regional scale, the WMW has acquired some visibility and legitimacy, despite the radicalism of its claims and demands in contrast to the prevailing machismo. In my view, this political legitimacy seems to be both a condition for and a result of the capacity of a critical number of women activists (from a critical number of localities in the region) to sustain participation and mobilization, and therefore to exercise more freedom of movement. In this case, there is also a multiplicity of scales of collective action, with many women, some of whom live in remote villages, involved in more than one scale simultaneously.

Changes in the lives of women from the rural areas of western RN who participate in the WMW are profound and multiple, and their participation in organized women's groups and in the WMW sometimes affords them opportunities in formal education, jobs, participation in economic development projects, and leadership roles in their communities. The women whom I interviewed voiced these changes in terms of meeting new women and making new friends, discovering new places, improved material life conditions, increased capacity to interact and negotiate (becoming less timid, acquiring a sense of self-worth and self-affirmation), decreased submissiveness, learning new knowledge and skills, changes in vision of their own place and women's place in the world, acquiring a sense of the possibility of being more independent from men and autonomous, changed relations with spouse and family members, acquiring the desire to fight for women's rights and against machismo, fostering new dreams and desires and new criteria for happiness, acquiring new ways of feeling, thinking, and acting, and so forth. Although these transformations can be clearly linked to participation in the WMW (which is the only feminist political articulation in the region), they cannot be attributed solely to going to meetings and geographical mobility. Nevertheless, women clearly express the central importance of geographical mobility and of meeting with other women for political purposes and solidarity building, since these are the most immediate and visible changes in daily routine that occur from the outset of participation. They also trigger questioning and contestation of the sexual division of labour and patterns of domestic oppression of women by men.

One of the key points here is that the symbolic and practical construction and articulation of simultaneous scalar collective action games contribute (at least potentially) to constructing new meanings and expanding women's political and social networks in a way that gives legitimacy and purpose to the very act of organizing, travelling near and far to go to meetings, and exposing one's political positions in the public space of concrete communities. The regional, national, and international scales of collective action all provide a concrete and legitimate reason for negotiating the right to travel, and time away from home, to go to protests or meetings. Furthermore, the different scales of collective action seem to reinforce each other: it is very unlikely that isolated groups would form and sustain their practices over time, let alone win some of their struggles, if they were not connected to and in solidarity with other groups, or if there were not political forces building up at other geographical scales.[11] Therefore, depending on the particular movement practices, organization of activist labour, and personal experiences within the movement (I am thinking mainly of empowerment and subversion of hierarchies, which has everything to do with particular ways of building and enacting solidarity), women begin to experience, embody, and think of their place in the world differently.

Conclusion

In this chapter I have proposed various conceptual tools to help make sense of some important transnational and multiscalar social movement and feminist practices in terms of contribution to social change and subversion of prevailing gender orders. The question that underlies the chapter as a whole is: What difference does transnational or multiscalar collective action make for specific women and for the transformation of gender relations in particular places? I have argued that to develop a feminist perspective on the social changes fostered by women's transnational and multiscalar collective action, we need an expanded vision of the political, one that goes beyond movements' relationships with states and with international institutions and norms, and that takes seriously the internal logics that inform movements' processes of mobilization and organization, strategies, goals, and fields of action – in other words, the whole range of social movement practices. As well, we need to go beyond studying the relationships between the national and supranational scales (mostly understood under the notion of the "boomerang effect"), and fully integrate into the study all the scales of collective action that are being produced and/or articulated with one another within the process of transnational organizing. As the examples drawn from the WMW in Brazil at least partially demonstrate, such a multiscalar and practice-oriented lens enables us to bring into focus the processes of subjectivity (trans)formations and reorganization of daily life, their particular characteristics in each place and time and at each scale of collective action, and the relationship between these processes and the social and gender orders that the movements purport to subvert.

It should be noted, however, that attention to the microsocial processes and forms of agency involved in production of alternative embodied subjectivities through innovative social movement practices is in no way a substitute for the political-economic analysis of people's positions within broader systems of oppression and exploitation and the dynamic balance of forces particular to each conjuncture. The multiscalar and practice-oriented lens should, to the contrary, foster a more systematic contextualization of the struggles for change within all the variously scaled social structures, processes, and unequal power relationships that make up the serious games of the hegemonic social and gender orders.

The conceptual approach that I propose here also raises methodological issues for the study of social movements. One of the points of interest in Ortner's (1996, 2006) approach to practice theory is that she provides a theoretically grounded unit of practice composed of sets of actors and their discursive and non-discursive practices in the context of the goals, rules, and differentiated positions of power and subject positions constructed by the serious game that they play, which is, in turn, a constitutive part of larger structured social orders. This metaphor can be applied to the social construction of space and scales through my proposed notion of scalar games. Using serious or scalar games as analytical units implies that discourse analysis alone cannot lead to an understanding of the concrete meaning and socio-political significance of social movements unless they are studied in relation to the whole range of the movements' practices. Such an understanding strongly advocates for ethnography as a privileged method of inquiry.

The study of transational and multiscalar movement activity calls, further, for innovative methodological approaches such as multi-sited ethnography, which is "designed around chains, paths, threads, conjunctions or juxtapositions of locations in which the ethnographer establishes some form of literal, physical presence, with an explicit posited logic of association or connection among sites that in fact defines the argument of the ethnography" (Marcus 1995, 105). This should be fairly straightforward, since it seems obvious that to study phenomena occurring in various places and at various scales, one has to conduct ethnographic research in more than one site. However, this does not exhaust the methodological issues at stake. Multi-sited ethnography involves a double methodological operation that consists of selecting sites and elucidating the nature of the relationship among them in relation to the object of study. A logical methodological choice for social and feminist movement studies would be to "follow the people" – their discourses and practices (Marcus 1995, 106-10) – both literally, in their living and working environments and as they engage in variously scaled activist practices, and figuratively, by mapping personal, political, and inter-organizational networks and interactions based on interviews and archival materials. This implies that the epistemological and methodological processes themselves are spatialized, which may complexify in subtle ways the analysis of spatialization of the practices being studied. Moreover, studying the relationship among scales of collective action in transnational social movements presents several practical challenges. First, the sheer extension and variability in space of the phenomenon under study may be daunting. For example, studying the relationship between the transnational and national scales of collective action of the WMW in Brazil does not tell us much about the relationship between the same scales in India, Spain, Burkina Faso, the Philippines, or any of the other countries involved in the WMW. Likewise, studying the relationship between the national and *estadual* scales in RN does not tell us how these relationships function in the twenty other states of Brazil where the WMW is present. A second challenge comes from the somewhat unpredictable changes to and reconfigurations of these relations in time. The multiplicity of interacting scalar games also makes it difficult, although certainly not impossible, to circumscribe smaller sections of these phenomena for the design of feasible empirical studies. In spite of these challenges, there seems to be reasonable ground to think that this approach lends itself to comparative studies; as long as the limitations of each study are clearly identified, the accumulation of circumscribed case studies could productively contribute to a better understanding of the relationships between social change and the multiplication of scales of collective action in feminist (or other) transnational social movements.

NOTES

1 For a more detailed discussion on the shortcomings of these paradigms in accounting for social change, see Beaulieu (2006).

2 There was a debate in the 1990s over whether students of social movements should define their variables and the object of study more restrictively or more inclusively.

Many leading scholars have chosen to argue for restrictive variables (for example, McAdam, McCarthy, and Zald 1996); others, for an expansion of the object of study from social movements to contentious politics in general, including strikes, wars, revolutions, social movements, and other forms of political struggle (McAdam, Tarrow, and Tilly 2001). In both cases, the result is a definition of the political that is restricted mainly to dynamics that directly include state actors.

3 Reflections and debates within social movements on the deconstruction of hierarchies and on the pros and cons of various organizing practices are far from new, but can be traced back to nineteenth-century anarchist traditions. In feminist movements, these debates have been voiced at least since the 1960s and 1970s. See, for example, Ti-Grace Atkinson's letter of resignation from NOW in October 1968 (Atkinson 1974, 9-11), and the early-1970s essays by Jo Freeman, "The Tyranny of Structurelessness," and by Cathy Levine "The Tyranny of Tyranny," both reproduced in Dark Star (2002).

4 Of course, I am not implying here that social movements are the only, or the most important, locus of subjectivity formation in society, or even of counter-hegemonic subjectivity formation. Nor do I wish to suggest that every social movement is necessarily involved in counter-hegemonic subjectivity formation. Rather, my argument is to the effect that social movements should be studied from that angle because they tend to be a privileged site of collective, highly intentionalized counter-hegemonic subjectivity formation in certain societies. Their capacity to create oppositional subjectivities and alternative patterns of relations, and the particular characteristics of these, can in turn explain their capacity to foster social changes in particular contexts.

5 See Crossley (2002, 168-91) for a discussion of Bourdieu's concept of *doxa* related to social movements and social change.

6 For a synthesis of work by Anthias on the issues of social stratification, see Kruzynski (2004).

7 For more detailed case studies of the WMW, see Dufour and Giraud (2005, 2007a, 2007b), Conway (2007, 2008, and in this volume), and Galerand (2007).

8 Here, I refer to the idea of diversity as related to space in a paragraph that invokes the image of the WMW as "global" and "transnational." But space can be thought of as the sphere of coexistence of multiplicity at any scale. In the case of social phenomena, it could range from the space occupied by two human bodies to the entire planet.

9 For the present purpose, I can only briefly sketch some elements of the WMW in Brazil, which, of course, leaves a great deal out of the picture. For a somewhat more detailed case study of the WMW in Brazil, see Beaulieu (2007).

10 These include meetings of women's groups in villages (and urban neighbourhoods), women's committees and women's assemblies in rural labour unions, regional networks of alternative development projects, street protests on various dates of the feminist calendar, regional seminars, training sessions, political debates, and other activities. CF8 organizes an annual WMW gathering for the nine states of northeastern Brazil, and in 2006 SOF organized the first large national gathering, which was attended by many women from western RN. In addition to these, rural women also attend regional, state, and, sometimes, national events held by alternative

agricultural movements and peasant movements, often wearing WMW tee-shirts and bringing WMW banners. Moreover, various organizations that play an important role in rural development in the region actively support the WMW and the rural women's organizational efforts. The WMW is also very active in regional coalitions and common social movement actions, such as the Grito dos excluidos (Cry of the Excluded) and the Forum Social Potiguar (Social Forum of the RN). It is also noteworthy that the WMW's major activities often receive coverage in local and regional newspapers and on television channels and radio stations (something notoriously difficult to achieve for feminist movements in most contexts).

11 Some rural women's groups fought with municipal authorities and won construction of better infrastructure for their villages, such as roads and phone lines. Others, through their organization, were able to obtain resources and technical assistance for agricultural infrastructure (such as wells for irrigation) and productive projects of their own (horticulture, apiculture, capriculture, and so on). Another important area of struggle is violence against women. There have been demonstrations against and public denunciations of domestic violence in some villages, and some women were able to separate from violent husbands. Other struggles consist of demanding and organizing the implementation of laws and progressive measures for gender equality that have been fought for and won at other scales (mainly the national scale) and that would not, without further struggle, have very much impact in the region. The WMW in western RN is also very active in producing general political education and public protests and discourses against free trade and its ill effects, capitalist developmental policies, and capitalist agribusiness, and for food sovereignty and an alternative, "solidary" economy.

REFERENCES

Alvarez, Sonia E. 2000. Translating the Global: Effects of Transnational Organizing on Local Feminist Discourses and Practices in Latin America. *Meridians: Feminism, Race, Transnationalism* 1 (1): 29-67.

Alvarez, Sonia E., Evelina Dagnino, and Arturo Escobar. 1998. Introduction: The Cultural and the Political in Latin American Social Movements. In *Cultures of Politics, Politics of Culture: Re-visioning Latin American Social Movements*, ed. Sonia Alvarez, Evelina Dagnino, and Arturo Escobar, 1-32. Boulder and Oxford: Westview.

Alvarez, Sonia E., and Arturo Escobar. 1992. Conclusion: Theoretical and Political Horizons of Change in Contemporary Latin American Social Movements. In *The Making of Social Movements in Latin America*, ed. Arturo Escobar and Sonia Alvarez, 317-29. Boulder, San Francisco, and Oxford: Westview.

Atkinson, Ti-Grace. 1974. *Amazon Odyssey: The First Collection of Writings by the Political Pioneer of the Women's Movement*. New York: Links Books.

Beaulieu, Elsa. 2006. Social Movements, Social Change and Transnationalization: Towards a Feminist Anthropological Framework. In *Transnationalization of Solidarities and Women's Movements (Conference Proceedings)*, ed. Pascale Dufour, 4-33. Université de Montréal. http://www.cccg.umontreal.ca/pdf/Actes %20de%20l%27atelier_document.last.pdf.

—. 2007. Échelles et lieux de l'action collective dans la Marche mondiale des femmes au Brésil. *Lien social et politiques* 58: 119-32.

Bertho, Alain. 2005. La mobilisation altermondialiste, analyseur du contemporain. *Anthropologie et Sociétés* 29 (3): 19-38.

Buechler, Steven M. 2000. *Social Movements in Advanced Capitalism: The Political Economy and Cultural Construction of Social Activism*. New York and Oxford: Oxford University Press.

Connell, R.W. 1987. *Gender and Power: Society, the Person and Sexual Politics*. Stanford: Stanford University Press.

Conway, Janet M. 2004. *Identity, Place, Knowledge: Social Movements Contesting Globalization*. Halifax: Fernwood Publishing.

—. 2007. Transnational Feminisms and the World Social Forum: Encounters and Transformations in Anti-globalization Spaces. *Journal of International Women's Studies* 8 (3): 49-70.

—. 2008. Geographies of Transnational Feminism: The Politics of Place and Scale in the World March of Women. *Social Politics: International Studies in Gender, State and Society* 15: 207-31.

Crossley, Nick. 2002. *Making Sense of Social Movements*. Buckingham and Philadelphia: Open University Press.

—. 2003. From Reproduction to Transformation: Social Movement Fields and the Radical Habitus. *Theory, Culture and Society* 20 (6): 43-68.

—. 2005. How Social Movements Move: From First to Second Wave Developments in the UK Field of Psychiatric Contention. *Social Movement Studies* 4 (1): 21-48.

Dark Star. 2002. *Quiet Rumours: An Anarcha-Feminist Reader*. Edinburg and New York: AK Press UK and USA.

Della Porta, Donatella, Massimiliano Andretta, Lorenzo Mosca, and Herbert Reiter. 2006. *Globalization From Below. Transnational Activism and Protest Networks*. Minneapolis and London: University of Minnesota Press.

Dufour, Pascale, and Isabelle Giraud. 2005. Altermondialisme et féminisme: pourquoi faire? Le cas de la Marche mondiale des femmes. *Chroniques féministes* (93): 9-15.

—. 2007a. Globalization and Political Change in the Women's Movement: The Politics of Scale and Political Empowerment in the World March of Women. *Social Science Quarterly* 88 (5): 1152-73.

—. 2007b. When the Transnationalization of Solidarities Continues: The Case of the World March of Women Between 2000 and 2006 – A Collective Identity Approach. *Mobilization* 12 (3): 307-23.

Dunezat, X. (1998). Des mouvements sociaux sexués. *Recherches féministes* 11 (2): 161-95.

Ferree, Myra Marx, and Silke Roth. 1998. Gender, Class, and the Interaction Between Social Movements: A Strike of West Berlin Day Care Workers. *Gender and Society* 12 (6): 626-48.

Flacks, Richard. 2004. Knowledge for What? Thoughts on the State of Social Movement Studies. In *Rethinking Social Movements: Structure, Meaning, and Emotion,* ed. Jeff Goodwin and James M. Jasper, 135-54. Lanham, Boulder, New York, Toronto, and Oxford: Rowman and Littlefield.

Frampton, Caelie, Gary Kinsman, A.K. Thompson, and Kate Tilleczek, eds. 2006. *Sociology For Changing the World: Social Movements/Social Research*. Halifax: Fernwood Publishing.

Galerand, Elsa. 2007. *Les rapports sociaux de sexe et leur (dé)matérialisation. Retour sur le corpus revendicatif de la Marche mondiale des femmes de 2000*. Montreal/Paris: UQAM/Paris VII.

Guidry, John A., Michael D. Kennedy, and Mayer N. Zald, eds. 2000. *Globalization and Social Movements: Culture, Power, and the Transational Public Sphere*. Ann Arbor, MI: University of Michigan Press.

Jordan, Glen, and Chris Weedon. 1995. *Cultural Politics: Class, Gender, Race and the Postmodern World*. Oxford, UK, and Cambridge, MA: Blackwell.

Kruzynski, Anna. 2004. Du silence à l'affirmation: Women Making History in Point St. Charles. PhD diss., McGill University and Université de Montréal.

Labrecque, Marie-France. 2001. Présentation. Perspectives anthropologiques et féministes de l'économie politique. *Anthropologie et Sociétés* 25 (1): 5-22.

Lovell, Terry. 2000. Thinking Feminism With and Against Bourdieu. *Feminist Theory* 1 (1): 11-32.

Marcus, George E. 1995. Ethnography in/of the World System: The Emergence of Multi-Sited Ethnography. *Annual Review of Anthropology* (24): 95-117.

Marston, Sallie A. 2000. The Social Construction of Scale. *Progress in Human Geography* 24 (2): 219-42.

Massey, Doreen. 1994. *Space, Place and Gender*. Minneapolis: University of Minnesota Press.

–. 2006. *For Space*. London, Thousand Oaks, and New Delhi: Sage Publications.

McAdam, Doug, John D. McCarthy, and Mayer N. Zald, eds. 1996. *Comparative Perspectives on Social Movements: Political Opportunities, Mobilizing Structures, and Cultural Framings*. New York: Cambridge University Press.

McAdam, Doug, Sidney Tarrow, and Charles Tilly. 2001. *Dynamics of Contention*. New York: Cambridge University Press.

Melucci, Alberto. 1989. *Nomads of the Present: Social Movements and Individual Needs in Contemporary Society*. Philadelphia: Temple University Press.

–. 1996. *Challenging Codes: Collective Action in the Information Age*. Cambridge: Cambridge University Press.

Mohanty, Chandra Talpade. 2003. *Feminism without Borders: Decolonizing Theory, Practicing Solidarity*. Durham and London: Duke University Press.

Nash, June. 2005. Introduction: Social Movements and Global Processes. In *Social Movements: An Anthropological Reader*, ed. June Nash, 1-26. Malden, MA; Oxford, UK; and Carlton, Australia: Blackwell.

Ortner, Sherry B. 1996. *Making Gender: The Politics and Erotics of Culture*. Boston: Beacon Press.

–. 2006. *Anthropology and Social Theory: Culture, Power and the Acting Subject*. Durham, London: Duke University Press.

Reger, Jo, and Verta Taylor. 2002. Women's Movement Research and Social Movement Theory: A Symbiotic Relationship. *Research in Political Sociology* 10: 85-121.

Roseberry, William. 2001. Political Economy in the United States. In *Culture, Economy, Power: Anthropology as Critique, Anthropology as Praxis,* ed. Winnie Lem and Belinda Leach, 59-72. New York: State University of New York Press.

Sewell, William H. Jr. 1992. A Theory of Structure: Duality, Agency, and Transformation. *American Journal of Sociology* 98 (1): 1-29.

Staggenborg, Suzanne, and Verta Taylor. 2005. Whatever Happened to the Women's Movement? *Mobilization* 10 (1): 37-52.

Taylor, Verta, and Nancy Whittier. 1995. Analytical Approaches to Social Movement Culture: The Culture of the Women's Movement. In *Social Movements and Culture,* ed. Hank Johnston and Bert Klandermans, 163-87. Minneapolis: University of Minnesota Press.

–. 1998. Guest Editors' Introduction. Special Issue on Gender and Social Movements: Part 1. *Gender and Society* 12 (6): 622-25.

–. 1999. Guest Editors' Introduction. Special Issue on Gender and Social Movements: Part 2. *Gender and Society* 13 (1): 5-7.

West, Guida, and Rhoda L. Blumberg, eds. 1990. *Women and Social Protest.* New York, Oxford: Oxford University Press.

PART 2

DEEPENING SOLIDARITIES AMONG WOMEN AND WOMEN'S ISSUES

Framing Transnational Feminism
Examining Migrant Worker Organizing in Singapore

LENORE LYONS

Although many scholars agree that the Beijing Women's Conferences of 1995 provided considerable impetus for the transnationalization of women's movements (see Basu 2000; Meyer and Prügl 1999; Moghadam 2000; Naples and Desai 2002; Sperling, Ferree, and Risman 2001), there is much less agreement on what impact this has had on the lives of women globally. A strong proponent of women's transnational organizing, Valentine Moghadam (2000, 80) posits that since Beijing, locally and nationally based women's rights and feminist organizations have engaged in new forms of transnational feminist activism that provide unprecedented opportunities for women to address issues as diverse as reproductive health rights, human trafficking, and legal rights under Muslim law. In an upbeat assessment, Moghadam claims that transnational feminist networks (TFNs) and alliances with international non-governmental organizations are the most effective forms of women's organizing to have emerged in the era of globalization.

In a much more critical review, Manisha Desai (2005, 319-20) argues that while transnational feminist activism has been most successful at the level of policy and discursive changes, it is less successful in redistributing material resources, with the result that "the ironic state of the feminist movements post Beijing ... is that (some) women's agency is visible everywhere even as (most) women's lives remain mired in multiple inequalities." In her critique, Desai makes an explicit link between cross-border activism and the transformatory potential of transnational feminist politics, and she suggests that there is nothing inherent in transnational feminist activism that makes it more effective in bringing about improvements in the lives of women than activism that occurs at the local or national level. She notes that transnational feminist movements can be very successful at engaging with the forces of globalization at the level of discursive power and yet remain depoliticized at the level of policy making (Desai 2005, 328). In other words, it is one thing to be critical of globalization and entirely another matter to bring about sustained improvements in the lives of women globally.

Desai's comments point to the tendency, present in much writing about transnational feminist activism, to adopt a celebratory tone that assumes that women's engagements beyond the local or national arena must necessarily be a positive phenomenon. Scholars and policy-makers, supported by international funding agencies, project a view that women's transnationalism will provide sorely needed ballast against coercive state power and its excesses, and will be a means to remedy the negative impacts of globalization on women's lives. On a cautionary note, however, Vera Mackie (2001, 188) reminds us that the "transnational public sphere, if it can be said to exist, is a gendered, raced, classed and ethnicized public sphere." In the rush to celebrate the emergence of global civil society, we must stop to remind ourselves that transnationalism does not transcend difference but is embedded within it. For this reason, in some contexts it may be politically safer for women's rights and feminist activists to restrict their transnational efforts or to avoid transnational interactions altogether.

These differing viewpoints about the effectiveness of women's transnational organizing partly reflect different understandings of what is meant by the term "transnational feminism." As outlined in the Introduction to this collection, there are two main strands within the literature: one that focuses on the nature of the transnational public sphere (particularly focused on the organizational structure and form of transnational feminist networks), and another that examines how women are connected to each other through geographic locations and how flows of capital, labour, and ideas influence knowledge production (see Mohanty 1991, 2003). Scholars writing within the first strand focus on the organizational forms that feminist practice takes and define transnational feminism as feminist activism that crosses national borders (see Moghadam 2000; Sperling, Ferree, and Risman 2001). While scholars writing within the second strand also employ this understanding of transnational feminist activism, their focus is much more on the ideological bases of feminist claims. By providing a critique of the racist, patriarchal, and heterosexist relations of rule that underpin global capitalism, this approach seeks to produce knowledge that is grounded in local specificity but at the same time takes account of global interdependencies (see Grewal and Kaplan 1994).

What is remarkable about the literature on transnational feminism is that although there is considerable overlap between these two strands, there has been little discussion about how transnational feminism as theory is translated into activist practices or whether cross-border feminist activism is the natural organizational form of transnational feminist theorizing. In one of the few studies that attempt to link theory to practice, Desai (2005, 319, emphasis added) defines feminist transnationalism as "both organising across national borders *as well as* framing local, national, regional, and global activism in 'transnational' discourses." Similarly, Sonia E. Alvarez (2000, 30) defines the transnationalization of social movements as "local movement actors' deployment of discursive frames and organizational and political practices that are inspired, (re)affirmed, or reinforced – though not necessarily caused – by their engagement with other actors beyond national borders through a wide range of transnational contacts, discussions, transactions, and networks, both virtual and 'real.'"

This is not a view, however, that is shared by all scholars or activists. Women engaged in cross-border activism, including involvement in TFNs, may not necessarily be engaged in local women's movements. Similarly, feminist activists whose work is grounded within transnational feminist theory may not engage in cross-border organizing.

These problems point to the need for greater precision regarding the meanings associated with the terms "transnational feminism" and "transnational feminist activism." Clarity of meaning, however, cannot be achieved by imposing top-down definitions of these terms or by using the experiences of well-known TFNs as the benchmark for the transnationalization of women's solidarities. Such a move risks alienating feminist scholars and women's activists who see themselves as part of a global women's movement, but whose activities do not fit the narrow understanding of cross-border activism. As Dominique Masson points out in her chapter in this volume, careful attention to the politics of transnational feminism requires a multiscalar approach in which we explore the links between transnational and other scales of women's activism. Attention to the spatial dimension of women's collective action provides the means with which to examine how transnationalism is materially and discursively constructed and to examine the impact that activism within the transnational public sphere has on the work of feminists engaged at the local and national levels.

To further our understanding of these processes, in this chapter I examine the multiple ways in which NGOs working to address the rights of female migrant workers in Singapore understand and articulate their activism in light of transnational feminist discourses. Migrant worker NGOs provide an important basis for considering the form and nature of transnational feminist activism because they are concerned with issues that are inherently transnational. They are part of an international social movement addressing the feminization of transnational labour migration in which millions of poor women from the global South migrate overseas in search of work to support themselves and their families. The vast majority of these women are employed in the domestic service sector (Anderson 2000; Chin 1998; Constable 1997; Parreñas 2001) or the commercial sex industry (Kempadoo 1999; Law 2000). Migrant women working in these industries face particular problems in relation to labour laws and citizenship rights. These problems are not unique to migrant workers in any one country; there is a remarkable consistency in the formal and informal regimes that regulate the work of lower-skilled migrant workers throughout the Asia-Pacific region (Huang, Yeoh, and Rahman 2005). This does not mean that the experiences of male and female migrant workers are the same, or that all female migrant workers are equally positioned within transnational labour markets. Gender, class, age, sexuality, ethnicity/race, and nationality all shape the experiences of migrant workers, and for this reason feminist scholars have paid particular attention to the way that migrant workers are positioned within prevailing gender, class, and race hierarchies (Wee and Sim 2003).

Sending and receiving states, as well as the traditional labour movement, have been slow to respond to the needs of these workers, and so there has been enormous growth in the number of organizations advocating on their behalf (Chin 2003; Ford 2006; Gurowitz 1999, 2000; Law 2003; Law and Nadeu 1999; Lyons 2005c; Piper and Uhlin 2002; Sim 2003). Given my interest in examining the nature of transnational feminist organizing, for this study I focus on migrant worker NGOs that have strong links with national-level women's movements, utilize a gender analysis in their work, and have dedicated programs addressing the needs of female migrant workers. In examining these organizations, I consider three interrelated issues: the ways in which they understand and portray the problems faced by female migrant workers (whether they understand these problems to be transnational in origin), the solutions that they propose to these problems (whether the solutions are transnational in character), and the extent to which they are able to organize and network transnationally (the extent to which their activism crosses borders). In teasing apart these issues and investigating the ways that NGO activists write and talk about transnational activism, I want to shed light on the intersection between transnational feminist theorizing and feminist activism and further the understanding of the meanings associated with transnational feminist organizing. This study reveals that the transnationalization of solidarities cannot be measured solely in terms of the number or frequency of cross-border engagements among various different actors, or of the extent to which women's NGOs employ a critique of globalization in their work. To restrict our understanding of transnationalization to these two ways of organizing risks our overlooking the very important work that local organizations perform in the establishment of solidarity. While cross-border organizing has the potential to *broaden* solidarity (in both geographical and conceptual terms), local-level organizing may be much more successful in *deepening* solidarity among differently placed actors.

The National Context

Singapore hosts a large migrant worker population, which represents approximately one-fifth of its total population of almost 4.5 million (Singapore Department of Statistics 2007). The Singapore government is extremely reticent about releasing data on foreign worker numbers due to perceived public sensitivity about their presence. It is estimated that 500,000 of these workers, of whom 150,000 are female domestic workers (Almenoar and Tan 2004), are unskilled or low-skilled. In addition to documented migrant workers, there are significant numbers of migrant sex workers, the majority of whom enter Singapore on short-term tourist passes from throughout Asia (Henson 2004).

Although Singapore is a major receiving country for female migrant labour in the region, migrant worker organizations are noticeably absent (Lyons 2005c). The activities of NGOs in Singapore are curtailed by strict rules governing the formal registration of associations and societies, a strong interventionist stance by the state, restrictions placed on the activities of international NGOs and other agencies, and often-fraught diplomatic relations with the two major migrant-sending countries, Indonesia and the Philippines (Koh and Ooi 2000; Singam et al. 1997). Singapore's ruling People's Action Party (PAP) has demonstrated little tolerance for public discussion of issues that cast its policies in a negative light and expects civil society organizations to support state-defined national values and accept that some subjects are always off-limits. Opportunities for NGOs to advance their causes depend in large part on the extent to which their goals are congruent with the state's own ideology and interests. Moderation, consultation, and consensus are key modes of operation as NGOs negotiate the constraints of relations between the state and civil society (Lyons 2000a).

In relation to transnational connections, while activist groups mobilize around international support and standards, the anti-West/anti-US position of the Singaporean government (as evidenced in the rhetoric surrounding "Asian values") has made such connections more complex. Locally based NGOs are wary of receiving funding from overseas sources for fear that this may result in government suspicion about their activities (Perera and Ng 2002). All NGOs are scrutinized closely to ensure that "foreign elements do not hijack [them] to serve a foreign agenda which is contrary to our national interests" (Ho Peng Kee, Senior Minister of State, Law and Home Affairs, quoted in Parliamentary Debates Republic of Singapore 2004, 37). In addition, foreign-based NGOs find it difficult to become formally registered, and without registration they cannot operate locally. This has resulted in a very small international NGO presence and very few transnational linkages among local, regional, and global groups.

Organizing on Behalf of Female Migrant Workers

It is against this backdrop that present-day activism in support of migrant workers can be understood. For many years, the rights of migrant women workers in Singapore have been identified as off-limits to civil society activists. Like many topics deemed too sensitive or taboo for activist intervention, the issue has never been publicly identified by the state in its official statements as an area that is out of bounds. However, the arrests of Catholic social workers and lay workers from the Geylang Catholic Centre for Foreign Workers in 1987 for allegedly threatening the state and national interests (commonly referred to as the Marxist conspiracy) cast a shadow over advocacy efforts in support of foreign workers for the next decade (Lyons 2005c).

The Association of Women for Action and Research (AWARE) is Singapore's key feminist organization. It was established in 1985 in response to a series of government policies, known as the Great Marriage Debate, aimed at encouraging graduate women to marry and have more children (Lyons 2004). Over the last twenty years, AWARE has waged a continuous campaign against the PAP's pro-natal policies, which, paradoxically, encourage women to have more children while at the same time insisting that Singapore's economy is dependent on women's participation in the labour force (Lyons 2005b). The introduction of a guest worker program for domestic workers is an integral part of the state's response to these competing demands – women can continue to work and also be "home managers" supervising a foreign domestic worker. AWARE argues that employing domestic workers is not the solution to the "crisis in the home"; instead, the government should encourage employers to introduce family-friendly policies and men to take greater responsibility for housework and childcare (AWARE 2004).

From AWARE's perspective, eliminating the foreign domestic worker program would be an indicator of the success of its campaigns to change traditional gender roles. Consequently, until very recently problems faced by female migrant workers were not in themselves conceived of as a feminist issue by the organization. Some members were caught up in the Marxist conspiracy, and many still believe that AWARE faced possible deregistration at that time (Lyons, 2008). The arrests of persons associated with the Marxist conspiracy were interpreted by AWARE's executive committee as a signal that domestic worker rights were clearly off-limits. This partly explains the group's reluctance to address the needs of foreign domestic workers (FDWs). Its failure to engage with this issue since the late 1980s cannot, however, be attributed solely to a fear of state power. The majority of AWARE members are middle-class, and many of them are employers of domestic workers. For these busy women, hiring a live-in domestic worker is a prerequisite for juggling their careers, family responsibilities, and involvement in community activities, including their work in AWARE. Engaging with the question of FDWs would require AWARE members to address the fraught topic of class location and demand for cheap domestic labour, issues that cut to the core of their own life experiences.

AWARE's silence is also consistent with its claim not to speak on behalf of "other" women. Out of respect, AWARE's executive committee argues that it has no right to speak about the rights or status of women in other countries – in other words, AWARE members can speak only about women like themselves (Lyons 2000b, 2001). Paradoxically, on one of the few occasions on which AWARE broke its self-imposed silence on women overseas, it found itself the target of a backlash against its own failure to take a stand on the conditions facing FDWs in Singapore. In 1998, AWARE presented a petition to the Indonesian Embassy decrying the treatment of ethnic Chinese women in Indonesia who were raped during a series of racial clashes that year. In receiving the petition, a spokeswoman for the Indonesian Embassy pointed out that Indonesian women were frequent victims of violent abuse while working as domestic workers in Singapore, an issue that AWARE had not addressed (Zakaria 1998). AWARE was put in the awkward position of having to explain why it had not included FDWs in its campaigns against violence against women. Following this embarrassing episode, AWARE began to make public statements in support of migrant workers, particularly in relation to the need to punish the perpetrators of violence against FDWs. These activities culminated in its support for the formation of a new organization – Transient Workers Count Too (TWC2).

TWC2 was formed in 2003 in response to media reports about the death in December 2001 of a nineteen-year old Indonesian woman, Muawanatul Chasanah, after months of brutal assaults by her employer. Her employer's neighbour was quoted in the media as saying, "Even if I knew, I wouldn't have called the police, it's not my business. He can do what he wants, that's his problem" (Ho and Chong 2002). These comments prompted a number of Singaporeans to meet informally with the goal of addressing attitudes toward and treatment of domestic workers in Singapore. The group originally called itself The Working Committee 2.[1] Several prominent members of AWARE were actively involved in establishing TWC2, and Braema Mathi was president of both organizations during 2004-05. For AWARE members who wanted to address FDW issues, their involvement in the establishment of TWC2 was a means to test the state's "out-of-bounds" markers without jeopardizing AWARE. It also provided them with the basis for establishing a broad-based movement of men and women and thus moving beyond the characterization of domestic work as a women-only – or, indeed, a feminist-only – issue. Keeping the two organizations separate in the eyes of the public was therefore very important.

The aim of TWC2 was to "promote respect for domestic workers through education, and secure better treatment of domestic workers through legislation and other means" (The Working Committee 2 2003a). Its initial focus was on FDWs because this group was perceived to be the most vulnerable of all documented (legal) migrant workers. Throughout 2003, TWC2 conducted a very successful media campaign aimed at raising public awareness about the range of issues faced by FDWs. The group was formally registered under the Societies Act in 2004 and renamed itself Transient Workers Count Too, retaining the original acronym (TWC2). In its constitution, TWC2 has signalled a broadening of its objectives beyond the needs and interests of FDWs to all "transient workers" (Gee and Ho 2006; Lyons

2005c); although it has continued its public awareness campaign and lobbying role, it moved its attention away from issues of abuse to focus on standardization of employment contracts, particularly the implementation of one rest day per week (the Day Off campaign). The organization's underlying objective is to address issues facing female migrant workers once they are deployed in Singapore. This focus was evident in an event that took place in late 2004, when members of the public accused TWC2 of damaging Singapore's international reputation by publicizing instances of violence by Singaporean employers. In justifying its anti-violence campaign, TWC2 claimed that its objective, as stated in an activities report the year before, had always been to raise awareness at the local level and that it had never initiated contact with non-Singaporean journalists (The Working Committee 2 2003b, 7). Furthermore, it asserted that although foreign journalists reported on its work, advocating beyond Singapore's borders was not part of its mission.

UNIFEM Singapore is quite different from AWARE and TWC2 – in terms of both its structure and its role in relation to female migrant worker issues. It was registered under the Societies Act in January 1998 and functions as a National Committee of the United Nations Development Fund for Women (UNIFEM). As is the case with TWC2, there is a significant membership overlap with AWARE, and two former AWARE presidents serve on UNIFEM Singapore's board of advisors. As a UN National Committee, UNIFEM Singapore is mandated to raise funds in support of UNIFEM's activities. Through its liaison with the UNIFEM Regional Office in Bangkok, UNIFEM Singapore's board identifies regional projects that it wishes to support and then runs fundraising activities such as film nights or benefit concerts in Singapore with the aim of assisting these programs.

Despite its limited role as a fundraising body, UNIFEM Singapore's executive has frequently overstepped this directive and initiated its own development programs in Singapore and the region. One of these programs, the Migrant Workers Reintegration Project, which ran from 2004 to 2006, provided Singapore-based training courses on small business planning, reintegration planning, and personal financial management skills for Filipina domestic workers. The year-long training program was premised on the idea that FDWs need financial literacy training so that they do not squander the money earned during their time abroad due to poor savings habits. The overall aim of the program, however, was to provide training and support in micro-entrepreneurship so that FDWs could start their own businesses in the Philippines. UNIFEM Singapore believes that such businesses are a panacea for labour migration since they provide the means for working-class women to stay at home with their families rather than travelling abroad for work. UNIFEM Singapore's response to these issues, however, is nationally based – it restricts its work to skills training in Singapore in the hope that this will make a difference when the women go home. In 2005, UNIFEM Singapore was criticized by the UNIFEM Regional Office for developing this and other aid projects (UNIFEM manager, personal communication, April 2006). Consequently, in July 2006 it facilitated the establishment of a new organization – Aidha – to continue its work in this area. Several members of UNIFEM Singapore sit on the Aidha executive committee.

With regard to activism around migration issues, FDWs are the main target of all three organizations. Although TWC2's brief is to address the needs of all migrant workers, it has had limited engagement with migrant sex workers. Until recently, AWARE was also silent on the issues facing women working in the sex industry. In 2005 and 2006, a number of cases of physical abuse of foreign sex workers in Singapore were reported in the local media, prompting a response by both TWC2 and AWARE to issues of sex trafficking. Much of the focus, however, has been directed at the trafficking of women and girls in the region, rather than the movement of sex workers into Singapore. For example, AWARE commissioned a study in 2006 on the introduction of an extra-territorial law to prosecute Singaporean men who engage in sexual acts with minors while overseas (AWARE 2006). At the official launch of the report, AWARE invited UNIFEM Singapore to discuss its work on HIV/AIDS training for sex workers and an anti-trafficking capacity-building program on the nearby Indonesian island of Batam. Each organization, however, continues to pursue a separate anti-trafficking agenda.

Despite the strong connections among the three groups, no formal alliances or joint campaigns have emerged. This lack of alliance-making reflects a separation between what are often considered local women's issues and migrant worker issues, as well as different understandings of the problems facing female migrant workers. In relation to the first issue, although all three groups agree that Singapore's pro-natalist policies have driven demand for FDWs, none has made a link between the state's interest in controlling the reproductive capacity of Singaporean nationals (a local women's issue) and its intrusive monitoring of FDW sexuality (a migrant women's issue). Under current labour laws, any FDW found to be pregnant or to have contracted a sexually transmitted disease during her employment contract is forcibly repatriated. The regulation of domestic worker sexuality is enforced through a program of compulsory medical checkups every six months. This issue, however, has largely been ignored by the two advocacy-oriented groups (AWARE and TWC2) because they recognize that the issue would gain little sympathy from either the government or the public, which is supportive of the restrictions placed on Singapore's guest worker program.

Similarly, while AWARE has voiced some support for those who argue that FDWs are a poor substitute for full-time care by a parent as part of its campaign for improved parenting leave for all Singaporean workers (a local women's issue), it has not joined with TWC2 to campaign for the rights of migrant workers to be involved in raising their own children (a migrant women's issue). Under current laws regulating the FDW program, women cannot bring their families with them to Singapore and must serve a minimum two-year contract before returning home. Many women spend years apart from their families and leave their children in the care of extended family. In failing to take up this issue, the two groups missed an opportunity to make an important connection between the reproductive rights and the employment rights of *all* women. UNIFEM Singapore's response to these issues is to focus on skills training as a means of reintegration that allows FDWs to be reunited with their families and earn a livelihood in the country of origin. This approach, however, is based on a paternalistic view of the savings habits of poor women and a belief that micro-entrepreneurship is a solution to widespread poverty.[2]

Although its understanding of the factors that have led to the feminization of labour migration may be limited, UNIFEM Singapore is the only one of the three organizations to focus on the reasons that poor women in the developing world travel abroad for work. In contrast, AWARE's and TWC2's activities remain narrowly focused on the common experiences of all migrant workers once they arrive in Singapore rather than the particular circumstances that lead them to migrate. I am not suggesting, however, that their work is not informed by transnational feminist discourses. The decision by all three organizations to describe maids as "workers" draws on international labour rights and women's rights campaigns on the issue of women's labour. In the case of TWC2, the use of the term FDW has another important outcome. By replacing the value-laden term "maid" with that of "foreign domestic worker," TWC2 seeks to highlight the common experiences of all domestic workers regardless of nationality. In an environment in which employment agents actively market "maids" on the basis of national characteristics (for example, Filipinas are good with children, while Indonesians are better at manual labour) and market differentiation has real consequences in relation to working conditions (particularly wages and rest days), highlighting the similarities among women migrant workers serves an important political purpose.[3]

This type of "trans-ethnic" advocacy is also crucial in situations in which strong Filipino transnational advocacy networks have had the greatest success in improving the conditions of employment for Filipina domestic workers (Piper 2005). Trans-ethnic advocacy is an important means of ensuring that all migrant women benefit from the gains made by different national groups. In a context in which the PAP government encourages Singapore's three official "racial" groups to be engaged in ethnicity-based social welfare programs, trans-ethnic advocacy can potentially make an important political statement about state-sponsored multiracialism.[4] For example, in its activist work on behalf of Singaporean women, AWARE has deliberately chosen not to divide its programs along ethnic lines. Following suit, TWC2 advocates for improvements in the working conditions of all foreign workers, while recognizing that some workers have specific needs because of the national circumstances that encourage them to migrate. It is often difficult, however, to translate these needs into specific policy outcomes, or to educate the public about the needs of different groups, without reinforcing existing stereotypes. The other risk in trans-ethnic advocacy efforts is that migrant women's particular experiences as national subjects may be ignored. This is evident, for example, in UNIFEM Singapore's tendency to see financial literacy training as a "one model fits all" solution to poverty in the region.

Not only are the links among the three organizations limited, but so, too, are their connections with organizations and networks outside of Singapore. Prior to 2007, no identifiable transnational feminist network linked activists working in support of migrant domestic workers in the Asia-Pacific region.[5] This does not mean, however, that there are no links among NGOs, international organizations, and government bodies interested in addressing the needs of female migrant workers. Examples of regional networking activities include conferences and workshops, formal cross-border alliances and campaigns between NGOs and international NGOs, and bilateral policy initiatives that involve NGOs and government bodies. Together, these activities constitute a dense fabric of migrant worker activism, some of which is feminist in orientation. The cross-border activities of AWARE and TWC2 are restricted mainly to attendance at regional and international conferences and workshops. These interactions take the form of education and information sharing rather than direct collaboration on campaigns. AWARE has strong links with ASEAN-based women's groups dealing with issues such as violence against women and reproductive health rights, but is not part of any regional feminist network addressing these issues in relation to migrant women. TWC2 has had even more limited contact with NGOs based overseas and until recently was not a member of regional migrant organizations such as Migrant Forum in Asia. This lack of formal links with international groups is consistent with the position of other Singaporean NGOs, which are wary of being perceived as being tied too strongly to non-Singaporean organizations or campaigns.

In comparison with AWARE and TWC2, UNIFEM Singapore's international links are very strong, reflecting its status as an affiliate member of UNIFEM. This status provides the organization with access to information and other resources not normally available to a nationally based women's organization. UNIFEM has a strong interest in issues facing female migrant workers, and a number of its projects in support of migrant women are based in the Asia-Pacific region, including the Empowering Migrant Women Workers campaign and its assistance of victims of trafficking.[6] However, UNIFEM's organizational regulations are very clear about who can participate in these campaigns and in what capacity. Although migrant women from the developing world may live and work in Singapore for many years, their collective needs and concerns are dealt with through a regional network based in Bangkok rather than by UNIFEM's Singapore office. Consequently, UNIFEM Singapore has been unable to access the resources of UNIFEM in establishing its own development programs. For example, UNIFEM Singapore developed its own materials for its financial literacy training program and did not draw on the experience or expertise of other organizations involved in reintegration schemes for FDWs. Thus, although it is part of an international NGO that, in turn, is part of a TFN working on issues faced by female migrant workers, UNIFEM Singapore occupies a fairly marginal position within this network.

Framing Transnational Feminism

My purpose in examining these three organizations is to demonstrate how transnational feminisms are framed at the local level. Each case study presents an organization that is engaged with transnational issues and whose work is informed by circulating transnational discourses on women's rights, migrant rights, and labour rights. Each organization sees itself as part of a global network of individuals, NGOs, international institutions, and government bodies working to support the needs of female migrant workers. And yet, if we use mode of organizing as the basis for determining what constitutes transnational feminism, it is difficult to describe the efforts of these three organizations as examples of transnational feminist activism. They have few cross-border ties and are not part of any concrete cross-border campaigns. Deploying a definition of transnational feminism that relies less on the form of organizing and more on the ideological basis of activism, however, proves no less problematic. Although all three organizations recognize that the problems faced by migrant women are not unique to Singapore (that is, they are global issues), their focus remains bounded by the national context. If, as Inderpal Grewal and Caren Kaplan (1994) argue, transnational feminisms produce knowledge that takes account of global interdependencies, then it could be concluded that AWARE, TWC2, and UNIFEM Singapore are not part of a transnational feminist movement.

Discounting the work of these groups as examples of local women's organizing, however, falls into the trap of methodological nationalism or the tendency to frame the understanding of social movements within the spatial boundaries of the nation-state (Conway cited in Masson, this volume). As Masson (this volume) argues, TFNs and cross-border campaigns occur not "in a void but as part of a multiscalar world of movement organizing and movement politics." To restrict our understanding of transnational feminist activism to cross-border collaborations or campaigns risks overlooking the dense fabric of women's organizing that enables TFNs to emerge and be sustained. Participating in regional conferences and communicating with overseas organizations are constitutive parts of women's transnational organizing – they are the vertical scaffolds that support the complex connections among differently located organizations, individuals, and institutions. Although AWARE and TWC2 engage in a limited way with migrant worker advocacy efforts at the international and regional levels, their participation in these events is crucial in shaping the ways that migrant worker issues are understood at the national level. Attending conferences and meeting with regional activists also ensures that locally specific understandings of conditions "on the ground" are filtered back up to transnational campaigns. In some circumstances, these informal cross-border connections may be more powerful than formal transnational links. As the example of UNIFEM Singapore demonstrates, formal cross-border ties with international agencies do not always ensure that national-level organizations are embedded within transnational advocacy efforts.

Paying attention to the vertical links and power relations that operate among different scales reveals that transnational feminist activism is not something that occurs on a two-dimensional plane "up there" above the local or national scale but is embedded within these scales. In other words, transnationalism is a process, rather than a location. If we see the activities of different local- or national-level organizations in these terms, then our understanding of transnationalization moves beyond an analysis of cross-border organizing to a consideration of the ways in which solidarity is established at different scales. Although they have limited engagement with actors and organizations located in other national sites, the NGOs in this study facilitate the deepening of solidarities between migrant workers and activists. The mutual understanding that may emerge from these interactions is an essential part of any activism that seeks to address entrenched discrimination and labour rights violations. These vertical ties are a necessary building block in developing sustained solutions to the problems faced by migrant women.

Abandoning a placed-based definition of transnational feminism allows us to move beyond the narrow study of TFNs and other transnational actors that dominate in the global North. In doing so, I am not suggesting that we simply discard the conceptual distinctions among scales by claiming that all forms of feminist organizing are transnational. The groups discussed in this chapter are local-level organizations that, given that Singapore is a small city-state, also operate at a national scale. However, their advocacy efforts involve a process of framing at multiple scales, and although they have limited engagement at the regional and global levels they are clearly engaged in processes of transnational framing.

Broadening our understanding of transnational feminist activism to include how the transnational is constructed within the activist practices of feminist organizations (how local feminists attempt to scale up), allows us to explore the ways in which ideas circulate among different scales and are translated into concrete practices within specific organizational contexts. While feminist scholars are beginning to look at the ways in which domestic struggles take up travelling feminist discourses and deploy transnational feminist frames (Silvey 2004), the theoretical issue here is one of expanding our definition of transnational struggles to include the work of (re)scaling frames. Such an approach provides a means for assessing the impact that transnational feminist organizing is having on women's lives at the local, national, regional, and global levels. As this study demonstrates, to focus on one scale in isolation is to tell only a partial story about how transnationalization of feminist campaigns addresses the rights of female migrant workers.

ACKNOWLEDGMENTS

The research on which this chapter is based is supported by a four-year grant from the Australian Research Council (ARC) for the project Transnational Activism: Organizing for Domestic Worker Rights in Southeast Asia (DP0557370). The project examines the role of NGOs and local and transnational networks that have developed in Singapore and Malaysia to address the rights of female domestic workers. I want to thank the editors and contributors to this collection, including participants at the International Workshop on Transnationalization of Solidarities and Women Movements, Université de Montréal, Montreal, 27-28 April 2006, for their feedback on an earlier draft of this chapter.

NOTES

1 This was a reference to the short-lived The Working Committee (TWC), formed in late 1998 and disbanded a year later (Lyons 2005c; Singam et al. 2002).
2 See Weekley (2004) for a critique of similar skills training and micro-entrepreneur schemes operating in Hong Kong.
3 For a discussion of the common stereotypes used to market maids to potential employers, see Lyons (2005a).
4 For a discussion of multiracialism in Singapore see Lai (1995).
5 The regional network United for Female Domestic Workers Rights was formed in November 2007.
6 For further information refer to the UNIFEM website (www.unifem.org).

REFERENCES

Almenoar, Maria, and Theresa Tan. 2004. Minimum Age for Maids Raised from 18 to 23. *The Straits Times*, 3 September.

Alvarez, Sonia E. 2000. Translating the Global: Effects of Transnational Organizing on Local Feminist Discourses and Practices in Latin America. *Meridians: Feminism, Race, Transnationalism* 1 (1): 29-67.

Anderson, Bridget. 2000. *Doing the Dirty Work? The Global Politics of Domestic Labour.* London: Zed Books.

AWARE. 2004. *Beyond Babies: National Duty or Personal Choice?* Singapore: Association of Women for Action and Research.

–. 2006. *Beyond Borders: Sex with Children – Implementing Extra-territorial Legislation for Singaporeans.* Singapore: Association of Women for Action and Research.

Basu, Amrita. 2000. Globalization of the Local/Localization of the Global: Mapping Transnational Women's Movements. *Meridians: Feminism, Race, Transnationalism* 1 (1): 68-84.

Chin, Christine B.N. 1998. *In Service and Servitude: Foreign Female Domestic Workers and the Malaysian "Modernity" Project.* New York: Columbia University Press.

–. 2003. Visible Bodies, Invisible Work: State Practices Toward Migrant Women Domestic Workers in Malaysia. *Asian and Pacific Migration Journal* 12 (1-2): 49-73.

Constable, Nicole. 1997. *Maid to Order in Hong Kong: Stories of Filipina Workers.* Ithaca: Cornell University Press.

Desai, Manisha. 2005. Transnationalism: The Face of Feminist Politics Post-Beijing. *International Social Science Journal* 57 (184): 319-30.

Ford, Michele. 2006. Migrant Worker Organizing in Indonesia. *Asian and Pacific Migration Journal* 15 (3): 257-71.

Gee, John, and Elaine Ho, eds. 2006. *Dignity Overdue.* Singapore: John Gee and Elaine Ho.

Grewal, Inderpal, and Caren Kaplan. 1994. Introduction: Transnational Feminist Practices and Questions of Postmodernity. In *Scattered Hegemonies: Postmodernity and Transnational Feminist Practices,* ed. Inderpal Grewal and Caren Kaplan, 1-36. Minneapolis: University of Minnesota Press.

Gurowitz, Amy. 1999. Mobilizing International Norms: Domestic Actors, Immigrants, and the Japanese State. *World Politics* 51 (3): 413-45.

–. 2000. Migrant Rights and Activism in Malaysia: Opportunities and Constraints. *Journal of Asian Studies* 59 (4): 863-88.

Henson, Bertha. 2004. Why Those China Girls Worry Me. *The Straits Times,* 3 July.

Ho, Karen, and Elena Chong. 2002. Starved Battered Dead ...: Nine Months of Maid Abuse Went Unnoticed. *The Straits Times,* 20 July.

Huang, Shirlena, Brenda S.A. Yeoh, and Noor Abdul Rahman, eds. 2005. *Asian Women as Transnational Domestic Workers.* Singapore: Marshall Cavendish Academic.

Kempadoo, Kamala, ed. 1999. *Sun, Sex, and Gold: Tourism and Sex Work in the Caribbean.* Lanham: Rowman and Littlefield.

Koh, Gillian, and Giok Ling Ooi, eds. 2000. *State-Society Relations in Singapore.* Singapore: Oxford University Press.

Lai, Ah Eng. 1995. *Meanings of Multiethnicity: A Case-Study of Ethnicity and Ethnic Relations in Singapore.* Kuala Lumpur: Oxford University Press.

Law, Lisa. 2000. *Sex Work in Southeast Asia: The Place of Desire in a Time of AIDS.* London: Routledge.

–. 2003. Sites of Transnational Activism: Filipino Non-Government Organisations in Hong Kong. In *Gender Politics in the Asia-Pacific Region,* ed. Shirlena Huang, Peggy Teo, and Brenda S.A. Yeoh, 205-22. London: Routledge.

Law, Lisa, and Kathy Nadeu. 1999. Globalization, Migration and Class Struggles: NGO Mobilization for Filipina Domestic Workers. *Kasarinlan* 14 (3-4): 51-68.

Lyons, Lenore. 2000a. The Limits of Feminist Political Intervention in Singapore. *Journal of Contemporary Asia* 30 (1): 67-83.

–. 2000b. A State of Ambivalence: Feminism and a Singaporean Women's Organisation. *Asian Studies Review* 24 (1): 1-24.

–. 2001. Negotiating Difference: Singaporean Women Building an Ethics of Respect. In *Forging Radical Alliances Across Difference: Coalition Politics for the New Millennium*, ed. Jill M. Bystydzienski and Steven P. Schacht, 177-90. London: Rowman and Littlefield.

–. 2004. *A State of Ambivalence: The Feminist Movement in Singapore.* Leiden: Brill.

–. 2005a. Embodying Transnationalism: The Making of the Maid. In *Corporeal Inscriptions: Representations of the Body in Cultural and Literary Texts and Practices*, ed. E. Lorek-Jezińska and Katarzyna Więckowska, 171-85. Torun: Wydawnictwo Uniwersytet Mikolaja Kopernika/Nicolas Copernicus University Press.

–. 2005b. *Making Citizen Babies for Papa: Feminist Responses to Reproductive Policy in Singapore.* Copenhagen: Asia Research Centre Copenhagen Discussion Papers.

–. 2005c. Transient Workers Count Too? The Intersection of Citizenship and Gender in Singapore's Civil Society. *Sojourn: Journal of Social Issues in Southeast Asia* 20 (2): 208-48.

–. 2008. Internalized Boundaries: AWARE's Place in Singapore's Emerging Civil Society. In *Paths Not Taken: Political Pluralism in Postwar Singapore*, ed. Michael Barr and Carl A. Trocki, 248-63. Honolulu: University of Hawaii Press.

Mackie, Vera. 2001. The Language of Globalization, Transnationality and Feminism. *International Feminist Journal of Politics* 3 (2): 180-206.

Meyer, Mary K., and Elisabeth Prügl, ed. 1999. *Gender Politics in Global Governance.* Lanham: Rowman and Littlefield.

Moghadam, Valentine. 2000. Transnational Feminist Networks: Collective Action in an Era of Globalization. *International Sociology* 15 (1): 57-85.

Mohanty, Chandra Talpade. 1991. Introduction: Cartographies of Struggle, Third World Women and the Politics of Feminism. In *Third World Women and the Politics of Feminism*, ed. Chandra Tapalde Mohanty, 1-50. Bloomington: Indiana University Press.

–. 2003. *Feminism without Borders: Decolonizing Theory, Practicing Solidarity.* Durham: Duke University Press.

Naples, Nancy A., and Manisha Desai, eds. 2002. *Women's Activism and Globalization: Linking Local Struggles and Transnational Politics.* London: Routledge.

Parliamentary Debates Republic of Singapore. 2004. *Official Report. Part 4 of First Session of Tenth Parliament.* Vol. 77 (18). Singapore.

Parreñas, Rhacel Salazar. 2001. *Servants of Globalization: Women, Migration and Domestic Work.* Stanford: Stanford University Press.

Perera, Leon, and Tisa Ng. 2002. Foreign Funding: Managing Conflicting Views. In *Building Social Space in Singapore: The Working Committee's Initiative in Civil Society Activism*, ed. Constance Singam, Tan Chong Kee, Tisa Ng, and Leon Perera, 93-96. Singapore: Select Publishing.

Piper, Nicola. 2005. Rights of Foreign Domestic Workers – Emergence of Transnational and Transregional Solidarity? *Asian and Pacific Migration Journal* 14 (1-2): 97-119.

Piper, Nicola, and Anders Uhlin. 2002. Transnational Advocacy Networks and the Issue of Female Labor Migration and Trafficking in East and Southeast Asia: A Gendered Analysis of Opportunities and Obstacles. *Asian and Pacific Migration Journal* 11 (2): 171-96.

Silvey, Rachel. 2004. Transnational Migration and the Gender Politics of Scale: Indonesian Domestic Workers in Saudi Arabia. *Singapore Journal of Tropical Geography* 25 (2): 141-55.

Sim, Amy. 2003. Organising Discontent: NGOs for Southeast Asian Migrant Workers in Hong Kong. *Asian Journal of Social Science* 31 (3): 478-510.

Singam, Constance, Tan Chong Kee, Tisa Ng, and Leon Perera. 2002. *Building Social Space in Singapore: The Working Committee's Initiative in Civil Society Activism.* Singapore: Select Publishing.

Singam, Constance, Simon Tay, Kwok Kian Woon, and Yang Razali Kassim. 1997. *The Future of Civil Society in Singapore.* AMP Occasional Paper Series. Singapore: Association of Muslim Professionals.

Singapore Department of Statistics. 2007. *Latest Indicators: Population (Mid Year Estimates) and Area 2007.* http://www.singstat.gov.sg/keystats/annual/indicators.html#Population%20Indicators.

Sperling, Valerie, Myra Marx Ferree, and Barbara Risman. 2001. Constructing Global Feminism: Transnational Advocacy Networks and Russian Women's Activism. *Signs: Journal of Women in Culture and Society* 26 (4): 1155-86.

Wee, Vivienne, and Amy Sim. 2003. *Transnational Labour Networks in Female Labour Migration: Mediating between Southeast Asian Women Workers and International Labour Markets.* Vol. 49. Hong Kong: Southeast Asia Research Centre Working Paper Series.

Weekley, Kathleen. 2004. Saving Pennies for the State: A New Role for Filipino Migrant Workers? *Journal of Contemporary Asia* 34 (3): 349-63.

The Working Committee 2. 2003a. *Our Objectives.* www.aware.org.sg/twc2/who.shtml.

—. 2003b. *The Working Committee 2: Activities and Impact.* Singapore: The Working Committee 2.

Zakaria, Zuzanita. 1998. Surprise Invite for AWARE as Petition Delivered. *The Straits Times,* 10 September.

The International Women and Health Meetings
Deploying Multiple Identities for Political Sustainability

SYLVIA ESTRADA-CLAUDIO

The International Women and Health Meeting (IWHM) has become one of the largest series of gatherings of women's health advocates, academics, funding institutions, and other women's networks involved in women's health and reproductive rights. Its ten successive international meetings represent a twenty-eight-year process that has shaped and been shaped by the global feminist health movement. Organizing practices developed throughout the life of the IWHM have allowed feminist activists engaged in the meetings a large amount of flexibility and a capacity to adapt to political changes across time. This can best be traced to the inclusion and deployment of various identities over the lifetime of the meetings. Such inclusions have been made possible by specific governance mechanisms and practices within the IWHM that express its commitment to building transnational solidarities. In this chapter, I trace how the recognition, negotiation, and deployment of women's multiple bases of political identification have allowed the IWHM to survive and flourish organizationally, and how they have been an integral part of a process of establishing and deepening solidarities across a variety of borders that are not limited to national frontiers. Increased internationalization and the changing locations of the international meetings, I argue, have played a key role in this process, as has the IWHM's engagement with intersectional identity politics. Attempts to deepen solidarities through inclusiveness, however, are not without pitfalls, and I highlight the political and organizational tensions posed by efforts to cope with fractured identities at the IWHM. In the conclusion, I outline some of the consequences of such complexity for transnational feminist politics.

Methodological Caveats

As a feminist writing from within Third World academia, I am aware that there is a risk that the lived experiences and struggles of the marginalized might become the material that legitimizes and advances academic careers. Feminism (and transnationalism, if it is to be true to its progressive impulse) requires that I interrogate a variety of power relationships, including my own involvement in the global processes of knowledge production. In short, from where do I speak?

I have been a part of the IWHM process since I helped organize the Manila meeting in 1990. Since then, I have attended each meeting except one, and I have served on the international advisory committee (IAC) of several of the meetings, including the tenth one, in New Delhi in 2005. Because these meetings are a non-institutionalized process, no single set of persons serves as leadership, no one person can be spokesperson, and no institution can be seen to represent participants. My attempt to "gain permission" to speak about the IWHM has thus been to notify as many other women as possible who have been involved in the process of my desire to write about parts of it. I received no objections and was helped by several women in writing an earlier workshop paper on the IWHM (Estrada-Claudio 2006). However, this chapter and its analysis are by no means a collective undertaking. They are entirely my own and, as such, remain limited and open to contestation. Finally, it must be noted I focus here only on elements that have led to sustainability of the IWHM process over time, and not on those that have led to discord or setbacks. I also deal essentially with processes internal to the IWHM and do not discuss other health-related meetings, feminist or otherwise, in which transnational activists and their organizations have intervened on the basis of common understandings developed at IWHM meetings.

The International Women and Health Meeting: Feminist Organizing Processes

After the first IWHM meeting was held in 1977 in Rome, meetings were scheduled every two to three years.[1] The IWHM had no group of leaders to ensure continuity, no constitution or bylaws; there was no permanent office, nor was there a repository of finances or documents. Yet, the process survived, despite the fact that it was non-institutionalized.

The themes and stated purpose of the IWHM have varied with each meeting, reflecting changes in both political realities and political theory. The purpose of the third meeting, held in Geneva in 1981 (the earliest meeting for which documentation is currently available), was "to exchange knowledge, experience and ideas among women working in self-help health" (Third IWHM Organizing Committee 1981, 3). While "self-help" remained a value for feminist activists at the meetings, it became limited as a vibrant international women's health movement progressively redefined international human rights standards to include sexual and reproductive rights. The IWHM's focus shifted from self-help to rights over the years, signalling a broader change in discourse. The statement of purpose of the ninth meeting, held in 2002, for instance, retained the idea of providing a forum for exchange among activists, but the meeting was described as "a venue for women's health activists from around the world to gather ... in order to take stock of the gains and setbacks in the area of women's health and reproductive rights" (Canadian Organizing Committee 2002, 1).

Indeed, tracing the changing themes of the meetings is an effective way to track the discourses that feminists have developed around the issues of health and reproduction over the last thirty years. It is also a good indication of the broad scope and political flexibility of the IWHM. The location of meetings and themes (when information is available) are summarized in the figure below.

This political flexibility was made possible by novel organizing and governance processes. From the outset, the IWHM has followed feminist principles of non-hierarchical and inclusive leadership. As will become apparent in the other sections of this chapter, these processes have interrogated power along structural axes such as class, race, and ethnicity.

Feminists looking at global social movements stress the feminist and transnational nature of this type of organizing. For example, Cynthia Cockburn (2005, 6, emphasis in original) notes about women's organized responses to militarism that "women are quite clear that they organize as women in order to be *in control of process*. They say they have developed distinctive methodologies of organization and action with which they can be comfortable." One such distinctive organizational methodology in the IWHM process is that each international meeting is governed by a different national organizing committee (NOC). Each NOC has final authority over all aspects of that particular meeting, but has no further authority beyond it. Available documents seem to show that this form of governance was not consciously planned from the outset. Nonetheless, it has become a tradition.

Figure 1: LIST OF IWHM MEETINGS AND SUMMARY OF THEMES

1st IWHM – Rome, Italy, 1977
Women from Europe involved with the abortion campaign and broader issues of women's health met in Rome, which, in retrospect, was called the 1st IWHM.

2nd IWHM – Hanover, Germany, 1980

3rd IWHM – Geneva, Switzerland, 1981
Workshop Topics:
1. Health, Poverty and Racism
2. The Role of Paramedics
3. Abortion
4. Imperialism and Population Control
5. Sexuality
6. Contraception
7. Pregnancy and Childbirth
8. Breastfeeding and Nutrition
9. Women and Madness
10. Women's Research into Natural Medicine
11. Menopause, Lesbian Health, Dental Self-Help
12. "Women from the Third World"
13. International Information, Documentation and Networks
14. Yoga as a Method of Contraception and Abortion
15. Women and Violence

4th IWHM – Amsterdam, Netherlands, 1984
Theme: *No to Population Control, Women Decide*

This meeting was organized in the form of a tribunal. Many issues were discussed and positions taken on:
1. Contraception, Abortion and Sterilization (the slogan was: "Our Bodies, Our Lives, Our Right to Decide")
2. Drugs (a multinational issue)
3. Sexual Politics (for different groups: Muslim, lesbian, women with children, etc.)
4. Population Control or Women's Control (from different countries' viewpoints)
5. Women and Disability
6. Racism

►

◄ Figure 1

5th IWHM – Costa Rica, 1987

It was at this meeting that May 28 was designated the "International Day of Action for Women's Health." This day has gained widespread currency, not just among feminist health networks and women's groups. For example, in 1999 the government of South Africa recognized this day. It was also referenced in the 2006 Global Health Newsletter of the USAID – an organization that received scathing critiques at various IWHMs for its population control policies.

6th IWHM – Quezon City, the Philippines, 1990

Theme: *In Search of Balanced Perspectives and Global Solidarity for Women's Health and Reproductive Rights*

Main plenary themes:

1 Women's Health and Development
2 Women's Health and Reproductive Rights
3 Violence (militarist, religious, institutional) Against Women
4 Sexuality

7th IWHM – Kampala, Uganda, 1993

Theme: *United We Stand to Solve the Global Problem of Women's Health and Reproductive Rights*

Sub-themes:

1 Addressing cultural and religious obstacles to improve health practices
2 Generating broader political support and understanding for women's causes
3 Integrating women's perspectives and priorities more fully into government and donor funded population health
4 Encouraging and supporting women in their efforts to improve their health and well being.
5 Ensuring adequate attention is paid to often neglected health issues such as sexually transmitted diseases, cancer, violence against women's health after menopause
6 Broadening the linkages between child survival and family planning programs
7 Increasing women's input into the development and dissemination of reproductive and health terminologies
8 Protecting women against AIDS
9 Coping with causes and consequences of unwanted pregnancies.

►

◄ Figure 1

8th IWHM – Rio de Janeiro, Brazil, 1997
Theme: *Women's Health, Poverty and Quality of Life*
The theme was discussed using gender, race, and social class approaches.

9th IWHM – Toronto, Canada, 2002
Themes:

    1 Women's Reproductive Rights
    2 The Impact of Violence (state and family) on Women's Health
    3 The Impact of the Environment (natural and built) on Women's Health

10th IWHM: New Delhi, India, 2005
Theme: *Health Rights, Women's Lives: Challenges and Strategies for Movement Building*

Sub-themes:

    1 Public Health, Health Sector Reforms
    2 Reproductive and Sexual Health
    3 The Politics and Resurgence of Population Policies
    4 Women's Rights and Medical Technologies
    5 Violence (of state, militarism, family and "development") and Women's Health

---

Source: Revised by the author from a document provided by the Indian Organizing Committee (2005b). Significant input also came from Loes Keysers and Martha de la Fuente.

Beginning with the fifth meeting in Costa Rica, in 1987, and until the ninth meeting in Canada, in 2002, the locale for the next meeting was decided upon at the end of each one, based on voluntary bids by participants from the countries that wanted to host it. Once selected, that country (more specifically, the volunteering individuals and organizations) became fully responsible for pushing the process forward.[2]

The host country's NOC is responsible for all aspects of its meeting. Naturally, each NOC is composed of an entirely new set of persons, drawn from women's networks, NGOs, academic and research settings, and a pool of interested individuals. This has resulted in a variety of political standpoints, assessments of political situations, organizational approaches, and prioritization of issues. The practice of rotating organizational responsibility has allowed the IWHM to remain current and cutting-edge in discourse. It has also kept the process democratic, because moving the meeting around countries and regions has prevented the dominance of any single perspective.

The IWHM has also survived and remained meaningful over the years because organizing the meeting has galvanized women's health groups within each respective host country, helped them empower their advocacy both locally and internationally, and given them opportunities to do global analysis. Conversely, women attending from many countries have had a concrete opportunity to grasp both similarities and differences in women's health issues across national and regional boundaries. It would seem, therefore, that the IWHM is a non-institutionalized, non-hierarchical solidarity process that finds its relevance in transnationalism as an ideological or political project (Kearney 1995).

Non-institutionalization has its drawbacks, however. Aspects of institutional memory – such as best practices and lessons learned – are difficult to pass on. The control of each meeting by an NOC also increases the danger of falling into parochialism. These pitfalls have been addressed in various ways. For example, for the sixth IWHM meeting in 1990, Filipina activists started a process that internationalized decision-making somewhat, by creating an international advisory committee (IAC) (Philippine Organizing Committee 1992). At that time, the IAC was composed of representatives of several women's and health networks, including the Argentine Commission of the Fifth Feminist Encuentro of Latin America and the Caribbean, Catholics for a Free Choice, the Feminist International Network for Resistance Against Reproductive and Genetic Engineering, the International Women's Health Coalition, Isis International, the Latin America and Caribbean Women's Health Network, the Women's Global Network for Reproductive Rights, and the organizing committee of the First African Regional Meeting on Women and Health. The formation of the IAC to counsel the NOCs has continued as a practice for subsequent IWHM meetings. Its composition, however, has changed over time; recent committees have been composed of women from different regions instead of networks. While the composition of these committees remains fluid, several women have served repeatedly on them, and they bring a large store of experience to the organizing process of each meeting.

Recognizing Identities in Struggle

One of the central propositions of this chapter is that the success of the IWHM lies in the negotiation and recognition of various political identities of feminist activists. The successful governance mechanisms described above have arisen as a result of adjustment to the fluidity of women's identities. The IWHM has been able not only to adapt to the range of national and regional identities of women active in the organization, but also to respond in flexible and open ways to the emergence of concerns about intersectionality and multiplicity that have traversed women's action and movements over the last decades.

Transnational Organizing Practices and National Identities

The practice of giving responsibility for each IWHM meeting to a nationally based organizing committee recognizes the plurality and importance of national identities. Having participated in making the choice for the next "national" feminist movement to host the meeting over the years, I can state that we indeed "negotiate" a national identity for a particular group of women who will do the organizing work. Once negotiated, however, belief in this identity is so strong that the organizing committee of the host country has unilateral control over process, programming, fundraising, allocation of financial subsidies, and venue – thus reflecting the values of non-interference, autonomy, and sovereignty of nation-states that guide international relations.

The efficacy of this practice within a transnational organization such as the IWHM may seem dubious in the context of the need to present a common front against transnational practices or institutions that threaten women's health. As well, some political theorists of globalization doubt that national organizations are the appropriate sub-units of transnational ones (Hardt and Negri 2000), and activists have noted the erosion of the role of the state in protecting its citizens in an era of globalization. But the continuing assertion of national identities can serve some of the political goals of the international women's health movement. It can also be congruent with the role of the state in the area of social services under globalization. Whereas the World Trade Organization appears as the primary enemy for large sectors of the poor today, the most significant actors over the past few decades in the health sector have been the International Monetary Fund and the World Bank, whose austerity programs, health sector reforms, user fees, and budget cuts for social services have had catastrophic effects for the world's poor. These policies are still negotiated bilaterally between national governments and international institutions. They are still being enacted through the surrender (forcible or otherwise) of state sovereignty and are often legitimized by allegedly democratically mandated governments.

Furthermore, because health is a social service, the state remains primarily accountable when there is absence or neglect. Repressive state practices in some parts of the world are also manifested in the violation of reproductive and sexual rights and freedoms. Repressive laws on sexual orientation, marriage and family relations, and contraception are promulgated and enforced by national governments.

IWHM organizing practices, while initially suited to internationalism and the anti-patriarchal and anti-imperialist struggles of the second half of the twentieth century, have nevertheless taken account of the need to go beyond nationalism. Feminists have long understood the limitations of nationalism and national identity for women's struggles.[3] As I have noted, in plenary sessions and personal conversations, theoretical discussions and practical actions, IWHM organizers and participants understand the arbitrariness of national identity. At the sixth meeting, banners of participating countries were put up in the main plenary hall. However, the countries were based on women's identifications rather than on the prevailing geopolitical ones. One woman, for example, asked to have her banner show the country Eritrea, much to the dismay of a participant from Ethiopia, who complained to me that she was a government official and would run into difficulties back home. It will be recalled that at that time, Eritrea had not yet won its struggle of independence, and was considered by Ethiopia to be a part of its national territory. Similarly, several indigenous women's homeland names were identified on the banners along with the names of countries that claimed these homelands as part of their national territory. Furthermore, at various IWHM meetings, participants have been cognizant of the situations in which nationalism is used against women and in which violence is perpetrated against women in the name of nationalism. There is also recognition that religious fundamentalism can conflate its interests with national patriarchies to the detriment of women's sexual and reproductive rights. However, the IWHM would never have survived if meeting organizers did not understand that women are differentially positioned in interlocking systems of oppression.

Deploying Other Identity Positions

Apart from national identities, the recognition of the various social relations of power that shape women's bodies and of the multiple identities that go with them has also played an important role within the IWHM process. As Josefa Francisco (2005, 1) writes,

As feminist movements we are conscious of the fact that our bodies are replete with cultural and social meanings. Equally important is our understanding and experience that women's bodies are key arenas upon which many moral and political battles are being fought. It is through women's bodies that the community, state, family, fundamentalist forces (state and non-state), religion, the market and male identity seek to define themselves. Through a plethora of patriarchal controls these forces and institutions transform women's bodies into expressions of power relations. Women's bodies are in this way, at the center of authoritarian or democratic projects.

Francisco's comments point to the need for taking into account and recognizing other identities because power over women's bodies has multiple foci. Over the years, members of organizing communities have shown their awareness of this. The highlighting of an increasingly wide range of identity positions is a key ingredient in the continuing relevance of the IWHM process. The increased internationalization and the geographic travels of the meetings played a key role here.

The first IWHM meeting, in Rome in 1977, was a meeting of European groups and was labelled "the first" only in retrospect (Indian Organizing Committee 2005b). The second meeting, in Hanover, was still very largely dominated by participants from Europe. Loes Keysers (personal communication, 12 March 2006), participant in the third meeting, in Geneva, recalls the beginnings of the process of wider internationalization of the IWHM, in terms of both its participants and the emergence of issues regarding race and imperialism:

It was international in a small way at least ... at least one South African, a Sri Lankan, a Bangladeshi, a Thai and an Indian woman got travel grants. Moreover it is quite likely that some refugees from South America participated in this meeting. In any case, I remember that the very presence of non-European women raised questions about structural racism and imperialism in population control interventions, [operating] under the then "innocent" guise of family planning.

The real work of networking in order to internationalize the IWHM began for the fourth meeting: in February 1982, in an International Contraception, Abortion and Sterilisation Campaign coordination meeting, there was a proposal to organize the next meeting. At the meeting in May 1982, a

decision was made to break the precedent of the first three meetings by trying to work with groups outside of Europe.[4] Various organizing difficulties,
however, led to the fourth meeting being held in Amsterdam. The fifth
meeting, in Costa Rica in 1987, was the first to be held in the Third World.

"In Search of Balanced Perspectives and Global Solidarity for Women's
Health and Reproductive Rights," the theme of the sixth meeting, held in the
Philippines in 1990, reflected the need to bring the perspectives of Third
World women into the feminist health movement. Filipina organizers established quotas to ensure that subsidies went to women in Africa and Asia, as
well as to women from poor communities in the First World. There was
even an attempt to ensure that only a fourth of the participants would come
from Europe and North America. This was to be achieved not by limiting
the number of women from these countries, but by ensuring a proportion-
ate number of subsidies for women from other regions.

Organizers of the sixth IWHM meeting believed that lesbians and their
organizations had to be given more space and recognition within the heterosexist feminist movement. One of my clearest memories as an organizer was
our effort to ensure that there would be a lesbian speaker at the plenary session on sexuality and workshop spaces for lesbian caucuses, even though
rooms and time were in short supply.[5] In addition, members of the Philippine Organizing Committee attended the initial lesbian caucus as a sign of
support.[6]

Since then, there has been a trend toward recognizing an increasing
number of identity positions at successive IWHM meetings. Such recognition has resulted from and contributed to the various discourses that have
arisen in transnational women's movements. For example, at the eighth
meeting, held in Rio de Janeiro in 1997, the organizing committee ensured
that the theme, "Women's Health, Poverty, and Quality of Life," was discussed in the light of gender, race, and class oppressions. This added identities such as "poor" and "woman of colour" to the mix of national and
regional identities. These positionings have allowed the meetings to make
connections with many emerging struggles and the social movement sectors that represent them. Finally, for the tenth meeting the Indian Organizing Committee (2005a, 1) both reiterated and added to the categories of
race, class, and gender: "It is now widely accepted that health is dependent
on age, class, race, caste, ethnicity, culture, location, disability, marital status
and sexual orientation; and that it is also intrinsically linked to the production and reproduction roles that women play."

Networks that actively participate in the IWHM processes are yet another example of how identities are recognized, inscribed in practice, and mediated. Many plenary and workshop speakers are chosen on the basis of network representation, and they are from international networks such as Women Living under Muslim Laws, and Catholics for a Free Choice – affiliations that, in this case, highlight women's religious identities. Speakers from the International Lesbian Information Service and the International Gay and Lesbian Association are also asked to speak, to give a voice to identities based on sexual orientation.

Coping with the Tensions of Fractured Identities

At the ninth IWHM meeting, I was asked to assist the Canadian Organizing Committee in running a conference-long workshop that would eventually come up with recommendations for organizing the next meeting. One recommendation that emerged from this workshop was to expand the IAC to accommodate more regional representatives; another was to include "sectoral" representatives. Whereas the Canadian IAC had only one representative for Europe, for example, it was suggested that the Indian IAC should add a second representative for Eastern Europe. Similarly, it was recommended that Latin America and the Caribbean be treated as two separate regions instead of one. In this way, a total of sixteen world regions were identified. To the sixteen regional representatives would be added sectoral representatives for women with disabilities, young women, indigenous women, lesbians, and elderly women. There were also suggestions that the major networks be involved (again) in the process.[7]

I bring up this particular issue to illustrate the tensions and pitfalls that arise from identity politics. It was repeatedly pointed out during the workshop that the size of such an IAC would be impractical. However, no solution could be found to this generally acknowledged problem. Indeed, this long list of identities achieved easy consensus precisely because it tried to be all-inclusive and despite its lack of practicality.

As I reported the long list of suggested IAC representations to the closing plenary session of the Canadian IWHM meeting, there was laughter, followed by yet more suggestions for categories. It was obvious to everyone that no matter how inclusive was the listing of categories by region, country, sector, class and caste, age group, ethnicity, sexual orientation, disability, and so on, each individual participant or group of participants would still be tasked with "being the voice" of millions of others.

Cognizant of these recommendations, the Indian Organizing Committee for the tenth IWHM meeting had to find a way to (partially) solve the problem. The committee's members achieved this by taking advantage of the fact that individual women have access to multiple identity positions. Thus, the Indian IAC was composed of a large group of women (seventeen in total) who somehow managed to come from various world regions and "sectors." It is important to note that such attempts at constructing representation around multiply held identities may succeed for some purposes, yet there are instances in which they do not. Thus, while the capacity to conflate the identities of "young woman from Vietnam," for example, may be helpful in forming reasonably small IACs, the conflation of "woman from the Third World" with "poor woman" must be criticized because it stands in the way of increasing grassroots participation.

Early and consistent efforts at inclusiveness at the IWHM meetings anticipate the insights of Maylei Blackwell (in UCLA International Institute 2005, 11) about emerging feminist transnational networks:

> First there was a kind of a more celebratory tone of the possibilities and challenges of so-called global civil society, in which myself and several other scholars who work in social movement organizing saw how these spaces were actually fraught with unequal power relationships and exclusions along some lengths that have been already talked about – class, sexuality, race, gender. And how when we talk about who can participate in NGOs, who has access to the international arena, that we have to remember that as much as those are spaces or possibilities of liberation, they're also spaces where power operates.

Blackwell's point about differential access to transnational networks and the NGOs that often comprise them is well taken. Despite a commitment to the grassroots, the poor, and the marginalized, these types of participants remain underrepresented at IWHM meetings. I am but one of many who have tried for years to overcome this problem by attempting to bring more grassroots women to the meetings. But these efforts have often been stymied by lack of funding or, when funding was available, the lack of personal documents for passports, bank certificates for visa applications, and so on. The more sweeping statements about an increasingly connected world and global community do not take into consideration the systematic bias against the free migration of the poor.

Furthermore, power operates in international/transnational networks not just through who gets to come to network activities and meetings. The fact that meetings usually feature plenary speeches, papers, and workshops tends to disenfranchise women without higher levels of formal education or facility in at least one major European language. The Philippine organizers of the sixth IWHM meeting ensured that the plenary sessions had simultaneous interpretation into Filipino, a feat that required some political will to allocate the rather large additional budget for the service. There were also "echo meetings" conducted for Philippine women's NGOs after the main meeting. Similarly, the Indian Organizing Committee conducted a series of sub-regional pre-meetings and ensured that a large contingent of Indian women attended the IWHM meeting in New Delhi.

For the tenth IWHM meeting, in India, there was a conscious effort, as well, to be reflexive about the pedagogy of the conference by encouraging more alternative sharing and communication strategies and more creative approaches, in order to move away from the usual speeches, papers, and workshops that privilege women with formal educational backgrounds. For example, there was an impressive international film festival that ran for the duration of the meeting. There were also art exhibits, booths, performances, and so forth. This consideration of pedagogical issues did not start at the tenth meeting. I remember a similar call being made in one of the plenary sessions of the eighth meeting in Brazil, when one of the speakers suggested that we belly dance!

The capacity to recognize multiple identities comes about because a theoretical understanding has evolved that sees identities as neither singular nor stable. Janet Price, a participant in the tenth IWHM meeting and member of its IAC notes that even the seemingly most stable of identities underlying the concept of "woman" – the biologically female body – has been directly challenged at the IWHM (personal communication, 15 March 2006). At this meeting, a male-to-female transgendered group from Malaysia gave a performance of songs and dances. Price comments on the controversy that this caused:

> Alongside this, is the question of "Woman," which in the early days of the IWHM was a very untroubled notion. We all "knew" who women were. But with intersectionality playing a stronger role in our practice and with the very powerful attack on the natural, biological basis of womanhood, attacks that emerged with notions of cultural construction of gender and that have

become more complicated with the rise in postmodern thinking, the question about the position of transgender and transsexual people within this space is opened up in a different way. It was addressed in India in a sideways fashion by the presence of the performing group from Malaysia. A small number of conference participants walked out, refused to watch as they weren't "women" performing, but the majority were only too happy to sit and watch and cheer. This would not, could not have happened with feminism as it was ten years ago. But today, links are being made, not only in the complications of what "women" are, but also in respect of the alliances being made in relation to sexuality and reproductive justice/rights.

The organizers of the tenth IWHM meeting (Indian Organizing Committee 2005a, 5) show a sophisticated grasp of the politics of identity that anticipates these dilemmas:

> Identity politics has given the scope for the articulation of concerns of "invisibility," "marginalization," "representation," etc. At this point, how do we explore the possibilities of a common agenda for advocacy, struggles and campaigns? Women from many parts of the world questioned language that homogenized experiences and universalized "sisterhood." Can we now explore the possibility of evolving global feminist concerns that accommodate and respect difference and diversity?

Conclusion

This chapter shows that the deepening of solidarities in transnational networks and events, such as the IWHM organization and meetings, is neither simple nor straightforward. Rather, it has required conscious political work, involving representation and decision-making, as well as strategic inventiveness in governance mechanisms and political practice. Crucially, this political work has been sustained by feminist understandings of intersecting oppressions and of the multiple and competing bases for identification to which they give rise. The questions posed at the tenth IWHM meeting indicate that even as activists are successful in recognizing multiple identity positions, they are not unaware of the problems that arise from such attempts. Mutual recognition "in and through difference" is not easily accomplished. All of the IWHM meetings have been marked by tensions along lines of class, race, heterosexism, and other biases. Many meetings, for example, have been marred by accusations of homophobia, racism, and elitism against participants and even organizers. Tensions have become especially strong when the discrimination has been attributed to the organizers or to their inability to ensure the existence of procedures that prevent it from occurring. And all this has happened despite the seeming consensus that the IWHM is ideologically opposed to these very oppressions.

Yet, the IWHM has survived because its organizers have been able to recognize and overcome (at least partially) some of these problems for specific political ends. Public statements made at opening ceremonies and other key moments signal to all participants that the IWHM is intended to result in the equitable sharing of symbolic space. The geographical travels of the meetings, the negotiation of national and regional identities in early meetings, and the list of regions and "sectors" included in the redrafting of the composition of the IAC for the ninth meeting illustrate organizers' attempts to concretize the IWHM's "imagined community" (Anderson 1991).[8] Organizational methodologies and alternative pedagogies have been devised or adopted to achieve greater inclusiveness. Some difficulties, however, have proven to be trickier to solve, most notably issues of differential access to participation linked to lack of funding and systemic barriers to the spatial mobility of the poor.

Feminist politics is enriched by the insights that come from exploring the world of reproduction and sexuality in settings such as IWHM meetings. Such an engagement leads to a politics that is cognizant of the tenuous nature of subjectivity, resulting from the fact that women and men engage with various foci of power as they lead their everyday lives. The increasing entanglement of power in our daily existence is part of the process called globalization, which has brought about not only increasingly tight linkages in production, reproduction, and consumption but also an increasing capacity on the part of transnational capital to reach into our most intimate spaces and extract value. The IWHM process has engaged these power/subjectivity matrices by accepting that organizing work cannot be done around the concepts of class and nationality alone. This has meant recognizing the struggles of women of differing abilities, ethnicities, classes, castes, ages, nationalities, sexual orientations, marital statuses, and religions within the larger political goal of women's health, sexual, and reproductive rights.

However, feminists must not only dialogue among themselves but also engage with other social movements. This is critically important at the present time, when global activism is growing. One of the difficulties presented by attempts to engage with other social movements – by the "stretching" of solidarities beyond feminist and women's constituencies and issues – is that taking simple political positions runs contrary to the complexity of the emergent feminist politics.[9] This complication has a long history in feminism because, for many activists, feminism involved the rejection of the master narrative of class analysis as a basis for political engagement. The development of increasingly complex analyses based on several positionalities makes the engagement with other movements an even more difficult process. Nonetheless, it is crucial that feminists do engage with them. Certain currents of the environmentalist movement, for example, have accepted demographic arguments that bolster population control, with major consequences for women's reproductive freedoms. In many local and transnational settings, labour movements are deeply patriarchal. Nationalist discourses can also mean wars that have devastating effects on women and their children, especially because women's bodies can become cultural markers for "the enemy." I believe that this means that feminists must sharpen their ability to work within a feminist politics that is grounded in the materiality of our bodies, the boundlessness of our desires, the multiplicity of our passions, and the bedrock of our capacity to make commitments and to act.

ACKNOWLEDGMENTS

I would like to thank the following women who served as resource persons or helped in other ways to make this paper possible: Lyda Canson, Junice Demeterio-Melgar, Martha de la Fuente, Josefa "Gigi" S. Francisco, Manisha Gupte, Anissa Helie, Anuj Kapilsharami, Loes Keysers, Nuzhath Leedham, Ana Maria Nemenzo, Janet Price, and Neha Suri.

NOTES

1 There is a discrepancy in the documents regarding the dates of the first meeting in Rome and the second meeting in Hanover. The proceedings of the third IWHM meeting, published in 1981, state that the first meeting was held in 1977 and the second in 1980. The proceedings of the tenth IWHM meeting state that the Rome meeting was held in 1975 and the Hanover meeting in 1978. I have retained the dates from the older document.

2 Manisha Gupte of the Indian Organizing Committee (personal communication, 17 September 2006) indicated that there was a variation in this pattern at the tenth IWHM meeting, at which the next host country was not chosen at the closing plenary session. This was based on the recommendation of the IAC. The Indian Organizing Committee and the IAC are managing the process of selecting the next host through networking with possible host organizations, thus signalling a return to pre-1987 practice.

3 Virginia Woolf stated this as early as 1938: "In fact, as a woman, I have no country. As a woman I want no country. As a woman my country is the whole world" (2007 [1938], 125).

4   Martha de la Fuente (personal communication, 29 October 2007). De la Fuente is citing documentation from the fourth IWHM meeting.
5   Our ignorance on this matter was amazing because until the last minute, those of us working on the program, myself included, did not know whom to ask. This led to a number of awkward situations until Rina Nissim finally saved us from disaster by agreeing to talk on short notice.
6   Our support was unnecessary, however, as the room was packed to capacity, mostly by Filipinas. I credit the sixth IWHM meeting and those lesbian caucuses with providing great impetus to the Filipina lesbian feminist movement at a time when it was just emerging. The effect of the solidarity exhibited by lesbians from other countries who patiently answered questions and revealed their personal struggles cannot be overstated.
7   I am reciting these facts from memory. Having been tasked to write up and report the recommendations at the final plenary of the ninth IWHM meeting, I am confident of their general outlines.
8   That this is indeed an imagined community is illustrated further by the fact that it actually has a foundational myth. The organizing committee of the third IWHM meeting (1981, 1) writes that over five hundred women from thirty-six countries participated and that for the first time funds were "especially secured to bring women from Asia, Africa and Latin America to enable a truly international exchange."
9   I am grateful to Janet Price for this insight.

REFERENCES

Anderson, Benedict. 1991. *Imagined Communities: Reflections of the Origin and Spread of Nationalism.* Rev. ed. London and New York: Verso.

Canadian Organizing Committee. 2002. *Concept Paper for the 9th IWHM.* Toronto, Canada.

Cockburn, Cynthia. 2005. Feminist Antimilitarism: Scope, Problematic and Difficulties in a Global Social Movement. Lecture for the Colloquium *Intended and Unintended Suffering: The Legacy of Meg Stacey's Ideas and Works,* 29 June, University of Warwick, Coventry.

Estrada-Claudio, Sylvia. 2006. The International Women and Health Meetings: Catalyst and End Product of the Global Feminist Health Movement. Paper presented at the Transnationalization of Solidarities and Women Movements Conference, 27-28 April, Political Science Department, Université de Montréal, Montreal.

Francisco, Josefa. 2005. Concept Note for the Feminist Dialogues. Unpublished document, Porto Alegre, 23-25 January.

Hardt, Michael, and Antonio Negri. 2000. *Empire.* Cambridge, MA, and London, UK: Harvard University Press.

Indian Organizing Committee. 2005a. Health Rights, Women's Lives: Challenges and Strategies for Movement Building. *Proceedings of the 10th International Women and Health Meeting,* 21-25 September, New Delhi.

–. 2005b. IWHM-History. Unpublished document.

Kearney, Michael. 1995. The Local and the Global: The Anthropology of Globalization and Transnationalism. *Annual Review of Anthropology* 24: 547-65.

Philippines Organizing Committee. 1992. *In Search of Balanced Perspectives and Global Solidarity for Women's Health and Reproductive Rights: Proceedings of the Sixth International Women and Health Meeting.* Quezon City: Philippines Organizing Committee.

Third IWHM Organizing Committee. 1981. Editorial. *Isis International Bulletin* 20: 3.

UCLA International Institute. 2005. *Transnational Feminism: A Range of Disciplinary Perspectives.* Transcript of a roundtable sponsored by UCLA's Center for Modern and Contemporary Studies, Center for the Study of Women and the Research Group on Transnational and Transcolonial Studies. http://www.international.ucla.edu/cms/files/060518_transnational_feminism.pdf.

Woolf, Virginia. 2007. *Three Guineas.* New York: Penguin Books.

5 Transnational Activism and the Argentine Women's Movement Challenging the Gender Regime?

DÉBORA LOPREITE

The Argentine gender regime is being challenged, especially with regard to its reproductive policies, by the emerging global gender equality regime and by domestic actors. Over the last three decades, a new gender regime framing women's demands at the global and regional (Latin American) scales has emerged as a result of key UN conferences that have enabled the transnational women's movement to create solidarities and frame shared understandings of women's issues (Desai 2005; Friedman 2003). Although the emergent international gender norms are not obligatory for member states, the multiplication of norms and institutions has helped to empower women's movements and strengthen women's networking. The participation of national actors in the international arena has contributed to the global formation of gendered policies (Kardam 2004; Zwingel 2005) and has also helped these actors in their efforts to improve women's status at home. As is argued in this book, the transnationalization of solidarities not only enables solidarities to travel beyond national borders, but also deepens these solidarities. This process opens up opportunities for a better, shared understanding of situations, issues, and potential solutions (see the Introduction to this volume). In this chapter, I argue that this has had empowering effects on Argentine women's groups, enabling them to advance women's interests, especially on reproductive rights.

The empowering of national women's movements is very apparent in Argentina, a country long characterized by a conservative gender regime.

While democratization and the subsequent debate on human rights provided an initial opening to women's movement politics in the 1980s, it was
not sufficient to achieve a breakthrough. In the 1990s, however, major UN
conferences (Cairo 1994; Beijing 1995) contributed to the formation of a
global gender equality agenda, with a particular emphasis on reproductive
rights. In Latin America, a regional gender equality agenda emerged among
Latin American women activists through UN-related regional conferences
and new transnationalism practices (Encuentros), which provided Argentine women's groups with new discourses and strategies for challenging the
domestic gender regime. At the same time, developments at the national
scale provided new openings. In light of these developments, the formulation of the new gender agenda in Argentina needs to be understood in relation to both new opportunity structures at the global, regional, and national
scales and the use that Argentine women's groups have been able to make of
these, especially through their ability to jump across scales.

In the first section of this chapter, I examine changes in the domestic
political opportunity structure arising from democratization, in 1983, and
the subsequent emergence of a human rights framework. I analyze the
establishment of the Consejo Nacional de la Mujer (CNM), the women's
policy machinery, in belated compliance with the UN Convention on the
Elimination of All Forms of Discrimination Against Women (CEDAW),
adopted in 1979. In the second part, I look at the emergent global and
regional gender regimes and women's organizing at the regional scale. This
is followed by an analysis of the intersection between the national, global,
and regional scales focused on issues of reproductive rights and abortion.
Information was collected from Argentine government and UN documents.
I conducted interviews with members of women's organizations, members
of the National Congress, and government officials in Buenos Aires between
2005 and 2007.

The Gender Agenda in Argentina: Democratization and a New Political Opportunity Structure

The Argentine gender regime had long been conservative, committed to a
traditional family form, and very limited with regard to reproductive rights.
There were inequities with respect to women's access to contraceptive services and a lack of abortion services (Lewis 1992). Democratization in 1983
offered a favourable opportunity structure to begin challenging this conservative gender regime. During the 1980s, however, the debate was dominated by the need to expand women's political and civil rights, and the most

significant gender equality reforms were in the domain of civil law – such as the new family law, which included divorce and *patria potestad compartida*.[1] The new democratically elected government was also more responsive to gender equality developments on the global scale. For example, while the military junta (1976-83) had failed to ratify CEDAW, the new government was quick to do so in 1985 as part of a broader move to recognize human rights. Following the ratification of CEDAW, the then president, Raúl Alfonsín, created the first women's office in Argentina in 1987, the Subsecretaría de la Mujer (Women's Sub-secretariat). As these institutional reforms came into effect, Argentine women started to hold their regular annual Encuentros de mujeres (women's national conferences) in 1986. Each conference took place in a different province and was attended by fifteen to twenty thousand women from all over the country. At these gatherings, women started to build common discourses questioning the basis of the gender regime.

While the sub-secretariat remained under the control of the Ministry of Social Action and did not play a central role in addressing gender equality issues, the CNM – created in 1992 as an initiative of women within the governing Peronist party – reflected the openness of the Argentine state to the global push to instal women's policy machineries in state bureaucracies in order to promote and monitor a "gender perspective" across all public policies (mainstreaming). These agencies were, however, usually understaffed and lacked material resources. Anne Marie Goetz (1997) and Nüket Kardam (1997) note that, paradoxically, this very lack of resources in developing countries motivates the leaders of such agencies to establish links with civil society organizations and become more receptive to women's demands. This was only partially true in the Argentine case, however. As we shall see, the CNM was gradually deflected from its initial goals and isolated from women's organizations and their demands. Its poor performance and political weakness also reflected the political instability of the new Argentine democracy and the consequent lack of continuity of staff and policy orientation.

Since 1983, the political opportunity structure has been changing as a result of the government's efforts to adjust domestic policies to the new global directives on gender equality provided by the UN, CEDAW, and the Beijing Platform (1995). While the global gender regime helped to shape the Argentine gender regime, this process took place without the explicit mediation of the women's movement until the 1990s, when the global gender regime became more fully developed. Although Peronist women activists promoted the creation of the CNM, during the 1990s conflicts arose over reproductive rights, and changes in government and party politics affected the opportunities to advance a gender agenda.

The CNM in the 1990s: State Modernization and a Women-Friendly Policy

In Argentina, the creation of a women's policy machinery was part of a state modernization process aimed at improving administrative performance in the bureaucracy. Its specific mission was to implement the new quota law of 1991 – which stipulated that women must hold a minimum of 30 percent of the seats in the National Congress – and the Plan for Equal Opportunities for Women and Men. However, its establishment, through a presidential decree by Carlos Menem, coincided with the adoption of the neoliberal agenda promoted by the Washington Consensus on structural adjustment. The simultaneous adoption of these agendas was problematic for the women politicians who envisioned the CNM in a more progressive way.[2]

Under the presidency of Virginia Franganillo (a key person in the Peronist women's movement), the CNM promoted ongoing interaction with women's organizations, established a number of programs to increase women's political participation, and played an important role in the 1995 Beijing conference (Waylen 2000). During this period, the National Congress passed a bill to combat domestic violence, and in 1993 the president issued a decree against sexual harassment in public departments and agencies. Furthermore, since its creation, the CNM has been involved in advancing reproductive rights; together with a group of women members of the National Congress, it developed the first law to address reproductive rights in the National Congress (personal communication with former CNM leader, 27 October 2005).

The Menem government's main agenda, however, blended neoliberal economic ideas with a strong dose of social conservatism. Therefore, with respect to reproductive rights, the CNM found itself up against the emerging alliance between Menem and the Catholic Church, which aimed to stop all attempts to legalize abortion.[3] Menem also attempted to introduce an anti-abortion clause into the constitutional reform of 1994, which led to a clash between him and Franganillo, under whose direction the CNM had become heavily involved in the campaign against the anti-abortion clause. Ultimately, Franganillo was forced to resign from the CNM in 1994. In 1995, a group of women members of the National Congress close to Franganillo attempted to pass a bill that addressed family planning, but it was never debated in the Senate.

In 1995, Menem created an ad hoc commission in the Ministry of Foreign Affairs to follow up on the Beijing Platform for Action, but he made it clear that his position on reproductive rights had not changed by appointing Esther Schiavone, an enthusiastic Menemist activist who also opposed abortion, to the presidency of the CNM. During this period, the organization's role shifted toward a technocratic agenda committed to implementing women-friendly policies but excluding reproductive rights. Under Schiavone's leadership, the CNM's agenda was reoriented mainly toward measures promoting gender parity in the workplace and the reconciliation of work and family life. After introducing equal treatment for workers of both sexes in the public sector in 1997, Menem issued a decree addressing equality of opportunities for men and women in the workplace. The decree found its antecedents in CEDAW and the Beijing Platform for Action, but also in Treaty 156 of the International Labour Organization on the equality of treatment and opportunity for men and women workers – in particular, workers with "family responsibilities."[4]

With these two decrees, Menem's government moved to selectively implement the Beijing and CEDAW directives, in an attempt to place Argentina among the group of democratic countries promoting gender equality and the reconciliation of work and family life. Yet, this agenda was ambiguous from a gender perspective, because Menem's policies did not attempt to transform gender relations within the family. As in the European directives to advance gender equality (Stratigaki 2004), "reconciliation" has been interpreted as improving women's ability to combine paid work and family responsibility rather than changing gender relations within the family itself.

This narrow gender agenda was not well received by women's organizations. Despite the move to define a women-friendly policy, Argentina's official opposition to the reproductive rights agenda in the Cairo (1994) and Beijing (1995) conferences and Menem's isolation from women's groups resulted in the CNM's losing legitimacy as a means of advancing gender equality. This explains the radicalization of the reproductive rights debate that started in the 1990s. While Menem's agenda explicitly excluded this topic, Argentine women's organizations worked together to develop and advance a reproductive rights discourse. Indeed, Menem's international alliance with the Vatican and other conservative states incited the women's movement to focus on challenging the Argentinean government's position on reproductive rights in the international arena (McIntosh and Finkle 1995).

Successive changes in institutional location and political importance further weakened the CNM's position within the executive branch of government.[5] In 1999, a moderate, internally fragile centre-left coalition (Alianza UCR-Frepaso)[6] led by Fernando De La Rua took power during a period of deep economic recession. Politically and technically bound to introduce macroeconomic reforms to overcome the financial crisis, De La Rua's government collapsed in December of 2001. The women of the Alianza were divided on how to proceed with a gender agenda, and tensions between women from the UCR and Frepaso political parties weakened the CNM's position within the government. Moreover, Carmen Storani, the new head of the CNM and an activist in the UCR, was considered by the women's movement to be too close to the executive branch. For autonomous feminist activists with no party affiliation, the CNM was seen as a hostage to partisan strife. At the same time, women politicians felt that the CNM lacked a feminist perspective on women's affairs.

In 2001, Argentina's economic crisis prompted the government to default on loans and devalue the currency, giving rise to massive protests across the country. The crisis contributed to the marginalization of the CNM. More important, however, was the CNM's increasing isolation from the women's movement and from its original mandate to oversee gender equality compliance across all public policies. Nevertheless, the need to rebuild state capacity and alleviate the negative social consequences of the economic crisis opened new opportunities to discuss reproductive rights in the context of reproductive health and poverty-reduction policies.

A Shift to the Left and a New Social Agenda: Implications for Gender Policy

The centre-left government of President Néstor Kirchner, elected in 2003, developed a dual gender policy. On the one hand, the CNM was downgraded and lost its original mainstreaming purpose. It was relocated to the National Council for Social Policy Coordination. The new president of the CNM, Maria Lucila Colombo, was an activist from the Movimiento de Amas de Casa (housewives' social movement). She had explicitly supported anti-abortion positions during the legislative debate on reproductive health (2000) when she was an elected representative in the Buenos Aires city legislature. As a Catholic left-wing activist, she favoured family planning but rejected abortion. The new mission of the CNM was thus based on a social agenda focused on the need to strengthen the role of the family in a context marked by economic and social fragmentation, while reformulating traditional gender roles (PROFAM 2001).

On the other hand, Colombo addressed several women's issues brought forward as part of the international and regional gender agenda. The CNM was actively involved with issues such as domestic violence and the Economic Commission for Latin America and the Caribbean (ECLAC) recommendations on the value of women's unpaid work. Although Colombo self-identified as being part of the women's movement, she kept at a distance from its organizations. The lack of a feminist perspective in the CNM is crucial to understanding its limitations as an agency for advancing a comprehensive gender equality agenda within the national bureaucracy (personal communication with Socialist Party [PS] national legislator, 23 May 2007).

In a context in which it was proving difficult for women to penetrate the state's bureaucratic structure, some women's organizations looked to the UN's international human rights system for support. Indeed, uneven state support for the gender agenda, the weaknesses of female civil servants and politicians divided along party lines, and the isolation of women's organizations incited women's groups to "jump scales." This was possible because of the emergence of a global gender regime and the increasing transnationalism of the Argentine women's movement.

The Global and Latin American Gender Regimes: Opportunities for Argentine Women's Organizing

The global gender regime is composed of a set of formal principles, norms, legal rules, mechanisms for monitoring the compliance of state members, and shared understandings that form a gender equality discourse (Kardam 2004). CEDAW is one important legal instrument for gender equality. Yet, nation-states are not simply executors of this new international framework, as international conventions such as CEDAW do not force them to obey the regulations. Indeed, ratification of treaties is voluntary, which creates potential tensions among the emergent international legal framework, national governments, and internal forces that want to see these norms adopted in their countries.

CEDAW has adopted a monitoring process that involves the submission of periodic reports (every five years) by member states. The reports must list actions "taken to eliminate discrimination against women and specify factors and difficulties met in fulfilling their treaty obligations" (Kardam 2004, 90). The reports are scrutinized in public meetings at which government representatives face questions. Although this monitoring process does not result in the imposition of sanctions, mandatory participation in the public hearings may exert moral pressure on government representatives when they are exposed to international scrutiny. In addition, national women's organizations have the right to present an alternative report. This so-called hidden or shadow report plays an important role, providing other sources of information for the UN officials who question the national representatives in the public hearings.

Although the international gender regime involves a gender equality discourse, the way in which international agencies have interpreted women's needs has not been uniform. Definitions of gender issues vary according to each agency's goals. In her research conducted on three international donor agencies, Kardam (1997, 48) concluded that the World Bank's goals are shaped largely by financial standards, oriented "to promote economic growth for developing countries (with reliance on market mechanisms)." For instance, the World Bank adopted the issue of reproductive rights following the recognition of its role in the reduction of fertility rates and population growth, which in the South is seen as a brake on development. In recent years, it has developed "poverty reduction" as a policy paradigm and has shifted its focus by providing targeted social assistance and health services.[7]

Women's organizations have played an important role in the development of the regime through more than two decades of advocacy and network building. The UN system constituted an important site for the coming together of governmental and non-governmental organizations to define a global gender agenda. Over successive international conferences, participating women's organizations gained new technical and political skills (see also Díaz Alba, this volume). The alliance among leaders of the global women's movement within the UN system is seen as central to the codification of gender equality norms, and to the development of collective understandings of such norms (Kardam 2004, 90-91).

In these international conferences, women's organizations worked to empower women to achieve fundamental changes in gender relations and in the political, economic, and social structures that underpin them. Sonia E. Alvarez (1999) argues that the plurality and diversity of feminist practices contributed to a redefinition of the feminist agenda for social change. The emergent global regime brought new pressures to bear on national and local states to move forward with a gender equality agenda, implementing gender-focused programs in which the technical assistance and participation of women's organizations became a major requirement for accessing financial assistance from multilateral agencies (Alvarez 1999; Kardam 1991). To be sure, participants have had to frame their demands in accordance with the predominant discourses and goals of existing international institutions. Nevertheless, they have also contributed to a reshaping of the pre-existing institutional structure (Kardam 2004).

Regional Political Opportunity Structures and Latin American Women's Organizing

Historical legacies of military regimes are critical to interpreting the transnationalization of the Latin American women's movement and the consolidation of a convergent gender equality agenda in Latin America. Most of the military regimes of the 1970s, in countries such as Argentina, Brazil, and Chile, attempted to reinforce a conservative model of gender relations, including repression of women's reproductive freedoms. In Argentina, contraception was prohibited. In this context, it is not difficult to understand why democratic transitions and women's activism in Latin America were accompanied by demands for democracy, rights, and citizenship. As Georgina Waylen (2003, 168) points out, "Some women activists hoped that the return to democracy would bring with it a number of progressive gender reforms." Consequently, it was easy for Latin American women activists to find commonalities with international discourses on gender equality and to influence the international agenda through their participation in international organizations and international and regional women's conferences (Waylen 2003, 172). Internationalization of human rights and the democratization processes in the region gave women activists new legal tools within nation-states. Gerda Wekerle (2000, 205) observes, "Based on these international agreements, signed by national governments, women's movements argue that human rights cannot be constrained or revoked by nation-states."

For the most part, the global gender equality agenda reached Argentina through the regional formulation of platforms for action. For example, within the UN system, Latin American states developed their own regular conferences (Regional Conference about Women of Latin America and the Caribbean) organized by ECLAC. Through these conferences, Latin American states came to an agreement on the development of a regional platform for action (RPA) to complement existing instruments for the advancement of women, such as the Beijing Platform for Action. The 1995-2001 RPA for the Women of Latin America and the Caribbean identified priority areas such as gender equity in economic and social development; women's equitable share in decision-making and power in public and private life; elimination of poverty; human rights, peace, and violence; shared family responsibilities; and international support and cooperation (RPA 2004). Successive regional women's conferences have been held in different Latin American countries, resulting in three documents – the Santiago Consensus, the Lima Consensus, and the Consensus of Mexico City – that aim to translate general purposes into practical policies. In all of these regional conferences, member nation-states have agreed to implement the RPA.

Although UN-related regional conferences have played an influential role, their resolutions are not backed by sanctions for states that do little to address gender inequality. There are no explicit monitoring mechanisms. In other words, although national governments may have agreed to platforms for action at the regional level, they are not obliged to implement them rigorously. Nevertheless, the new Latin American regime at least provides women's movements in the region with discursive tools with which to pressure national governments to advance a gender equality agenda. As such, the new regime has clearly provided an important space for political activism and communicative action, which has contributed to the formulation of a shared discourse denouncing the economic injustice arising out of structural adjustment policies implemented in the region. Indeed, the formation of collective understandings at the regional level opens an intermediate scale of action for women's organizations. The creation of regional organizations and the development of regional conferences offer opportunities for grassroots groups with limited access to international conferences (due to lack of geographical and linguistic proximity) to participate in the global process of institutionalization of women's interests.

Latin American women's organizing and strategizing, however, had had an earlier start, in the feminist Encuentros, at which women from different backgrounds and identities have come together since the 1980s to discuss the issues at stake. The Encuentros are heterogeneous, polycentric, and expansive (Alvarez 2000). Alvarez (2000, 35) suggests that women "continue to view the Encuentros and other alternative transnational arenas, such as the regional networks, as crucial sites in which to re-view and refine their feminist discourses and practices, in dialogue with others in the region."

Jumping Scales: Monitoring, Compliance, and the Role of the Argentine Women's Movement in the UN System

In transnational contentious politics, social movement actors may decide to "jump scale" – to change scales (by moving upward or downward) in search of more favourable political conditions (Smith 1992). As Sidney Tarrow

(2005, 145) points out, "Domestic actors, frustrated at their inability to gain redress from their own governments, have long sought the support of external allies." By providing information to UN officials, women's organizations have been able to denounce the existing status of Argentine women and to press the national government to move ahead with the gender equality agenda.[8]

Argentine women's advocates' strategy of jumping scales can be seen in the hidden reports submitted to UN officials and in the role that these reports have played, in turn, in monitoring the Argentine state's performance in its implementation of CEDAW rules and conventions. While the development of a gender equality agenda entails several issues, one salient topic has caught the attention of women's advocates, Argentine representatives, and UN officials: reproductive rights and abortion.

Although international conventions such as CEDAW do not force nation-states to comply with all of the regulations stated in the norms, "a certain level of international pressure and the desire to avoid embarrassment in an international arena may prompt state representatives to go along with decisions taken at international conferences" (Kardam 2004, 8). Susanne Zwingel (2005) points out that over the CEDAW committee's last twenty years of work, its professionalism and global profile have risen significantly. In addition, there has been an improvement in the reports submitted to UN officials by member states as they have learned to provide reliable data. In this regard, domestic women's organizations make an important contribution to addressing issues (Alvarez 1999), revealing the growing role of women's organizations in Argentina (and in other Latin American countries). Hidden reports provide a detailed analysis of the status of women in Argentina. Among the topics of importance in the reports are the need to implement policies that deal with violence, including sexual harassment and domestic violence; cuts to social and health insurance and reductions in family allowances; and the lack of regulation of domestic workers. Particular attention is given to deficiencies in the health sector and to the reproductive rights of women.

Hidden reports have been written and submitted by six Argentine women's organizations: Asociación de Especialistas Universitarias en Estudios de la Mujer (ADEUEM), the Latin American and Caribbean Committee for the Defence of Women's Rights (CLADEM) Argentina, Fundación para el Estudio e Investigación de la Mujer (FEIM), Instituto Social y Político de la Mujer (ISPM), Feministas en Acción, Asociación Mujeres en Acción, and Centro de Estudios Legales y Sociales (CELS) (a broader human rights advocacy group). Some of these organizations (CLADEM, FEIM, and CELS in particular), with highly professionalized staff, have better access to the international system and strong links with other international activists, while other organizations are composed of women active in both political parties and grassroots-level associations.[9]

These organizations differ in terms of both access to international and domestic funding and links with international experts and UN officials. Yet, all of them are part of an extensive network that addresses women's issues. They also offer a feminist perspective to gender mainstreaming at the different institutional scales (personal communication with ADEUEM and CLADEM leaders, 22 November 2005).

Argentina first submitted official reports in 1988, during Raúl Alfonsín's presidency; further reports were made in 1997, 1998, 2002, and 2004 (CEDAW 1997, 1998, 2002, 2004a, 2004b), reflecting the increasing globalization of women's issues. UN officials' concerns were divided into three types of issues, which were pursued by the women's organizations through the hidden reports. These three areas also reflect the kinds of problems that were exposed in the Argentine reports.

The first set of issues were related to women's welfare in light of the consequences of structural adjustment policies implemented in Argentina and the rest of Latin America. In 1997, for example, the principal areas of concern for CEDAW were the increasing levels of female unemployment after the implementation of structural adjustment policies, gender segregation in the labour market, and the lack of special legislation to penalize sexual harassment in the workplace. In addition, CEDAW addressed the high levels of maternal mortality and morbidity due to childbirth and the fact that abortion rates remained high "despite the economic and social development of the country" (CEDAW 1997). It recommended actions to reduce maternal mortality, including modifying the legislation to decriminalize abortion.

The second area of concern was the institutional instability of CNM – an issue of particular relevance to the six women's organizations submitting the hidden reports to CEDAW after the financial crisis of 2001. For example, the hidden report submitted in 2002 articulated concern with increasing levels of poverty and the lack of coordinated national policies on reproductive health and rights, together with the ongoing disempowerment of the CNM as the main mechanism to coordinate and monitor the implementation of a gender equity agenda across all public policies. This report (CONTRAINFORME CEDAW 2002, 4) informed the CEDAW Committee that the CNM had "suffered an institutional and financial downgrading becoming, in January of 2002, a program of the National Council of Social Policies. Since 1998, the CNM experienced ongoing budget reductions and the loosening of management autonomy, a situation that has been aggravated since 2002."

The hidden report also revealed that "there are no mechanisms of coordination of the different state agencies, in particular between the CNM, the Women's Office in the Ministry of Foreign Affairs and the women's movement" (CONTRAINFORME CEDAW 2002, 4). In response to the concerns expressed by women's organizations, UN officials (CEDAW 2002) alerted the Argentine government in the public hearings held in 2002 to the "attempt to downgrade the CNM and the lack of a formal strategy for coordination of the different State agencies" and noted the importance of continuity, autonomy management and coordination of the national mechanism for the advancement of women at this time of crisis in the country and recommends that they should be strengthened."

The third area of concern was related to reproductive rights, an issue that shaped Argentina's gender agenda in the 1990s. This issue surfaced thanks to the outcomes of the Cairo Conference on Population and Development held in 1994, and was also due to the emergent global gender equality regime on reproductive rights. Yet, women's organizations played an even more critical role in addressing this issue through their hidden reports. In particular, observations were made regarding the Menem government's policies on reproductive rights.

Specific questions were asked of the Argentine state's representatives in several sessions in which the reports were discussed. During one of the 1998 sessions (CEDAW 1998, Art. 12), the Assembly chairperson, Ms. Castillo, asked if "the government intended to review its policy of allowing the sterilization of women only with the express consent of their husbands or partners and only in life-threatening situations, and if not, what its reasons were to continue to permit such legal obstacle to the exercise of women's reproductive rights." She was also "alarmed that abortion and obstetrical complications were the principal cause of death among Argentine women." The Argentine government representative and president of the CNM, Esther Schiavone (CEDAW 1998, Art. 16) responded, "Women had the right to decide how many children they had and the spacing between them. However, there were disparities in the information and counselling services available as, owing to the decentralization of health care, as such programs were implemented at the municipal and provincial levels."

In contrast to the answers provided by the Argentine government, the hidden report by the women's organizations emphasized the lack of reproductive rights and the role that old demographic policies still played in government decisions. Women's organizations noted that the situation had not changed since 1997:

> Historically, Argentinean women have seen their free choice of having children or not, how many, when and how to have them restricted. Despite CEDAW and other international instruments of human rights, the situation has not changed. The Argentinean state has a persistent pro-natalist tradition and it is sensitive to the pressures of conservative groups inside and outside of the Catholic Church. As a result, the Argentinean State has not been able to carry out comprehensive and persistent public policies to guarantee reproductive rights. Since the last report submitted to CEDAW in 1997, this situation has not changed. (CONTRAINFORME CEDAW 2002, 16)

The hidden report also noted, "According to official data, in Argentina there are 400,000 abortions performed every year. Obstetrical complications for abortions are the first cause of hospitalization in gynaecological services" (CONTRAINFORME CEDAW 2002, 18). Based on this information, CEDAW representatives questioned the Argentinean representatives about the asymmetries of reproductive health policy implementation. UN officials also recommended that the Argentine government take action on issues such as the quantification of unpaid women's work, parental sharing of common duties and responsibilities in the household, regulation of childcare, regulation of domestic employees, and violence against women, including sexual harassment in the workplace.

An analysis of the hidden reports and the CEDAW monitoring process reveals that during the 1990s women's organizations used a critical tool, jumping scales, to articulate global and local discourses and pressure the national government on key issues, such as obeying international rules on gender equality. Moreover, the participation of feminist advocates in Néstor Kirchner's government, elected in 2003, helped to shift Argentine positions on reproductive rights in international arenas.

Through the representation of Ambassador Juliana Di Tulio, Argentina took a position in favour of reproductive rights for women according to the Beijing Platform for Action and CEDAW. It also took a more active role in the Latin American Conferences of Women by becoming the voice of the

Rio Group at the 49th Session of the UN Commission on the Status of Women. In this context, the active participation of women activists from Latin America was important in pushing national governments to ratify their commitment to Beijing 1995. Indeed, all Latin American member states approved the Consensus of Mexico City in June of 2004 during the 9th Women's Regional Conference of ECLAC held in Mexico City. The Consensus of Mexico City constituted a landmark for the advancement of women in Argentina, since the Argentine government, for the first time, committed to all of the elements without reservation, including reproductive rights and the CEDAW optional protocol, an instrument that provides access to justice for women who have been denied their rights in the national arena by permitting them to have their claims reviewed at the international level by the committee of independent experts that monitors compliance with the Convention.[10] The new government also deepened the regional integration of MERCOSUR, and femocrats[11] of the Southern Cone Countries held regular meetings in the context of MERCOSUR + Chile.[12]

Conclusion

In this chapter, I argue that a change in the Argentine gender regime has been taking place, visible notably in the domain of reproductive rights. This redefinition of the national gender regime is happening in a multiscalar world, in which different interconnected political structures provide opportunities for Argentine women's advocates to challenge gender relations at the national scale. The emergence of a global gender equality regime and the increasing transnationalism of the women's movement – in Latin America, in particular – have provided the Argentine women's movement with discourses and strategies with which to frame women's reproductive rights in the direction of women's equality within their country's borders. In this new context, women have been able to build solidarities across borders by reframing a sensitive women's issue in a new way. In other words, deepened solidarities across scales have had empowering effects for local activists, including in their ability to jump scales.

There were important changes in the Argentine political opportunity structure, especially after democratization was initiated in 1983. The extended debate on human rights favoured the adoption of CEDAW and the translation of the global gender equality regime into domestic politics. The creation of the CNM was the result of the adoption of these international norms. Yet, changes in party politics and governments highlighted the limitations on advancing a gender equality agenda at the national scale.

Moreover, in 1994 a major controversy caused the government to halt the advancement of reproductive rights within the country.

The partial adoption of the global gender equality agenda in Argentina reveals the peculiarities of the agenda's domestic adoption and translation. While Argentina has ratified international conventions on women's rights in the larger context of democratization, the reception of this agenda within national borders through the explicit adoption of policies and programs has been mitigated by the different political projects of various democratic governments since 1983. Thus, the Argentine gender equality agenda in the 1990s was shaped by the neoliberal project that predominated in that decade, as well as by the selectivity of the elements in the Beijing agenda and its reinterpretation in relation to the neoliberal paradigm. The later "new social agenda" addressed some other aspects of the international gender discourse, but with gender equality subsumed within a discourse focused on the need to reconstitute the family and adjust changing gender roles. Moreover, the emergence of reproductive rights at the international scale created a conflictual scenario in Argentina. Finally, the changing role of the CNM resulted, to a great extent, from the different positions of the national actors – governments and the women's movement – regarding reproductive rights.

While at the national scale women's groups were constrained in their efforts to advance gender issues, their ability to jump scales was critical to challenging pre-existing power relations at the national scale. Indeed, issues discussed in the UN arenas – poverty, inequality, CNM's institutional weakness, and reproductive rights and health – were the consequence of the domestic tensions created by attempts to translate a global gender regime into varied projects adjusting national interests to new gender equality goals. An excellent example of scalar strategies is the way that women's organizations provided information to UN officials and forced the Argentine government to be held accountable, during UN hearings, for its previous commitments to enforce women's rights. International monitoring mechanisms and the contribution of the different actors to the framing of the debate at the international, regional, and national political scales are thus central to understanding the formation of a gender equality agenda in Argentina.

NOTES

1 The new family law acknowledged equal rights and duties for women and men and the possibility for children born either outside marriage or to parents married to other people to be recognized as legitimate by their biological fathers or mothers.

During this period, women's social rights were also extended with pensions for women in conjugal relationships but not legally married. In the domain of political rights, women politicians advocated for the inclusion of quotas for women in party lists.

2 In fact, there were three different phases in the creation of the CNM. First, a presidential decree created the Consejo Coordinador de Políticas Públicas para la Mujer (Coordinating Council of Public Policies for Women) in 1991. One year later, in 1992, the National Women Council was created as a sub-secretariat dependent upon the executive. The following year, the CNM acquired Secretariat of State status.

3 In 1994, Menem publicly revealed for the first time his anti-abortion position in accordance with the goals of UNICEF on protection of mothers and children (personal communication with former CNM leader, 27 October 2005).

4 Both plans were only partially implemented, due in part to the structural constraints of the labour market.

5 Actually, at first the CNM was part of the presidential office. According to Georgina Waylen (2000, 779), however, "it was part of the government of the day and not ... a permanent part of the state apparatus."

6 The Alianza was formed by the merger of UCR (Unión Cívica Radical) and FREPASO (Frente País Solidario).

7 This is particularly relevant in the Argentine case, as the recent Sexual Health and Responsible Procreation Program, funded by the World Bank, fits within the broader agenda of poverty alleviation adopted after the severe fiscal crisis of 2001.

8 Argentina and other Latin American countries, such as Chile, have a tradition of externalizing calls for action in the human rights domain. In particular, during recent military dictatorships, several domestic actors were able to denounce human rights violations in the country. Sidney Tarrow (2005) calls this path information transmission and monitoring.

9 One of the particularities of Latin American women's organizing, highly noticeable within Argentina, is the "double activism" of the women working in networks. Women participate in political parties while identifying themselves as part of the women's movement *(movimiento de mujeres),* or they are members of the trade unions as well as activists *(militantes)* in the women's movement.

10 Thanks to pressure by the women's movement and the initiative of some women MPs, the Argentine National Congress has recently ratified the optional protocol. The main argument against the protocol is that it affects national sovereignty and opens the door to abortion.

11 Femocrat is a term used to refer to women working in the state bureaucracy representing women's interests.

12 MERCOSUR is the economic block composed of Argentina, Brazil, Paraguay, and Uruguay. Chile is an associated member state.

REFERENCES

Alvarez, Sonia E. 1999. Advocating Feminism: The Latin American Feminist NGO "Boom." *International Feminist Journal of Politics* 1 (2): 181-209.

–. 2000. Translating the Global: Effects of Transnational Organizing on Local Feminist Discourses and Practices in Latin America. *Meridians: Feminism, Race, Transnationalism* 1 (1): 29-67.

CEDAW (Committee on the Elimination of Discrimination against Women). 1988. *Concluding Observation on Argentinean First Periodic report.* United Nations.

–. 1997. *Fifteenth and Seventeenth Sessions Report.* United Nations.

–. 1998. *Consideration of Reports Submitted by State Parties. Second and Third Periodic Reports of Argentina.* United Nations.

–. 2000. *Fourth Periodic Report of State Parties. Argentina.* United Nations.

–. 2002. *Fifth Periodic Reports of States Parties. Argentina.* United Nations.

–. 2004a. *Follow-up to the Fourth and Fifth Periodic Reports of States Parties. Argentina.* United Nations.

–. 2004b. *Concluding Observations on the Fourth and Fifth Periodic Reports. Argentina.* United Nations.

CONTRAINFORME CEDAW. 2002. *Derechos Humanos de las Argentinas: Asignaturas Pendientes del Estado.* Convención sobre la Eliminación de todas las formas de discriminación contra la mujer.

Desai, Manisha. 2005. Transnationalism: The Face of Feminist Politics Post-Beijing. *International Social Science Journal* 57 (184): 319-30.

Friedman, Elisabeth Jay. 2003. Gendering the Agenda: The Impact of the Transnational Women's Rights Movement at the UN Conferences of the 1990s. *Women's Studies International Forum* 26 (4): 313-31.

Goetz, Anne Marie, ed. 1997. *Getting Institutions Right for Women in Development.* London and New York: Zed Books.

Kardam, Nüket. 1991. *Bringing Women In: Women's Issues in International Development.* Boulder: Lynne Rienner.

–. 1997. Making Development Organizations Accountable: The Organizational, Political and Cognitive Contexts. In *Getting Institutions Right for Women in Development,* ed. Anne Marie Goetz, 44-60. London and New York: Zed Books.

–. 2004. The Emerging Global Gender Equality Regime from Neoliberal and Constructivist Perspectives in International Relations. *International Feminist Journal of Politics* 6 (1): 85-109.

Lewis, Jane. 1992. Gender and the Development of Welfare Regimes. *Journal of European Social Policy* 2 (3): 159-73.

McIntosh, Alison C., and Jason L. Finkle. 1995. The Cairo Conference on Population and Development: A New Paradigm? *Population and Development Review* 21 (2): 223-60.

PROFAM. 2001. Argentina: Family Strengthening and Social Capital Promotion Project. World Bank Document.

RPA. 2004. Regional Programme of Action for the Women of Latin America and the Caribbean. ECLAC, Economic Commission for Latin America and the Caribbean, 1995-2001.

Smith, Neil. 1992. Homeless/Global: Scaling Places. In *Mapping the Future: Local Cultures, Global Change,* ed. Jon Bird, Barry Curtis, Tim Putnam, George Robertson, and Lisa Tickner, 87-119. London and New York: Routledge.

Stratigaki, Maria. 2004. The Cooptation of Gender Concepts in EU Policies: The Case of "Reconciliation of Work and Family." *Social Politics* 11 (1): 30-56.

Tarrow, Sidney. 2005. *The New Transnational Activism*. Cambridge: Cambridge University Press.

Waylen, Georgina. 2000. Gender and Democratic Politics: A Comparative Analysis of Consolidation in Argentina and Chile. *Journal of Latin American Studies* 32 (3): 765-93.

–. 2003. Gender and Transitions: What Do We Know? *Democratization* 10 (1): 157-78.

Wekerle, Gerda. 2000. Women's Rights to the City: Gendered Spaces of a Pluralistic Citizenship. In *Democracy, Citizenship and the Global City*, ed. Engin F. Isin, 203-17. London: Routledge.

Zwingel, Susanne. 2005. From Intergovernmental Negotiations to (Sub) National Change: A Transnational Perspective on the Impact of CEDAW. *International Feminist Journal of Politics* 7 (3): 400-24.

PART 3

STRETCHING THE SCOPE OF SOLIDARITIES

Troubling Transnational Feminism(s) at the World Social Forum

JANET CONWAY

The World Social Forum (WSF) is rightly celebrated by many feminists as an autonomous space for the convergence of an unprecedented array of emancipatory movements, including a great variety of women's movements, from all over the world.[1] This chapter is an exploration of the contemporary contours of transnational feminist politics against this backdrop. There are plural and competing transnational feminist projects apparent at the WSF. This plurality, and the complexity of the relationships among the projects, enormously complicates general theories of transnationalism and transnationalization.

While the transnational feminisms discussed here appear broadly convergent, they lead largely parallel lives in the WSF, suggesting an uneasy coexistence. The study that is the subject of this chapter arose from my experience at the 2007 WSF in Nairobi, at which I detected the presence of two distinct feminist camps, each mounting a series of events that was largely ignored by the other. The WSF is so large and pluralistic that this was not, in and of itself, necessarily significant. However, as I followed each of these feminist pathways, I began to discern distinct feminist projects, as well as sharpening differences and palpable tension between them. This chapter is an exploration and mapping of that conflictual political terrain.

Many activists are reluctant to discuss such tensions for fear of needlessly polarizing a difficult situation. I share that concern and have sought to constructively analyze the plurality, complexity, and contradictions of these feminisms. The leaders of these networks recognize each other as friends and fellow feminists who "do some things together [but] basically don't find affinity" (Phumi Mtetwa, personal communication, 24 January 2007). I likewise find that feminisms in anti-globalization spaces are in broad alliance but manifest significant differences arising from distinct histories and political orientations, with implications, both political and analytical, for the future of feminism and its imbrication with the worldwide convergence of movements for global justice.

In this chapter, I focus initially on two distinct expressions of transnational feminism at the WSF, the Articulación Feminista Marcosur and the World March of Women, but the main analytical focus is on a third, the Feminist Dialogues.[2] The Feminist Dialogues is an episodic initiative of a coalition of twelve transnational feminist networks that first appeared at the 2004 WSF, oriented primarily to fostering transnational feminist dialogue. It did not appear as an entity on the WSF program until 2007 in Nairobi. In order to understand the historical emergence and specific character of the Feminist Dialogues in Nairobi, and to situate it vis-à-vis the World March of Women, I have opted to back up historically to well before its first appearance to focus on one of its founding networks, Articulación Feminista Marcosur. As will become clear, there is significant continuity between the Articulación and the Feminist Dialogues that makes tenable the comparison between them and the World March of Women, although it is important not to conflate the first two.

The Articulación Feminista Marcosur and the World March of Women have been the most prominent and influential transnational feminist networks in the WSF. From the beginnings of the Forum, each has had sustained involvement in the political struggles in both its events and its governance structures, notably its International Council. Other feminisms, large and small, come and go in the Forum, depending on the political conjuncture and geographical location of the global events. Each major feminism is a transnational network composed of a number of constituent feminist groups based in different countries, although the scale and geographic grounding of each is quite distinct. The Articulación is a regional-scale transnational network based in Latin America, composed of nine networks in eight countries, most of them in the Southern Cone. The March, on the other hand, can justifiably be called global, with six thousand groups active in 163 countries and present on all continents. The Articulación (and the Feminist Dialogues, of which it is a founding member) readily uses the language of transnationalism to describe what it is and the politics that it seeks to advance. There is no evidence that the March rejects this designation, but it more readily calls itself global or international.

In the WSF, each of these networks, the Articulación and the March, belongs to a distinct cluster of allied feminist groups. The groups in each cluster regularly collaborate in mounting events and supporting one another's initiatives in the WSF. Until recently, the clusters were informal and barely visible to the casual observer. However, beginning in 2004, a more formal collaboration, composed of groups that agglomerated around the Articulación's highly visible Campaign Against Fundamentalism, began to appear. By the time of the 2007 WSF in Nairobi, this collaboration, the Feminist Dialogues, had consolidated. It projected a highly internationalized, coherent transnational feminist presence as an alternative to that of the World March of Women.

The chapter begins by troubling discourses of the transnational in feminist politics and scholarship. In the spaces and processes of the WSF, every feminism present is arguably transnational or transnationalizing, simply by virtue of its engagement with the Forum, but some are more transnationalized than others. The variable scales, modalities, organizational forms, geographic groundings, and political content of claims to the transnational in feminist practice need to be disaggregated and problematized, studied empirically and comparatively – an agenda to which this book and this chapter will, I hope, contribute.[3] After exploring these conceptual issues, my subsequent use of the term "transnational feminism" simply refers to networks that self-identify as feminist and have constituent groups in two or more countries.

Following this conceptual overview, I introduce the Articulación and the March and their convergent efforts to make the Forum feminist. A major objective of this narrative is to historicize the emergence of the Feminist Dialogues as a distinct initiative but one in continuity with the political and cultural orientations of the Articulación. By the 2007 WSF in Nairobi, axes of difference appeared more sharply drawn, particularly between the Feminist Dialogues and the World March of Women. Through a comparative study focused on transnational feminist practices in Nairobi, I contend that these feminist encounters in, over, and around the WSF involve contestations not only over the WSF but *over the character of feminism itself.*

A Feminist Genealogy of the Transnational

Historically, the descriptor *transnational feminism* emerged in the context of the UN-sponsored conferences of the late twentieth century. By the mid-1980s, major debates had erupted between "Third World" and "Western" feminisms, the latter signifying the globally dominant, liberal feminism of US-based white, class-privileged women and of the aid and development establishments. Third World feminists accused Western feminists of projecting putatively universal understandings of women's oppression based on their own culturally specific experience. Instead of Western liberal feminism masquerading as global sisterhood, Third World feminist critics advocated a transnational and cross-cultural feminist praxis, committed to combating inequalities among women while being sensitive to differences arising from cultural, social, and global geopolitical locations. They envisioned the possibility of transnational feminist solidarity that was also anti-imperialist, anti-colonial, anti-racist, and anti-capitalist (Alexander and Mohanty 1997; Mohanty 2003; Mohanty, Russo, and Torres 1991). In these discourses, then, invoking the transnational involved recognizing (the possibility of) connection without erasing differences or ignoring inequalities, especially those rooted in histories of colonialism. In feminist usage, the term *transnational* often carries this ideological content and normative weight beyond its geographical or scalar connotations.

Increased use of the term *transnational* by feminist theorists has also implied a critique of the centrality of nations, nationalisms, and the national scale in political life, including in feminist political imaginaries. The transnational became a way of naming the circulation of feminist discourses across various kinds of difference without reinscribing national(ist) boundaries or invoking a global-to-local hierarchy among scales of activism. In these feminist discourses, then, the transnational refers to relations and flows across national frontiers while avoiding claims to the universal that accompany the term *global* and the historical project of global sisterhood (Grewal and Kaplan 1994; Kaplan, Alarcón, and Moallem 1999).

In recent years, the use of *transnational* with reference to contemporary feminist practices has become ubiquitous, such that it also has less theoretically laden, more simply descriptive meanings. Valentine M. Moghadam (2000) uses it to designate issue-based networks working in two or more countries. Angela Miles (2000) uses "transnational feminism" interchangeably with "global feminism" to describe the phenomenon of localized feminisms around the world whose members are increasingly aware of each other and the global context of their struggles and are building dense networks of collaboration. Manisha Desai (2005) understands it as describing cross-border organizing and as an analytic that can refer to all scales of activism. Until very recently, almost all feminist scholars and activists used the term approvingly. Desai (2005, 319) claims that since Beijing "transnational feminist practices ... have become the dominant modality of feminist movements around the world." The transnational is so often invoked, by both scholars and activists, in so many different ways that it is essential to distinguish how it is being deployed in any particular context.

These debates about the possibility and character of a feminist ethic of solidarity across difference clearly undergird the overlapping but variable transnational feminist praxes at the WSF. However, there is also a growing unease about the "transnational" emerging in feminist scholarship. In particular, political developments at the United Nations over the last decade have provoked growing ambivalence. By the mid-1990s, contentious issues included mainstreaming gender at the UN and in national and international institutions; the resulting "NGO-ization" of feminism and the creation of cadres of expert consultants, or femocrats; and the complicity of the UN with free trade agendas and conflicts with feminists increasingly identifying opposition to neoliberalism and structural adjustment as central to women's struggles worldwide. As these issues became combined with a generalized crisis in multilateralism and the rising strength of conservative and fundamentalist religious forces, growing numbers of feminists saw engaging in UN processes as both increasingly risky and ineffectual.[4] The emergence of the World March of Women in the late 1990s and the Articulación Feminista Marcosur in 2000 can be understood in this context as a critical feminist reaction and expression of the search for alternative politics and practices.

Political critiques of UN-focused feminist advocacy have over-determined analytical work on the more heterogeneous phenomenon of transnational feminism because so many of the movement practices that travel under that label are intertwined with the history of UN activity. Many questions are being ever more sharply posed by feminist scholars: To what extent is "transnational feminism" code for feminist politics that has been domesticated by its interpolation with the UN processes? To what extent is it a feminism of cosmopolitan elites, urbanized and educated in the terms of Western academia, whether geographically located or politically identified with the global South or the global North? Does the signifier *transnational feminism* denote, implicitly or explicitly, a specific cluster of practices and discourses with particular political content, carried by particular agents, reproduced through particular political cultures, and rooted in particular histories but projecting itself as a universal – a revived global sisterhood project carried by the high politics of a new, multicultural, highly mobile, well-resourced, and globally visible feminist vanguard? Can we even speak of a single phenomenon, transnational feminism, with specific modalities, as Desai (2005) seems to imply? Or are other transnational feminisms possible? We will return to these questions.

Transnational Feminisms at the World Social Forum

In the Latin American iterations of the WSF, the World March of Women and the Articulación Feminista Marcosur have been two particularly visible streams of feminist participation. The origins of the March lie in the organizing of a ten-day mass march in 1994 to protest deepening poverty in Quebec. It was so successful, both as a grassroots mobilization and as a pressure campaign, that Quebec feminists introduced the idea of a world march at a workshop in Beijing in 1995. A series of actions orchestrated by local- and national-scale committees around the world, unified by a shared platform of demands focused on poverty and myriad forms of violence against women, constituted the World March of Women. The actions began on 8 March 2000 (International Women's Day) and continued over the next eight months, culminating in an action at the United Nations on 17 October 2000 (International Day for the Elimination of Poverty), at which a petition with over five hundred thousand signatures was presented. Six hundred groups from 163 countries participated. By 2003, fifty-five hundred women's groups were participating; by 2005, over six thousand (Dufour 2005, 2, 6; World March of Women 2004, 234).

Since 2001, the March has become a prominent presence on the international scene: in spaces of social protest, it was active at anti-G8 protests in Evian (June 2003), the People's Forum for Alternatives to the WTO in Cancun (September 2003), and major anti-Iraq war demonstrations, as well as UN conferences against racism in Durban (August-September 2001), Alternative Finance for Development in Monterrey, Mexico (February-March 2002), global feminist encounters such as the Association of Women in Development (AWID) conference on alternatives to globalization in Guadalajara in October 2002, the World and Regional Social Forums, and the World Assembly of Social Movements.

At the 2002 WSF, the March contingent included women from twenty countries. Their lavender flags and T-shirts were everywhere, especially in the WSF's massive street demonstrations. In the Assembly of Social Movements, one of the self-organized groupings of the WSF, the March was a visible and vocal feminist presence. Its slogan, "The world will not change without feminism; and feminists cannot change women's lives unless we change the world," met with roars of approval at the closing ceremonies of the 2002 WSF. In 2003, the March was even more in evidence, with a large booth and a full program of gender-related events, including a major one in the youth camp on feminism and a new political generation (World March of Women 2003c, 5-6).

The March's commitment to grassroots mobilization, street action, and the claiming of public space resonates with many other iterations of anti-globalization movements, especially among young people, and also characterizes its presence in the WSF. Drumming, chanting, singing, and theatrics have enriched and disrupted the spaces of the Forum, especially in Brazil, and "question the practices, codes and consciousness of those who are our 'partners' in the daily fight to make another world possible" (World March of Women, Globalization and Alliances Collective 2005).

In 2005, the March launched its second global-scale initiative, the Women's Global Charter for Humanity. Through an elaborate year-long process of articulation and negotiation among its members, the March sought to generate a collective vision, rooted in the seventeen demands of the 2000 World March Platform but oriented to alternative proposals (World March of Women 2003b). The charter targeted governments and international institutions (UN, IMF, World Bank, WTO), as well as the March's allied movements and local communities (World March of Women 2003b, 3).

A world relay in which the charter was handed from one women's group to another, "from one world region to another, one country to another, and one village to another" (World March of Women 2003a, 2) traversed political borders, bio-regional boundaries, and cultural differences. It began in Brazil on 8 March 2005 and ended in Burkina Faso on 17 October 2005 with stops in fifty-three countries and territories. The round-the-world journey of the charter concluded with "twenty-four hours of global feminist solidarity," a rolling sequence of one-hour actions beginning in Oceania and following the sun westward around the globe. The relay march was accompanied by the creation of a massive quilt. Women were invited to illustrate their vision with pieces of cloth that were then carried with the charter, constructing the Global Patchwork Solidarity Quilt over the course of the charter's world journey.

The Articulación Feminista Marcosur is a Latin American feminist initiative, a "space for feminist intervention in the global arena," born more explicitly as a response to the limitations and contradictions of the UN-focused transnational feminism of the 1990s. Specifically, the Articulación confronts *"pensamientos unicos"* (unitary ways of thinking that suppress pluralism) that appear in oppositional movements and among neoliberals (Vargas 2003, 914). As feminists, members of the Articulación insist on the centrality of the politics of the body in order to make visible suppressed aspects of the struggles against neoliberalism, militarism, and fundamentalism (Virginia Vargas, personal communication, 17 December 2007).

At the 2002 WSF, the Articulación's feminists spearheaded the Campaign Against Fundamentalisms, linking the economic fundamentalism of neoliberalism with rising ethnic and religious fundamentalisms. Cardboard masks depicting giant lips were sported by thousands of participants in the WSF's many street demonstrations. The accompanying slogan was "Your mouth is fundamental against fundamentalisms." In a single symbol, the masks captured the realities of people silenced by fundamentalisms, people who can speak but are afraid to, and those who raise their voices in protest. This mobilization reappeared at the WSFs in 2003 and 2005 in Porto Alegre, in 2004 in Mumbai, and in 2007 in Nairobi, and it involved other feminist networks, including AWID and the Women's International Coalition for Economic Justice (WICEJ). Carol Barton (quoted in Duddy 2004) of WICEJ commented, "We see it as a very powerful campaign for bridging differences in what have sometimes been different universes within global feminist organizing. It addresses issues around women's rights to control their bodies and their lives as well as women's economic and social rights. It has brought these two strands together."

The Articulación has organized numerous sessions in the WSF program, notably cross-movement dialogues that convene speakers from different WSF movements to explore their differences and foster mutual understanding and recognition. In a similar way, the Articulación has recognized the need for dialogue across difference among feminists. In 2003, 120 feminists from a dozen networks primarily from Latin America gathered in a pre-WSF strategy meeting, the immediate precursor of the Feminist Dialogues. This meeting was convened by the Articulación, hosted by the Brazilian Women's Coordination, and co-sponsored by the Latin American and Caribbean Committee for the Defence of Women's Rights, the Women's Popular Education Network, the Latin American and Caribbean Health Network, the Network of Women and Habitat, the September 28th Campaign, and the Campaign for the Convention on Sexual and Reproductive Rights, all of which were co-sponsoring the Articulación's Campaign Against Fundamentalism (Articulación Feminista Marcosur 2004). According to participants, there was widespread agreement on the importance of carrying feminist perspectives into global movements for social change and assuming greater leadership roles, particularly at the WSF. The participants saw feminist analyses on the intersections of race, class, gender, sexuality, nation, and so on, as critical contributions to global social justice movements, including the movement against neoliberalism. Likewise, in their foregrounding of fundamentalism, militarism, and patriarchy, feminist analyses and politics had much to contribute to the discourses of more narrowly focused economic justice movements.

An informal follow-up meeting at the conclusion of the 2003 WSF saw these feminists planning how they might bring the Campaign Against Fundamentalism to India and make links with Indian and Asian networks (Eschle and Maiguashca 2010). This was followed up with a meeting, a Metaforo arranged by the Articulación in August 2003 to foster dialogue with Indian feminist organizers represented by Nandita Shah from the National Network of Autonomous Women's Groups. Following these initiatives, the Articulación and the Latin American and international networks aligned with the Campaign Against Fundamentalism, now joined by several groups in India and Sri Lanka, agreed to collaborate on fewer but larger-scale feminist events targeted to audiences of one thousand to four thousand participants at the 2004 WSF. They further agreed to hold a pre-WSF women's event, the first Feminist Dialogues. The leading groups were the Articulación Feminista Marcosur, Development Alternatives with Women for a New Era-South East Asia (DAWN), the African Women's Development and Communication Network (FEMNET), INFORM Human Rights Documentation Centre (Sri Lanka), Isis International, the National Network of Autonomous Women's Groups (India), and WICEJ. These seven groups went on to constitute the Co-ordinating Group of the Feminist Dialogues, and in 2006 they were joined by five more.

In 2004, the fourth WSF, and the first to be held outside of Brazil, took place in Mumbai, India. The Indian National Network of Autonomous Women's Groups hosted Building Solidarities: Feminist Dialogues prior to the WSF. It took place over two days, involved 140 women, and successfully broadened regional diversity. For the feminist organizations and networks not rooted geographically in South Asia, the WSF in Mumbai was an occasion to build knowledge of and relationships with the feminisms of the region, as well as with the political parties of the Indian left and other Indian social movements (Barton cited in Duddy 2004), although it is important to note that the initiative was built on a twenty-year history of contact between key Latin American and Indian feminists, especially through the UN con-ferences (Virginia Vargas, personal communication, 17 December 2007). Several women from the March participated in and reported on the event, but the March was not involved in its organizing (World March of Women 2003d, 2).

In the spaces of the WSF itself, the March once again mounted multiple events, many of them in collaboration with other feminist networks, including Agencia Latino Americana de Información, Red Latinoamericana Mujeres Transformando la Economía, South-LGBT Dialogue, and Women of Vía Campesina. These distinct clusters of feminist collaboration – the Latin American and international groups endorsing the Articulación's Campaign Against Fundamentalism; the cluster associated with the Feminist Dialogues after 2004, which overlaps with the first; and the grouping, also heavily Latin American, working in collaboration with the March – reappear repeatedly before and after Mumbai in the WSF program.

With broadening participation, accumulating experience, and ongoing experimentation with format and process, the Feminist Dialogues has been rightly celebrated by some participants as a unique forum within which feminists may explore sensitive issues in the global women's movement: North-South dynamics and inequalities; differing priorities around such issues as reproductive rights, violence against women, and economic justice; differing choice of scales, institutional venues, and sociocultural terrains for feminist work; differing assessments of human rights perspectives and strategies; women's engagement with religion; and understandings of religious fundamentalisms in different cultural settings.[5] The Dialogues is also seen as an opportunity to advance feminist understandings of the linkages among neoliberalism, fundamentalisms, neoconservatism, communalism, and militarism in the present conjuncture and what this means for women's rights and feminist strategies (Barton cited in Duddy 2004).

From its inception, the Feminist Dialogues has been intended to assert a feminist identity. Manisha Desai (2005, 325), a scholar and participant in the 2005 Dialogues, understands this as a reaction to the co-optation of the human rights agenda by conservative forces, including non-feminist (even anti-feminist) women's movements. She also notes that all of the groups organizing the Dialogues reflect urban and autonomous tendencies in their respective contexts and associates this with their feminist identity.

Although the Feminist Dialogues was originally imagined as a way to strengthen the feminist presence in the WSF, its agenda quickly shifted to critical issues across regions and issues in global feminism, including linkages with other social movements. The Feminist Dialogues in Mumbai was deliberately ambivalent vis-à-vis the WSF, with feminists actively participating in the WSF while remaining organizationally autonomous in order to mount pressure from outside (Gandhi and Shah 2005).

In terms of the WSF, fostering cross-movement dialogue and breaking down sectoral silos did emerge as key shared priorities among some leading organizations of the Feminist Dialogues. In Mumbai, the Articulación and the National Network of Autonomous Women's Groups hosted an intermovement dialogue involving two speakers from each of four movements: women's, sexuality rights, labour, and dalit rights/racial justice. Each was asked to speak to how her or his movement had incorporated class, gender, race, and sexuality questions, the dilemmas and problems confronted, and the strategies employed. Activists from the other movements were asked to respond. Then the second speaker from the original movement was asked to comment, refute, or clarify. This moderated dialogue proceeded through four rounds. The format was repeated the following year in Brazil (Gandhi and Shah 2006). From Mumbai to the WSFs in Porto Alegre in 2005, Bamako, Mali, in 2006, and most recently Nairobi in 2007, the Feminist Dialogues has continued to grow in terms of absolute numbers, regional diversity, and increased participation by young women.[6]

Transnational Feminisms in Nairobi: Axes of Difference

By the 2007 WSF in Nairobi, the Feminist Dialogues had taken shape as a transnational feminist project with its own particular politics and aim to make specific and coherent feminist interventions in the 2007 WSF program. For the first time, the Co-ordinating Group of the Feminist Dialogues appeared as an entity in the WSF program, sponsoring a number of activities, including workshops on building anti-globalization alliances against fundamentalisms and feminist movement building, and it organized a wonderfully dynamic women's rally that attracted hundreds of women in a noisy march through the WSF grounds. Many of the marchers sported the cardboard lip masks of the Articulación's campaign against fundamentalisms. The Articulación did not mount its own events but was prominent in those organized under the banner of the Feminist Dialogues. The March was notable for its absence, both from the women's rally and from these events.

The March sponsored events on migration and violence against women; on food sovereignty and the need for alliances between rural and urban women; on women and work; and on its Global Charter. In addition, the March worked in coalition with other feminist and non-feminist groups in a variety of ways. It co-sponsored the IV Social Forum on Sexual Diversity with LGBT Dialogo Sur-Sur and its allied Latin American feminist organizations, although notably not with the Articulación or its Latin American allies. The March collaborated with a diverse group of organizations, including Transform Italia, Focus on the Global South, Campaign for the Welfare State, G10 Solidaire, and several other Italian labour groups, to host two events on labour and globalization, and it took the lead in organizing the WSF's Social Movements Assembly.

Based on a sampling of these groups of events, I observed some differences. The Feminist Dialogues' events attracted almost exclusively female audiences, many of them self-identified feminists whom I recognized from the pre-WSF Feminist Dialogues event. The March's events were more mixed in terms of gender and class. Both sets of events attracted international, multilingual and racially diverse audiences, but the women at the Feminist Dialogues events, especially the Africans, appeared to be largely professional or upper-class. One of the March's events, focused on its Global Women's Charter, began with the activists displaying the March's gigantic quilt and succeeded in attracting a different constituency, including many men and some of the women vending fruit and drinks, in addition to featuring women activists from poor people's movements in Kenya in a public effort to build the March in that country. The difference in the class and gender composition of the two groups of events was striking even as the substantive foci of the events were, at first glance, broadly convergent – certainly not at odds.

The status of "place" and "the local" in the practices and discourses of both the World March of Women and the Feminist Dialogues appeared as another noticeable difference. The March is a coordination of place-based "grassroots" feminisms, concretely engaged in specific geographies, around context-specific struggles pertaining to poverty and violence against women, in place-specific terms. The Feminist Dialogues is composed primarily of self-described transnational feminist networks. In their everyday activities, these networks may be embedded in place-specific ways, but their discourses and practices, as they instantiate the Feminist Dialogues, largely eschew place-based specificities. While speakers associated with the Dialogues may identify themselves by world region, their discourses about neoliberalism, fundamentalism, and militarization tend to be globalist in nature and abstracted from particular struggles on the ground anywhere. A focus on place and the local are preconditions for, although not the equivalent of, a grassroots praxis and, I suggest, a significant factor in explaining the distinctive political cultures of the feminisms under discussion.

While the Feminist Dialogues is thoroughly international, its leadership in Nairobi, especially in terms of who facilitated and spoke in its WSF events, was far more Latin American and South Asian than African. In their political culture, the Feminist Dialogues' events had the character of international meetings that could have been taking place anywhere in the world. Being in Africa seemed largely irrelevant. The World March of Women (2007), on the other hand, engaged in a thorough-going place-based internationalism:

> We knew from the outset that the absence of a World March National Coordinating Body in Kenya would be problematic for the organization of our activities at the Forum. Fortunately, we were assisted by a young woman who belongs to a feminist theatre troupe that treats various issues of importance to Kenyan society ... Thanks to their hard work, the March delegation included women from the poorest neighbourhoods of Nairobi and we now have the foundation to form a March coordinating body in Kenya ... We wanted to use the opportunity presented by the WSF to give a voice to the women's movement of Africa and reinforce its leadership within the World March of Women. Women from some 10 African countries who are active in the March attended the WSF.[7]

For all its internationalism, the Feminist Dialogues is strangely monocultural – a product, I suspect, of the particular transnational circuits of feminist activism produced by the UN processes in the 1990s. Despite its critique of and desire to break with the limitations of those practices, the Feminist Dialogues reflects the circulation of people and discourses among academia, UN agencies, donors, and international NGOs that feminist critics of UN-focused advocacy have repeatedly observed (see, for example, Wilson 2007). In an interview at the pre-WSF Feminist Dialogues event, Fatma Aloo (personal communication, 19 January 2007) of FEMNET, a co-sponsor of the Dialogues, had this to say:

> I was in the process toward Beijing. I hear the same things here. The biggest challenge for the feminist movement is to link with grassroots, the not-privileged. The feminist movement has not even started ... they're [gesturing to the room where the event was underway] still stuck in NGOism ...

also, it's the way this is organized ... you would think that being in Kenya –
as if there are no feminists in Kenya! – that it would be led by the Kenyans
... I am sitting here with Wahu [Kaara, head of the Kenya Debt Relief Net-
work]. Did you see her on a panel?

The Feminist Dialogues' more abstract, academic, and, often, placeless
discourses clearly resonate with educated women inculturated in the transnational discursive and organizational circuits of feminist advocacy. The
discourses of the Feminist Dialogues are more analytically sophisticated
than are those of the March. They are clearly informed by debates and developments in feminist scholarship and theory. One may readily discern this
at its events but also by exploring its website. Although there are references
to the state of the global feminist movement and instances of political ex-
hortation, there is little attention paid to the concrete practices of organizing or coalition-building. With the March, the opposite is true: its organizing
practices are the substantive focus of both its events and the largely descriptive discourses that its activists produce about it.

Both the March and the Dialogues claim to be (re)building the feminist
movement and cultivating anti-globalization alliances – and both are, although in quite different modes, on different terms, and on somewhat different terrains. The inter-movement dialogues promoted by the Articulación
and its allies are communicative practices that are critical in fostering intelligibility across difference and are themselves constitutive of movement-
building across issues, sectors, and regions. In the context of the WSF, I
think they are among its most interesting and important initiatives. However, these dialogues proceed largely on the terms set by their feminist
organizers. This became clear to me when I reviewed a video of the inter-
movement dialogues after having been at the Feminist Dialogues. It was
striking how the same discourses of intersectionality, often carried by the
same individuals, set the terms for the dialogue across movements.[8]

The March is more inclined to get its hands dirty through coalition work
on concrete issues involving a fuller range of activist partners and practices,
in which it is a strong feminist partner but does not set the rules of engagement. This has been evident repeatedly in its role in the Assembly of Social
Movements. Both the March and the Articulación, and now the Feminist
Dialogues, are interlocutors in the WSF, but the March is placing itself
squarely and consistently in the ambiguous spaces of the anti-globalization
movement, actively and concretely building trust and partnerships in practice with non-feminist but broadly emancipatory movements in and beyond

the WSF, including through its involvement in international campaigns and mobilizations.

The Feminist Dialogues is fostering convergence among self-identified feminists, cultivating anti-globalization feminist alliances across issues, sectors, and regions, building on the pre-existing transnational feminist circuits, cultures, discourses, and ways of doing things developed through exposure to the UN processes, international donor agencies, NGO-ization, and politics waged in terms of human rights. In contrast to the Feminist Dialogues' strongly articulated and explicitly feminist bases of unity, particularly on rights to abortion and sexual choice, the March is proceeding in practice to build another kind of feminist internationalism through its concrete attention to issues of particular concern to poor and marginalized women in specific places and with less regard as to whether they call themselves feminist, agree on abortion rights, or share the same discourse on sexual rights.

In understanding these differences in political orientation, it is also important to recognize that the Feminist Dialogues is not institutionalized. It is an episodic initiative by a coalition of networks primarily for the purpose of dialogue, and it piggybacks on the WSF. The March, on the other hand, has a sizable, globally dispersed social base, a permanent secretariat, and institutionalized representation and decision-making structures. The March's raison d'être is mass mobilization, and it exists as a powerful and autonomous movement beyond the WSF. However, both entities, in their discourses and practices, are seeking to intervene as feminists in the World Social Forum. Without rushing to political judgment about either, I want to further analyze what I perceived in Nairobi as political cultures and discourses of distinct feminist projects.

Desai (2005) critiques what she perceives as a focus on the discursive in transnational feminist practices at the expense of attention to structural and material inequalities among women and women's movements.[9] She characterizes transnational social movements as employing particular modalities, including reliance on cyber-connectivity and travel, that privilege urban, middle-class, and educated elites. In the case of women's movements, she notes the circulation of activists from the academy to UN agencies to international NGOs (Desai 2005, 320-21). She supports making a distinction between "transnational feminist networks" such as DAWN, WIDE (Women in Development Europe), and the Women's Environment and Development Organization, composed of educated middle-class women working on economic policy issues, and "grassroots networks," also transnationalized but based demographically in communities struggling to defend livelihoods adversely affected by globalization. This is suggestive for understanding the distinct transnational feminisms represented by the Feminist Dialogues and the World March of Women.

Similarly, in a recent article Ara Wilson (2007) comments on the "traces of the UN-NGO experience" in the WSF and its feminisms, particularly the 2005 Feminist Dialogues in Porto Alegre. She suggests that although the geographic history of transnational feminism points to multiple geographic and institutional sites, scales, and strategies, its travel through the UN orbit has indelibly marked it, particularly through NGO-ization. Wilson also notes the preponderance of critique over alternative visions or concrete strategies in the 2005 and 2006 Feminist Dialogues in Porto Alegre and Bamako, respectively, and I noted the same thing in Nairobi in 2007. She proposes that this may be an effect of years of working in the highly politically constrained world of the UN and its NGOs. Many of these feminist organizations are now turning to alternative transnational political spaces such as the WSF. Analyzing the nature of these histories and their contradictory effects in the present is critical for understanding the emerging plural forms of transnational feminism and the relations among them, which are intermittently co-operative and conflictual, and with other emancipatory movements and the WSF.

While the March has had its own occasional points of contact with the UN system, its historical roots and trajectory are quite different.[10] From its beginnings, the March represented a different kind of feminist transnationalism, oriented to movement building among women and feminists but also across sectors with mixed and non-feminist movements with which political alliances against neoliberalism could be constructed. Its leaders have been acutely conscious of building a global network of place-based activists and the challenges of negotiating place-based difference. In the diversity of its constituent groups in terms of sectors, scales, and modes of activities, in its reliance on "contentious politics" more than lobbying, and in its articulation to the anti-globalization movement, especially through its involvement with the WSF, the March represents novel developments in the field of transnational feminist politics (Conway 2007b; Dufour 2005, 3).

Contesting the Future of Feminism at the World Social Forum

Commentaries produced by activists in all of these networks recognize the importance of the WSF as a space for feminists. In the wake of the growing contradictions and limitations associated with the United Nations, the WSF has created conditions of possibility for feminists that they could not produce alone. Women active in the Articulación Feminista Marcosur, the World March of Women, and the Feminist Dialogues all testify repeatedly to the increased internationalization of their encounters in WSF contexts.

However, differences in emphasis among feminists on the meaning and strategic import of the WSF mirror larger tensions, both among feminists and within the WSF itself:

> For some actors, the WSF is a space of convergence of the anti-globalization struggle to coordinate an agenda of global mobilization; for others, it is a plural space in which to share and articulate democratizing alternatives and projects [*democratizadoras*]. For us, as Articulación Feminista Marcosur, the WSF is a space whose principal challenge is the development of new political cultures that guarantee the expression of a full range of actors emerging from the diversity and plurality [of the social reality] and create the possibility of dialogue among different movements, identities, and agendas. (Celiberti and Vargas 2003, 587-88, our translation)

Despite these tensions, there is ample evidence of feminists finding each other in and around the WSF, seizing the space provided by the WSF to mount activities for themselves and wider publics, and encountering other movements and feminisms. Feminists shape the public cultures of the WSF as they sing, dance, shout, and demonstrate in visible contingents and large numbers, and as they contest the organization, methodologies, and management of the Forum. Certainly, feminisms are also being transformed by these encounters.

As this chapter testifies, there is a plurality of transnational feminisms active in and over the WSF, emerging from different world regions, expressing distinct political histories and feminist politics, but appearing broadly convergent. With respect to the WSF, there are different feminist positionalities, but the feminist entities under discussion here all wage struggles, in their own distinct ways, over the feminist character of the WSF and the politics of its constituent movements.[11]

Emerging from post-dictatorship Latin America, the feminists of the Articulación are preoccupied with the question of democratization and draw explicitly on discourses of radical democracy. In the Forum, they recognize the tensions and contradictions arising from the different priorities, discourses, and logics of the various movements that are sharing the space. Their insistence on the multiplicity of oppressions and social subjects and the cross-cutting character of feminist issues has placed them at the centre of efforts to build discursive intelligibility across movements.

In the March's communications, there is consistent recognition of the effectiveness of the WSF in building convergence across different movements opposed to neoliberal globalization. Because its orientation is so clearly activist, the March's long-term commitment to the WSF is contingent on the strategic choices of other combative social movements. For Diane Matte (personal communication, 28 November 2005) and the March, feminism's unique contribution to the Forum and to the movement against neoliberal globalization has to do with "questions at the heart of capitalism, about the basic relationship between men and women and between individuals and our collective societal relationship." These feminists insist on attention to women's oppression as a fundamental feature of contemporary social order, central to capitalism even though it predates it. Feminist understandings of the omnipresence of violence against women and old and new forms of commodification of women's bodies and lives shift and stretch critical analyses of capitalism.

For the March, it has been important to be at the forefront of the WSF organizing process, where "it has been a struggle to get feminism recognized as an answer to neoliberal globalization ... as a social movement that is bringing something that is central" and not simply as one of an infinite number of groups, identities, and strategies. "The central analysis [operating at the WSF] is still Marxist" (Diane Matte, personal communication, 28 November 2005). In this view, feminism is itself a radical and egalitarian project of social transformation. It has its own specific and essential analytical and mobilizational resources to bring to a heterogeneous field of social struggles. The March's discourses and practices, with their strong emphases on anti-capitalism, anti-imperialism, and coalition-building with other movements of the left, draw clearly on the legacies of socialist feminism.

From the Indian pole of the Feminist Dialogues and somewhat convergent with the mass movement politics of the March, Nandita Ghandi and Nandita Shah (2005) contend that in the context of the anti-globalization and anti-war movements and the WSF, the Feminist Dialogues signal a return to movement activism. However, more broadly, the centrality of the body as a site of politics gives the Dialogues a more radical feminist appearance (Gouws 2007, 29). The interrelated axes of neoliberal globalization, militarism and war, and fundamentalisms are integrated through a focus on the body as a mediator of social relations (Vargas 2005, 110). The feminist networks of the Dialogues have been in the forefront of the struggle for the protection and inclusion of sexual and reproductive rights in the spaces, practices, and discourses of the WSF, most recently through a declaration following the WSF in Nairobi (Articulación Feminista Marcosur 2007). In some tension with the March, whose priorities in the WSF have been heavily oriented toward building political convergence against globalization, feminists of the Articulación Feminista Marcosur have seen the Forum primarily as a space for recognizing difference among the movements and advancing feminist-led inter-movement negotiations about these differences, premised on a transversal politics that incorporates the body as the site of intersecting social struggles.

Emerging from this study, a central question for the future of feminism is how open, plural, dialogical, and coalitional feminist movements will be, not just vis-à-vis each other but also in relation to movements that are recognized as broadly emancipatory in terms other than feminist. This includes grassroots women's movements that eschew the label of feminist and the array of social movements worldwide converging against neoliberal globalization. Despite a discourse of openness in the Feminist Dialogues, many of its participants seem reluctant to engage with non-feminist movements, fearful of having the specificity of feminism diluted or losing ground on contentious issues such as reproductive and sexual rights.[12] The militant focus of many in the Feminist Dialogues on women's control of women's bodies is absolutely essential; it remains a truism that if feminists do not insist on this, no one else will. However, feminists who stay in safe and shrinking feminist spaces risk irrelevance and sectarianism. Debates and tensions within the Feminist Dialogues, including about their ambivalent relationship with the WSF, testify to an awareness of this.

Those involved in transnational feminisms considered here are all acutely conscious of their movements' internal diversities, exclusions, and inequalities; these movements are aligned with each other and other movements of the WSF against neoliberal globalization. They recognize the importance of sustaining autonomous feminist movements and building anti-globalization alliances. However, questions persist about the terms of collaboration with non-feminist others and the weight of the body politics of sexuality and reproduction relative to those of food, water, land, and work.

A second question arises from the much-observed NGO-ization of feminism worldwide as an effect of the UN Decade and associated development strategies. Alvarez et al. (2002) argue that this has had contradictory political effects for feminist movements, including growing class, cultural, and strategic divergences between highly professionalized, internationalized feminist policy experts and advocates and grassroots women's, poor people's, and indigenous movements that have grown more combative in the face of aggressive neoliberalism. How feminist networks position themselves on the activist-femocrat continuum (recognizing that many move back and forth more or less successfully between these poles) is an essential question to pose in exploring feminist positionalities vis-à-vis each other, the WSF, and its constituent anti-globalization movements.

In conclusion, in comparing and analyzing some specific transnational feminist practices, it has become evident that feminist encounters at the WSF involve contestations *over the character of feminism itself.* Furthermore, contemporary "transnational feminism(s)" is an internally differentiated phenomenon that is better represented in the plural, with variable historical relationships with the cultures and practices of feminist advocacy that grew up around the UN. Some current expressions of transnational feminism demonstrate clear continuity with that tradition – built on its foundation, drawing on its strengths, while also reproducing some of its limitations. However, there are also genuinely new kinds of transnational feminist practices appearing, arising from different histories and legacies of feminist activism. This plurality requires that "transnational feminist practices" be empirically investigated, compared, and situated historically and comparatively in relation to one another and to a heterogeneous field of transnational and transnationalizing social movements with which contemporary feminisms, whether through conflict or cooperation, are changing the world.

ACKNOWLEDGMENT
This research was funded by the Social Sciences and Humanities Research Council of Canada.

NOTES
1 The World Social Forum was initiated in 2001 in Brazil to convene movements and civil society groups from around the world that share opposition to neoliberal globalization but are otherwise extremely diverse. The WSF is now a permanent global process composed of events and preparatory processes at every scale and on every continent. I have been researching the WSF since 2002, including tracking the presence of women and feminisms and particularly following the World March of Women (Conway 2007b, 2008). Key works on the WSF include Sen et al. (2004), Leite (2005), Whitaker (2007), and Santos (2006).
2 In representing these transnational feminist networks, I have relied on the websites, organizational publications, and writings by key activists; my participant-observation

of their activities at each WSF since 2002; and conversations, e-mail exchanges, and several formal interviews with leading activists.

3   See especially Masson's chapter in this volume.

4   See the chapter by Lyons in this volume for another review of these debates.

5   See Feminist Dialogues Co-ordinating Group (2006, 5-6) for an account of the historical emergence of the Feminist Dialogues. For an account of the developing organizational practices of the Feminist Dialogues, see Gandhi and Shah (2006b). For background documents, speeches, and reports of Feminist Dialogues events, including audio files and a photo gallery, see the Feminist Dialogues website, http://feministdialogues.isiswomen.org. See as well the Articulación website, www.mujeresdelsur.org.uy, for historical documents on the Feminist Dialogues and the Articulación's activities at the WSF.

6   For details, see Jones (2005a, 2005c) and Kinoti (2006). For analysis, see Gouws (2007), Wilson (2007), Vargas (2005), Jones (2005b), and Desai (2005). For an account of 2007 Feminist Dialogues, see Conway (2007a). Many features of the 2007 Feminist Dialogues carried over into its activities in the 2007 WSF, as discussed below.

7   In the summer of 2007 and flowing from this contact at the WSF, a chapter of the March was established in Kenya.

8   See Desai (2005, 327) for convergent observations.

9   The formulation "transnational feminist practices," Desai is aware, elides differences among NGOs, social movements, and social networks, reflecting real overlaps in organizational practices and resulting analytical difficulties.

10 See works by Dufour and Giraud (2007a, 2007b) analyzing the March's post-2000 shift away from the focus on the UN.

11 For a fuller analysis of the character and effects of feminist engagement with the WSF, see Conway (2007b).

12 This was evident, for example, in a debate among participants in the Feminist Dialogues in Nairobi about whether the march that was to take place on the WSF grounds would be a "feminist" or a "women's" march. The decision was ultimately made for the latter, but it was clear that there was a sizable constituency anxious that this was too politically undefined, especially in terms of the non-negotiable centrality of sexual and reproductive rights for a majority of those present.

REFERENCES

Alexander, M. Jacqui, and Chandra Talpade Mohanty. 1997. *Feminist Genealogies, Colonial Legacies, Democratic Futures.* New York: Routledge.

Alvarez, Sonia E., Elisabeth Jay Friedman, Ericka Beckman, Maylei Blackwell, Norma Stoltz Chinchilla, Nathalie Lebon, Marysa Navarro, and Marcela Ríos Tobar. 2002. Encountering Latin American and Caribbean Feminisms. *Journal of Women in Culture and Society* 28 (2): 537-79.

Articulación Feminista Marcosur. 2004. Building Solidarity – Feminist Dialogues. *Electronic Bulletin* 6 (1-10 January).

–. 2007. *Another World Is Possible in Diversity: Affirming the Struggle for Sexual and Reproductive Rights. An Open Letter to the International Council of the World*

Social Forum. Nairobi and Lima: Programa de Estudios sobre Democracia y Transformación Global. http://www.cadtm.org/article.php3?id_article=2473.

Celiberti, Lilian, and Virginia Vargas. 2003. Feministas en el Foro. *Revista Estudos Feministas* 11 (2): 586-98.

Conway, Janet. 2007a. Reflections on the 3rd International Feminist Dialogues: Notes from a Newcomer. *Journal of International Women's Studies* 8 (3): 211-13.

–. 2007b. Transnational Feminisms and the World Social Forum: Encounters and Transformations in Anti-Globalization Spaces. *Journal of International Women's Studies* 8 (3): 49-70.

–. 2008. Geographies of Transnational Feminism: The Politics of Place and Scale in the World March of Women. *Social Politics* 15 (2): 207-31.

Desai, Manisha. 2005. Transnationalism: The Face of Feminist Politics Post-Beijing. *International Social Science Journal* 57 (2): 319-30.

Duddy, Janice. 2004. *How is a Gendered Perspective Being Placed on the Agenda of the 2004 World Social Forum? An Interview with Carol Barton, Women's International Coalition for Economic Justice (WICEJ).* Association for Women's Rights in Development.

Dufour, Pascale. 2005. The World March of Women: Between Quebec and the World? *Workshop Claiming Citizenship in the Americas,* Chaire de recherche du Canada en citoyenneté et gouvernance, 27 May, Université de Montréal, Montreal, unpublished paper.

Dufour, Pascale, and Isabelle Giraud. 2007a. Globalization and Political Change in the Women's Movement: The Politics of Scale and Political Empowerment in the World March of Women. *Social Science Quarterly* 88 (5): 1152-73.

–. 2007b. When the Transnationalization of Solidarities Continues: The Case of the World March of Women Between 2000 and 2006 – a Collective Identity-Building Approach. *Mobilization: An International Journal* 12 (3): 195-210.

Eschle, Catherine, and Bice Maiguashca. 2010. *Making Feminist Sense of "the Global Justice Movement."* Lanham: Rowman and Littlefield.

Feminist Dialogues Co-ordinating Group. 2006. *Feminist Dialogues 2005 Report.* Quezon City: Isis International.

Gandhi, Nandita, and Nandita Shah. 2005. An Interactive Space for Feminisms. *Samyukta: A Journal of Women's Studies* 5 (2): 61-72.

–. 2006. Inter Movement Dialogues: Breaking Barriers, Building Bridges. *Development* 49 (1): 72-76.

Gouws, Amanda. 2007. Ways of Being: Feminist Activism and Theorizing at the Global Feminist Dialogues in Porto Alegre, Brazil, 2005. *Journal of International Women's Studies* 8 (3): 28-36.

Grewal, Inderpal, and Caren Kaplan. 1994. *Scattered Hegemonies: Postmodernity and Transnational Feminist Practices.* Minneapolis: University of Minnesota Press.

Jones, Rochelle. 2005a. The Feminist Dialogue: "Multidimensional Identities and Internal Diversities." Resource Net Friday File Issue 214, 18 February. http://www.awid.org/eng/Issues-and-Analysis/Library/The-Feminist-Dialogue-Multidimensional-identities-and-internal-diversities.

–. 2005b. Feminist Dialogues: Multidimensional Identities and Internal Diversities. *Development* 48 (2): 53-56.
–. 2005c. What Opportunities and Challenges Have Emerged from the Recent 2005 Feminist Dialogues? An Interview with Lydia Alpizar, Association for Women's Rights in Development (AWID). Resource Net Friday File Issue 214, 18 February. http://www.awid.org/eng/Issues-and-Analysis/Library/What-opportunities-and-challenges-have-emerged-from-the-recent-2005-Feminist-Dialogue.
Kaplan, Caren, Norma Alarcón, and Minoo Moallem. 1999. *Between Woman and Nation: Nationalisms, Transnational Feminisms and the State.* Durham and London: Duke University Press.
Kinoti, Kathambi. 2006. *The Feminist Dialogues at the Bamako Social Forum: An Interview with Roselynn Musa, African Women's Development and Communication Network (FEMNET).* Association for Women's Rights in Development (AWID), 10 February. http://www.awid.org/eng/Issues-and-Analysis/Library/The-International-Criminal-Court-A-model-for-gender-integration2.
Leite, Jose Correa. 2005. *World Social Forum: Strategies of Resistance.* Chicago: Haymarket Books.
Miles, Angela. 2000. Local Activisms, Global Feminisms and the Struggle Against Globalization. *Canadian Woman Studies – Les Cahiers de la Femme* 20 (3): 6-10.
Moghadam, Valentine M. 2000. Transnational Feminist Networks: Collective Action in an Era of Globalization. *International Sociology* 15 (1): 57-85.
Mohanty, Chandra Talpade. 2003. *Feminism without Borders: Decolonizing Theory, Practicing Solidarity.* Durham and London: Duke University Press.
Mohanty, Chandra Talpade, Ann Russo, and Lourdes Torres, eds. 1991. *Third World Women and the Politics of Feminism.* Bloomington: Indiana University Press.
Santos, Boaventura de Sousa. 2006. *The Rise of the Global Left: The World Social Forum and Beyond.* London and New York: Zed Books.
Sen, Jai, Anita Anand, Arturo Escobar, and Peter Waterman. 2004. *World Social Forum: Challenging Empires.* New Delhi: Viveka Foundation.
Vargas, Virginia. 2003. Feminism, Globalization and the Global Justice and Solidarity Movement. *Cultural Studies* 17 (6): 905-20.
–. 2005. Feminisms and the World Social Forum: Space for Dialogue and Confrontation. *Development* 48 (2): 107-10.
Whitaker, Chico. 2007. *A New Way of Changing the World.* Nairobi: World Council of Churches.
Wilson, Ara. 2007. Feminism in the Spaces of the World Social Forum. *Journal of International Women's Studies* 8 (3): 10-27.
World March of Women. 2003a. *World March of Women – Report of 4th International Meeting in New Delhi, March 18-22, 2004.*
–. 2003b. *World March of Women Newsletter* 6 (2 May). http://www.worldmarchofwomen.org/bulletin_liaison/en.
–. 2003c. *World March of Women Newsletter* 6 (1 February). http://www.worldmarchofwomen.org/bulletin_liaison/en.
–. 2003d. *World March of Women Newsletter* 6 (3 August). http://www.worldmarchofwomen.org/bulletin_liaison/en.

–. 2004. Perspective of Women of the World March of Women: Declaration at the 2003 World Social Forum. In *World Social Forum: Challenging Empires*, ed. Jai Sen, Anita Anand, Arturo Escobar, and Peter Waterman, 233-34. New Delhi: Viveka Foundation.

–. 2007. World Social Forum – Nairobi 2007: Change Women's Lives – Change the World. *World March of Women Newsletter* 10 (1 May). http://www. worldmarchofwomen.org/bulletin_liaison/en.

World March of Women. Globalization and Alliances Collective. 2005. Feminism and the Antiglobalization Movement: A Strategy Debate. In *The World March of Women in the Social Forum Process: CD ROM*. Montreal, Quebec.

Bringing Feminist Perspectives to Transnational Collective Action in Southeast Asia

DOMINIQUE CAOUETTE

The point of departure of this chapter is a set of observations made by feminist scholar Catherine Eschle (2005, 1750) regarding the pervasiveness of gender-blindness and built-in patriarchies that exist within the anti-globalization movement, in terms of analytical categories used and the participation of women in generating an alternative discourse to the neoliberal economic globalization:

> The common sense understanding of globalization clearly places economic processes center stage. In particular, most analyses focus on the role of corporations and international financial institutions such as the WTO, which push for a neoliberal agenda of "free trade," the reduction of state barriers to and intervention in trade processes, and the continuing integration of domestic markets ... Indeed, an emphasis on the determining impact of the global economy has become so widespread that it now dominates approaches to globalization in academia, activist circles, and the media and is characteristic of both neoliberal advocacy of globalization and critical opposition.

As Eschle (2005, 1747) further notes, commenting on what she considers to be the authoritative texts on the anti-globalization movement, "There is occasional, but usually limited, recognition of the participation of women ...

However, gender is not commented on or presented as relevant to motivations or styles of activism."

In Southeast Asia, as in many other regions of the world, there has been a growing tendency for social movements to organize and work transnationally to resist various expressions of economic globalization. The Philippines, Thailand, Malaysia, and, increasingly, Indonesia now host various forms of transnational activist organizations, including women's organizations (see Lyons, this volume).[1] Bangkok, Manila, and Jakarta act today as "nodes of transnational activism," places that "provide not only the practical infrastructure required by transnational NGO networks, but also a political climate that is not too hostile toward civil society activism" (Piper and Ulhin 2004, 14).

Within the constellation of Southeast Asian civil society organizations, activist networks involved in policy advocacy and knowledge production constitute an important component of transnational activism. By examining three regional activist organizations involved in research and advocacy on neoliberal economics and other processes associated with globalization, I explore how and to what extent women's issues and feminist perspectives are being integrated into such discourse and knowledge creation.

My goals are, first, to determine whether women, while being an object of advocacy, remain excluded from critical reflections, and second, to assess if the built-in patriarchies that exist within the dominant "malestream" international relations (IR) field (see the Introduction to this volume) are being echoed in anti-globalization policy advocacy circles. I will determine whether such exclusions are taking place by considering the advocacy statements, policy documents, research outputs, and publications produced by these three Southeast Asian networks.[2] I also conducted interviews with key members of the networks during two short field visits in May 2005 and July 2006, and with Northern NGO staff supporting them.

What I suggest is that much of the discourse and knowledge produced to feed and propel transnational activism in the region remain rooted in classic Marxist and neo-Marxist economic approaches to globalization, which constitute discourses and frameworks characterized by non-gendered perspectives. Despite a shared commitment to looking at and discussing women's issues, these regional Southeast Asian advocacy networks have yet to understand and better integrate feminist perspectives. This process of stretching, as described in other chapters in this volume (such as Díaz Alba's), reveals how challenging it is to bring a feminist perspective to non-feminist activist organizations. If integrated into the analyses of dominant global economic institutions and processes, such perspectives could help to disentangle the gendered dynamics and built-in patriarchies that are present within them.[3]

Southeast Asia has become increasingly integrated into the global economy through a model of rapid economic growth fuelled by export-oriented industries and economic and financial liberalization (Bello 2001; Fouquin 1999; Sundaram 1998). Most countries in the region are linked and affected by economic global processes – connections that were strengthened following the 1997 financial crisis. Such rapid economic transformation has not occurred without consequences for women in terms of health, labour conditions, legal and illegal labour migration (including for domestic work, sex, and entertainment), and trafficking. Unsurprisingly, issues related to human rights, election monitoring, environmental issues, regional integration, and economic globalization have become prominent themes in transnational organizing (Parnwell and Rigg 2001). Yet, up to now, Southeast Asia has remained relatively under-analyzed within the realm of transnational collective action literature. As Nicola Piper and Anders Uhlin (2004, 1) note, the region of East Asia and Southeast Asia "constitutes an understudied geographical area in the transnational social movement/civil society literature (as opposed to Europe, North America and Latin America)."[4]

Below, I discuss three regional organizations, Focus on the Global South, Asia-Pacific Research Network, and Third World Network, involved in alternative knowledge production. All three have played, and are still playing, important roles as nexuses of critical knowledge, policy advocacy, and regional networking within Southeast Asia and also more broadly within the alterglobalist movement, especially around issues related to trade and economics, and international financial agreements and institutions (among others, the GATT, the WTO, the IMF, and Asia Pacific Economic Cooperation [APEC]). First, I will outline each network's history and main activities; then, I shall turn to a detailed analysis of how women's issues and feminist perspectives have been considered, and at times partly integrated, into their advocacy and collective action framing.

Third World Network[5]

Third World Network (TWN) describes itself as "an independent non-profit international network of organizations and individuals involved in issues relating to development, the Third World and North South issues" (see the TWN website, http://www.twnside.org.sg/). Its international secretariat is based in Penang, Malaysia, where it was first established in November

1984. TWN also has offices in Delhi, Montevideo, Geneva, and Accra and affiliates in a number of countries, including India, the Philippines, Thailand, Brazil, Bangladesh, Malaysia, Peru, Ethiopia, Uruguay, Mexico, Ghana, South Africa, and Senegal.

The history of TWN goes back to the early 1980s. In 1984, Martin Khor, who was working as research director for the Consumers' Association of Penang, and other Penang-based activists organized a conference on development issues. The conference led to the creation of TWN with the goal of "link[ing] the local problems of communities in the South to the global policy-making arenas" (Commonwealth Foundation, n.d.). TWN was formed well before the latest wave of transnational social movement activism known as the anti-globalization movement. As two program officers from Inter Pares (a Canada-based social justice organization and one of the first international NGOs to support TWN) noted, the creation of TWN came about as a result of an international consultation that linked issues of public health and the environment with North-South relations (personal communication, Asia Program Officers, Inter Pares, 3 March 2005). The network's international advocacy orientation was not a coincidence, as it was partly a reaction to blocked channels of political expression at the national level. Malaysia's political system, despite its democratic façade, has had limited tolerance for direct political challenges, which is partly a consequence of the country's rapid integration into the global economy (Loh 2004, 2005; Verma 2002; Weiss 2004).

What distinguishes TWN from the other organizations examined here is its explicit commitment to working, whenever possible, with government officials to influence public policies. Through the years, TWN has been regularly involved with multilateral processes such as the United Nations Development Programme and the Association of Southeast Asian Nations (ASEAN) (Dropping Knowledge, n.d.). Beyond participation in official and parallel summits, TWN produces a wide range of publications (two magazines, its monthly *Third World Resurgence* and its bi-monthly *Third World Economics;* as well as books, monographs, and occasional briefing papers, many of which are circulated through the Internet). Its website has become its primary portal for the dissemination of its materials and analysis. TWN also plays an important role in supporting trade negotiators from the South and advising them about WTO issues, and it has been quite active with regard to the Cartagena Convention on Biosafety and the World Summit on Sustainable Development.

Women's Issues and Feminist Perspectives

Women's issues have always been on TWN's official list of concerns. The declaration that led to its establishment noted, "Among the most exploited people in the Third World are women," and "The development process has not generally improved the position of women in the Third World and in some instances it has even deteriorated as modernization in rural areas displaced the labour of women" (Third World Network 1985, 11).

However, as TWN developed, women's issues, and especially feminist perspectives on global economic processes, were often marginalized. This is evident in its key publication, *Third World Network Features* (TWNF), published at a rate of about 150 issues per year.[6] In 1993, subjects covered in TWNF were "environment, economics, health, human rights, biotechnology, development and many other issues affecting the Third World" (TWN Annual Report 1993). Ten years later, in 2003, women appeared for the first time as one of the themes covered, along with "terrorism, the Iraq crisis, health, safety, poverty, hunger, agriculture, human rights, finance, economics, globalization, development, war, environment, ecology, biotechnology, genetic engineering, information technology, human rights, etc." (TWN Annual Report 2003, 2). Of the 155 issues published that year, twelve dealt directly with women's issues, while several others covering health issues had implications for women. Key authors identified in those years (1993-2003) were both men and women, including well-known ecofeminist Vandana Shiva, although male-authored works always appeared more frequently (the balance being roughly two-thirds/one-third) (TWN Annual Reports 1993-2003).

In TWN's other publications, *South-North Development Monitor* (SUNS), *Third World Economics,* and *Third World Resurgence,* dominant topics have focused on "economic-related themes" (TWN Annual Reports 1993, 24), including the GATT, the IMF, the World Bank, the WTO, transnational corporations, trade, the environment, and development. In these publications, women's issues have not received much coverage. It should be noted, however, that in most of the issues of *Third World Resurgence* published since 2003, there has usually been one article dealing with women's issues as part of the publication's "Women" section. However, as discussed below, women's issues and feminist perspectives seem confined to this section rather than being addressed or applied transversally throughout the publication.

The focus on economics and global economic institutions has been consistent. A review produced in TWN annual reports between 1993 and 2003 shows more precisely the space and importance given to women's issues. As stated in its 1995 annual report, TWN (TWN Annual Report 1995, 30) has consistently given "high priority to economic related activities." This priority became even more central following the establishment of the WTO, the proposed Multilateral Agreement on Investment, and the 1997 Asian financial crisis. As TWN (TWN Annual Report 1996, 35) pointed out, "The year 1996 saw a great expansion in TWN's activities related to the WTO and related trade and development issues," especially around the time of the WTO Ministerial Meeting Conference held in Singapore in December 1996. While the environment, poverty, labour standards, intellectual property rights, and indigenous peoples' rights were discussed, women's issues did not officially appear on the agenda. Similarly, TWN's work on genetic engineering has been organized around "its environmental and social implications for developing countries" (TWN Annual Report 1995, 79), without specifying its differential impact on women.

Over the years, the TWN website has become a key component of its information-dissemination apparatus. In 2003, the website recorded a total of 8.2 million hits, an increase of 5 percent over 2002 (7.8 million hits) and of almost 100 percent over 2001 (4.8 millions hits). Interestingly, according to TWN's 2003 Annual Report (TWN Annual Report 2003, 36), "Among the top ten most requested web pages ... were web pages on trade/WTO issues, women's rights, the World Bank/IMF, the financial and economic crisis, biotechnology/biosafety and the TWN Online bookstore."

A final mode of TWN's knowledge dissemination and expertise has been through participation in and speeches delivered at various international gatherings, conferences, and workshops. Over a ten-year period (1993 to 2003), such participation grew steadily, from fifty events in 1993 to an impressive 185 events in 2002, ranging from high-profile UN-sponsored consultations to global civil society gatherings. A number of international consultations were related to women's issues, including for Preparatory Commissions and the International Conference on Population and Development.[7]

A key trigger for TWN's involvement in women's issues took place at the Fourth World Conference on Women held in Beijing in 1995. During a 1994 consultation on TWN's role at the Beijing Summit on Women, it was agreed that the network would be responsible for organizing "a one-day forum held in the NGO Tent as well as publishing a book on women's issues, issuing a statement, and distributing TWN briefings" (TWN Annual Report 1994, 79). A year later, in May 1995, TWN representatives made a second visit to Beijing to meet with the All China Women's Federation, an "NGO controlled by a group of elderly women who were very powerful in the government," to help plan TWN's participation in the Fourth World Conference on Women (TWN Annual Report 1994, 90). From 4 September to 15 September, four TWN representatives participated at the World Conference and TWN circulated a series of briefing papers.[8] A number of SUNS bulletins were also issued and a special issue of *Third World Resurgence* (September/October 1995) presented an analysis of the Summit and background articles.

Following the Beijing Summit, a small group discussion called African Women's Economic Activity took place during a TWN Consultative Meeting held in Accra, Ghana, in June 1996. However, no plenary discussion focused on this specific topic. TWN also became directly involved in Social Watch, a process involving "a network of NGOs to monitor the performance of governments following their Social Summit and Beijing Women's Conference commitments" (TWN Annual Report 1998, 39).

During the same period, TWN established a close collaboration with the Cordillera Women's Education and Resource Center (CWERC) in the Philippines in order to coordinate "the work and publications of TWN with the Philippines and in the Asia region" (TWN Annual Report 1995, 130). In 1997, CWERC, with MineWatch (London) and TWN, organized an international conference on the globalization of mining and its impact on women. Held in the Philippines, the conference was intended to bring "together women from all over the world who are affected by mining operations" (TWN Annual Report 1997, 90). From the exchanges and discussions, participants concluded that while mining had a "negative impact on those living in the mining communities in general and those who are affected by the mining operations, there are distinct impacts and added burdens on women because of the roles they play and their secondary status in most societies" (TWN Annual Report 1997, 90). Two years later, in August 1999, Victoria Tauli-Corpus, a former member of CWERC who had created the Tebtebba Foundation (Indigenous People's International Centre for Policy Research and Education) in 1996, organized, along with TWN, a workshop titled Economic Crisis, Social Consequences and People's Response in Manila to address the "gender aspects of the impact of the crisis and the response of women's groups" (TWN Annual Report 1990, 40, 84-88). The workshop led to a series of proposals for further research in the areas of economics, the environment, and gender, and to a "dialogue session" on possible collaborations between TWN and several women's organizations. According to TWN's 1999 Annual Report, the session was attended by thirty-five participants, most of whom were from women's organizations:

Among the suggestions was that TWN increase its dissemination of information, especially on global economic issues to women's groups: help to publicise and take up issues of concerns to women's groups; provide economic analysis or perspective on issues such as sex trafficking and violence against women; include a gender dimension in its research; and help provide alternatives. TWN agreed to take on these suggestions in its future activities, and also to consider its role in the follow-up to the workshop on women's and gender issues. (TWN Annual Report 1999, 88)

In line with this commitment, it seems, TWN staff attended the national strategizing meeting of the Women's Agenda for Change in June 2000 and participated in the organization of the People's Health Assembly held in Dhaka, Bangladesh, in December 2000, at which issues related to women's health were discussed. In 2001, TWN launched a Gender Series, which it described as consisting of "papers published by TWN on gender and development issues from a Third World perspective" and "highlights the obstacles that hinder women from enjoying secure and sustainable livelihoods, such as those posed by the process of globalization. It provides proposals aimed at gender justice and equality, and the empowerment and progress of women."[9] Two booklets were published in 2001, authored, respectively, by Victoria Tauli-Corpus *(Globalization and Impacts on Indigenous Women: The Philippine Experience)* and Noeleen Heyzer *(Globalisation, Gender Equality and State Modernisation)* (TWN Annual Report 2001, 41). The same year, during a workshop called Trade, WTO and Human Development, a paper titled "Gender, Poverty and Trade," written by Nilufer Cagatay of the University of Utah, was presented to the sixty-one participants from ten Asian countries in preparation for the WTO Doha meeting.

In parallel with these efforts, TWN has been part of the Tourism and Investigation Team (Tim-team), an organization located in Thailand "involved in tourism-development-environment-related issues," which has published the newsletter *New Frontiers* since its formation in the late 1990s. In 2001, Tim-team analyzed the impact of the expansion of "the tourism-related sex industry and cross-border trafficking of children and women" (TWN Annual Report 2001, 152).

Through both the series and the statements associated with the Women's Rights and Gender Issues section of its website, starting in the early 2000s, TWN's participation in meetings focused on women's issues gradually increased. For example, in 2003, not only did twelve of its 155 TWNFs deal with women's issues, but it also participated in a national-based meeting –

the Malaysian Association of Working Women Meeting held in March – at which it presented a paper titled "Gender Justice and Globalization" (TWN Annual Report 2003, 108). Furthermore, as mentioned above, the section of its website on women's rights was, according to its numbers, one of the most visited sections.

The challenge ahead for the organization seems to be developing feminist perspectives and applying them to its numerous analyses of WTO process-es. At this time, it appears that such perspectives remain marginalized in favour of a non-gendered progressive perspective on multilateral trade ne-gotiations. Currently, TWN does not use an explicitly feminist point of view in its writings on traditional knowledge, biodiversity-based agriculture, health issues, and pharmaceutical companies, or in its publications dealing with women's issues, but this could change.

Starting with the 1999 workshop called Economic Crisis, Social Conse-quences and People's Response, at which TWN committed to undertaking further studies and collaboration on gender issues, there have been signs of more openness to the possibility of developing a feminist outlook on a range of issues. For example, during a hearing on the review of the WTO Agree-ment on Agriculture held in Geneva in February 2003, TWN joined the other eighty NGOs present in arguing that the WTO Agreement failed "to recognize the central role played by women in food production and the nu-tritional well-being of the family and community" (TWN Annual Report 2003, 116).

Focus on the Global South

Conceived in 1993-94 by its first two co-directors, Kamal Malhotra and Walden Bello, Focus on the Global South was officially established in Bang-kok in January 1995 (Malhotra and Bello 1999). In many ways, the two founders represent archetypes of transnational activists. Bello, a Filipino political economist, had lived for years in the United States, where he was very active in the anti-Marcos dictatorship struggle and the international Third World solidarity movement and had worked with a Northern NGO, the Institute for Food and Development Policy – Food First. Malhotra, from India, had long been involved with an international NGO, Community Aid Abroad (CAA – Oxfam Australia) and many local NGOs. As noted in the first external evaluation of Focus, Bello and Malhotra agreed on a common set of ideas. Both were convinced that it was important to go beyond the existing North-South paradigm. They were also "skeptical about main-stream economic analysis, and the economics-culture-politics methodology"

(Kaewhtep 1999, 45) and thought that it was essential to strengthen the links between micro and macro perspectives. At the same time, they felt that it was important to build a bridge between activists mobilizing on the ground and progressive researchers and scholars. Finally, they recognized the importance of East and Southeast Asia as an emerging and dynamic socio-economic and political space that embodied the contradictory and often complex effects of globalization (Kaewhtep 1999, 45-46).

Malhotra and Bello sought to offer an alternative conception to the North-South divide since "North and South" were being "redefined as concepts to distinguish between elites and non-elites, and more importantly, those who are economically able to participate in and benefit from globalized markets and those who are excluded and marginalized from them in both developing and industrialized countries" (Focus on the Global South ca. 1994b, 1). The initial concept paper for Focus explained, "Focus does not see itself as just another think tank but as engaged enterprise, where analysis is meant to inform activism and vice-versa" (Focus on the Global South ca. 1994b, 2).

The reputations, track records, and networks of the co-directors were instrumental in obtaining seed money for the organization from a set of funding agencies. Thailand's relative political stability and the possibility of being associated with the Chulalongkorn University Social Research Institute were key factors in establishing the Focus head office in Bangkok. Beginning with a small staff (there were only six in 1996), Focus expanded rapidly: in 1999, it had close to twenty staff members, and by 2005 it had about twenty-five. It also opened two national offices: one in India and one in the Philippines.

Two types of factors help to explain why Focus was so successfully built and consolidated. The first type is endogenous and has to do with the capacity of Focus "to build networks and strengthen linkages between and among civil society organizations at the global, national and local level" (Sta. Ana III 1999, 6). Through the years, Focus staff not only have been involved in the production of research and policy analysis (Bello 2001), but have played a central role in organizing civil society networks within the region around a range of issues (food security, APEC, ASEAN, and Asia Europe Meeting [ASEM]) and been closely involved in many global processes, such as the World Social Forum, anti-WTO coalitions (for example, the Our World Is Not for Sale campaign) and the peace movement (Banpasirichote, Singh, and Van der Borght 2002, 2). The second type of factor is exogenous and has to do with global economics and international agencies. The Asian financial crisis that began in Thailand before spreading to the whole region increased the demand for analyses by Focus. As one of the external evaluators noted, "The Asian financial crisis and the role of the international financial institutions have undoubtedly become the burning issues of the day" (Sta. Ana III 1999, 24). Within a few years, Focus became a key reference for civil society organizations in Southeast Asia, as well as for the broader anti-globalization movement, interested in better understanding both the crisis and the role of the IMF and the World Bank.[11]

From its early days, Focus sought to combine analyses on the workings and impact of regional and global economic processes and studies of local resistance and initiatives with its two main programs: on the one hand, policy-oriented research on and analysis of critical regional and global socio-economic issues (the Global Paradigms Program) and, on the other hand, documentation, analysis, and dissemination of "innovative civil society, grassroots, community-based efforts in democratic, poverty reducing and sustainable development" (the Micro-Macro Paradigm Program) (Kaewhtep 1999, 46).

Women's Issues and Feminist Perspectives

While it has identified the limitations of the traditional North-South divide, Focus has not yet furthered its inquiry into inequality and the discrepancy of power relations in the household and how such processes might be affected by economic globalization. Although it recognizes and attempts to incorporate feminist insights into its publications, women's voices and feminist perspectives have not gained a significant place.

Gender hierarchies and the differentiated impact of globalization on women remain, at Focus as at TWN, broadly encompassed within the discourse around those excluded and marginalized by economic globalization in Southeast Asia – a discourse still, rather strangely, silent on women's participation and resistance. As it specified in its original concept paper, drafted in 1994, "Focus will address mainly economic, ecological, political and cultural developments with an approach that is multidisciplinary, grounded in empirical research, informed by activist engagement, and designed for intervention in policy debates" (Focus on the Global South ca. 1994b, 2).

In the vision of its founders, Focus constituencies are "grassroots" organizations based in the global South. Gender issues have been conceived in cultural terms, as part of what Focus defines as the cultural dilemma. For the organization, this dilemma raises the following questions: "What is a progressive Southern position on Islamic fundamentalist movements and especially women's status and the role of the community economy in these movements? And, also what is generically defined as 'Southern cultural perspectives on gender and development?'" (Bello and Malhotra 1994, 7). In an appendix to its concept paper, Focus further specifies that these issues would be analyzed through a network of cultural responses to globalization that would "include women's organizations" and "be focussed on a dispassionate discussion of the recent cultural responses to the deepening crisis of globalization" (Focus on the Global South ca. 1994a, 2). In an initial consultation made in India prior to the establishment of Focus, it was recognized that grassroots groups had already identified that attention needed to be paid to "liberalization or structural adjustment and its impact on marginalized communities and on women, and, related to the above, the changing relationship between the state, market, and civil society" (Focus on the Global South ca. 1994a, 4). In terms of its envisioned staff structure, the document states that a "conscious effort will be made to ensure gender equality, not only on staff but among fellows, activists and on the board" (Focus on the Global South ca. 1994b, 8).

Focus was formally founded in January 1995, and its first two-year work plan prioritized economic liberalization and sustainable development alternatives as key axes of research. As part of its goal of linking micro and macro issues, "Women's groups or those working on gender issues in the context of economic development and its impact [were] consciously sought in all cases" (Focus on the Global South 1995, 1). However, in the description of its various program activities, gender issues seemed to be subsumed under other research priorities and broader concerns framed around equity, community, and ecological sustainability. The exception was the Cultural Responses to Globalization Program, which was intended to examine women's empowerment alongside individual rights and pluralist democracy and to involve women's organizations in the research process (Focus on the Global South 1995, 5).

Three years later, in its 1998 work plan, Focus noted that it had "recruited experienced gender specialists" for its various programs and was trying "to integrate such perspectives" into all of its endeavours (Focus on the Global South 1998, 2). Similarly, with respect to its Micro-Macro Issues Linking Program, Focus stated that it was "attempting to integrate a gender perspective across the entire program" through the involvement of a Development Alternative with Women for a New Era (DAWN) board member and the hiring of staff with a gender perspective (Focus on the Global South 1998, 4).

As discussed earlier, Focus rapidly became a reference point for up-to-date analysis and policy documents, especially on global economic and political processes, such as APEC, ASEM, ASEAN, the WTO, and the 1997 financial crisis. While addressing issues similar to those of TWN, an evaluation report conducted by two external consultants, Lisa Jordan and Lori Udall (1999, 21), noted three differences based on a series of interviews with NGOs and individuals using knowledge produced by both organizations:

> The first interesting observation was that TWN generally used standard economic language to make arguments and did not necessarily challenge economists to think "outside the box," while Focus often challenged economists to incorporate social and cultural variables in an economic analysis ... Secondly, most interviewees cited the Micro-Macro program of Focus as the distinctive feature of Focus and where "value-added" is most clear. Third, even in arenas where both organizations are working, such as the WTO arena, the niches filled are different.

Surprisingly, the consultants did not address the issue of gender or the possibility that Focus might offer an analysis informed in part by feminist perspectives. Such an omission reveals that implementation of the professed goal of integrating a gender lens into various Focus programs proved to be challenging in day-to-day activity. All the more striking is the fact that this dimension was specified in the evaluation terms of reference; the evaluators were asked to look at the "social, gender, economic and environment impact of regional and global development and political processes" (Jordan and Udall 1999, 37).

Three years later, the 2003-05 Focus work plan still included gender equity as one of the components of its deglobalization project. Referring to this project, the document (Focus on the Global South ca. 2003, 5) explains, "This will involve a transition from a market-driven economy that puts the primacy on profitability – in the process creating severe class inequalities and sectoral imbalances such as the rural-urban divide – to a nature – and people-oriented economy that puts the emphasis on secure livelihoods, decent employment, and improved well-being based on social justice and dignity, gender equity, and ecological equilibrium."

As proposed, deglobalization would ensure the "diffusion of values and practices that reflect the universal values of equity, democracy, gender equality, and ecological sustainability" (Focus on the Global South ca. 2003, 9). Within such a perspective, women are considered one "sector" of society, alongside farmers, workers, the impoverished, and indigenous peoples (Focus on the Global South ca. 2003, 11). Written in the context of the US-led Iraq invasion and the World Social Forum, Focus emphasized its contribution to the "process of social building and strengthening of political space for people's organization," including the women's movement (Focus on the Global South ca. 2003, 11). However, beyond a generic commitment to gender equality, the descriptions of its India, Thailand, and Philippines programs did not refer to any research projects or intervention targeted specifically and concretely at this goal. In an adjusted 2004-05 work plan released a year later, in March 2004, following a two-day staff retreat and a two-day planning session, the only reference to women was in a discussion on "land and agrarian reform," in which a proposed joint publication with Food First and FIAN International looked at gender and land reform (Focus on the Global South 2004, 45; see also Thailand Land Reform Network, Focus on the Global South, Land Research Action Network 2004).

In the fall of 2007, Focus organized a workshop called International Course on Globalization and Social Movements for local and regional activists. In the workshop, gender equality was mentioned as one of the "spaces and opportunities for civil society advocacy for global or national economic justice" (Focus on the Global South and Chulalongkorn University Social Research Institute 2007, 1). Once again, while Focus remained committed to considering gender issues, it had difficulty situating specifically how such issues could be approached and whether feminist perspectives might be of use. This time, however, gender issues were approached from the point of view of class, social privilege, and race (5). Such attention to gender issues and feminist perspectives had been mentioned in the 1999 external assessment by Filomeno Sta. Ana III (1999) and Kanjan Kaewthep (1999, 88), who had suggested that new issues could be integrated into the direction of Focus, including a "gender perspective and feminist economy." The 2007 workshop may be an indication that specific steps are now being taken to mainstream women's issues, or at least develop a perspective that moves beyond a generic and sectoral conception of them.

Asia Pacific Research Network (APRN)

The third organization examined here is the Asia Pacific Research Network (APRN). Established in 1999, it was the product of a two-year process of consultation and exchange of materials among organizations from the Asia-Pacific region that were involved in research and documentation efforts. Spearheaded by a Manila-based research and data-banking centre, IBON (especially Antonio Tujan, its director), APRN's initial objectives were: 1) to build the research capacity of selected Asian NGOs; 2) to identify and strengthen one organization in each target Asian country that could act as the research-information and data-banking provider for local organizations; 3) to propose common research strategies by sharing experiences while enhancing capacities; and 4) to "develop capacity and a common research platform to support social movements in their respective countries on the emerging issues related to the WTO Millennium round, the IMF and the APEC" (APRN 1999, 3).

APRN's first annual conference, organized around the theme of trade liberalization, brought together eighty-five individuals from fifty organizations located in eleven countries and included ten of the seventeen founding organizations of the network (CI-ROAP 1999). Following the conference, a workshop on research methodologies identified specific activities for the network.[11]

Thereafter, APRN grew steadily. Through a grant from a Northern funding agency, it established a small secretariat, located in the IBON office in Manila, that was responsible for communications among network members, developing and maintaining a website and an e-mail forum, and coordinating publication of the *APRN Journal* (APRN 2000b, 1). In late 1999, APRN helped to organize the People's Assembly, a parallel summit held during the WTO Third Ministerial Conference in Seattle. Early in 2000, it conducted a series of workshops on information, documentation, and research training with regard to women and globalization, food security, and the WTO's Agreement on Agriculture. At the end of that year, APRN held its second annual conference in Jakarta, with the theme "Poverty and Financing Development." By then, the network had expanded its membership to twenty-three organizations based in twelve Asia Pacific region countries (APRN 2000a, 1).

During the following years, APRN continued to organize annual conferences that were co-hosted by at least one APRN member. Its sixth annual conference, on the theme of agriculture and food sovereignty, was held in Dhaka, Bangladesh, on 25-27 November 2004 and hosted by UBINIG (Policy Research for Development Alternatives), a long-standing member of the network. This time, organizers "decided to develop the APRN conference from a purely research and academic conference to a more open and public gathering of research institutions and people's organizations" (APRN 2004a, 1). The conference was well attended, with over five hundred participants from more than thirty countries, and it resulted in the adoption of the People's Convention on Food Sovereignty and a People's Statement (APRN 2004b).

Beyond its annual conferences, APRN organized a range of research activities. For example, during its 2002 General Council meeting, APRN members agreed to "embark on coordinated researches as originally envisioned at the start of the network in Manila" (APRN 2002a). Instead of financing individual research projects led by network members, APRN decided that research would be conducted jointly. The first two research projects dealt, respectively, with strategies for challenging multinational corporations (coordinated by GATT-Watchdog of New Zealand), and with issues of women and labour in Asia (coordinated by the Center for Women's Resources of the Philippines) (APRN 2001, 2002a, 2002b). The latter sought to document and reflect on the gendered impact of globalization, especially on women (Taguiwalo 2005).

More recently, APRN members also participated in the formation of the Reality of Aid – Asia network, thereby establishing an Asian counterpart to the Reality of Aid network aimed at monitoring and documenting international development assistance programs and projects. APRN also continued to be involved in global and regional activities, including a policy workshop on regional cooperation and human rights in Asia (June 2004), an international conference to commemorate the fiftieth anniversary of the Bandung Conference (April 2005), and a range of consultations and parallel forums on ASEAN and the WTO.

After almost ten years of existence, APRN has located itself as a key research and advocacy network primarily in Southeast Asia, but also within the broader Asia-Pacific region. It has expanded from seventeen to over fifty members based in nineteen different countries.[12] As with the two organizations discussed above, the presence of key individuals skilled at organizing networks, coordinating processes, and seeking financial assistance, coupled with the growing density of international and regional processes (economic integration, financial liberalization, the 1997 crisis) interacted positively to contribute to the rapid expansion of APRN.

Women's Issues and Feminist Perspectives

Somewhat reminiscent of TWN and its different research initiatives on women's issues, APRN has sought on various occasions to highlight how globalization might negatively affect women. At its July 2003 Research Conference on the Impact of Globalization on Women Labor, ARPN brought together various women's researchers from the region to share the results of sectoral research (agriculture, fisheries, processing industries, and migration). As described on its website, there were thirty-eight participants representing twenty-five different organizations from ten countries. Of those, twelve were APRN members, including three women's organizations (Asia Pacific Forum on Women, Law and Development, Roots for Equity, and Center for Women's Resources).[13] Another seven women's organizations that were not APRN members attended the conference. For APRN, "the fact that the Bangkok Conference pushed through, and its successful outcome, only emphasizes the importance that APRN gives to women and women's empowerment." As stated in the description of the conference, APRN "upholds the view that research can help in promoting advocacy, and organizing women in the end."[14] The Research Conference led, in 2005, to the publication of *Intensifying Working Women' Burdens: The Impact of Globalization on Women Labor in Asia* (Taguiwalo 2005), a collection of the various papers and presentations given during the meeting. As explained in the Introduction to that book, "While many of the conclusions are similar to those of previous studies on the impact of globalization on Asian women, the richness of the data, the variety of illustrations and the additional evidence of the adverse impact of globalization on women's work and on women's lives are unique and are possible only because of the broadness of the network and the close links of the research teams with the communities and women" (Taguiwalo 2005, 7).

However, the overall finding of the conference that "poor Asian women's liberation from poverty, hardship and inequality means challenging corporate globalization and struggling for a democratic path to development that will put an end to economic, political and gender inequalities" (Taguiwalo 2005, 14) is somewhat generic and vague and does not seem to put forward a specific feminist perspective on patriarchy and how economic globalization might be reifying and strengthening women's exclusion. Nonetheless, this research conference appears to have been a first clear attempt to strengthen women's advocacy around globalization. In fact, in the concept paper explaining the rationale for the conference, it was argued that "women are the preferred workers under globalization" and that "shaped by patriarchal cultures that regard women as secondary citizens, women in Asia are molded towards subservience, patience and docility, the qualities required for 'good workers'" (ARPN 2002a, 1).

In the book that came out of the conference, it is quite difficult to hear women's voices, in terms of revealing existing gender dynamics and power structures within organizations or between the researchers and the women's organizations that are being analyzed. Findings and figures are generally presented as objective realities, thus undermining the possibility of multiple interpretations and impeding a feminist reading. It seems just as difficult to find a feminist outlook in other APRN conferences and undertakings, despite a growing number of women's organizations within the network. For example, in the proposal describing the fifth APRN annual conference, "War and Terror: People's Right and the Militarization of Globalization," organized in 2003, women are back to being considered a "sector" along with labour, indigenous peoples, and peasants (APRN 2003, 2). In 2005, APRN organized a policy-research conference on trade, at which the focus was on issues related to WTO and major agreements (AoA [Agreement on Agriculture], TRIPS [Trade-Related Aspects of Intellectual Property Rights], GATS [General Agreement on Trade in Services], NAMA [Non-Agricultural Market Access]), trade-finance coherence, regional and bilateral agreements, and domestic and international trade. Once again, women's and feminist perspectives were absent, showing how difficult the inclusion of such perspectives has remained when dealing with issues that are not specifically considered to relate to women.

Conclusion

In this chapter, I have examined how three Southeast Asian research and policy advocacy networks have evolved since the mid-1980s, especially following the 1997 financial crisis. This form of transnational activism was first conceived by those who established the networks as a complement to local and national activism as well as an activist modality on its own. Transnational advocacy efforts initiated by TWN, Focus, and APRN have focused on generating research, policy documents, and common advocacy campaigns. The purpose of these undertakings has been to provide tools and methods with which social movements and people's organizations may challenge regional and international institutions and processes at both the international and national levels.

At the same time, as revealed by the analysis of the specific work of these networks on women's issues and with women's organizations, feminist perspectives are still very much at the margins. In fact, reaching out to mainstream activist organizations remains an important challenge for feminists and women's organizations within these networks or working in coalition projects. While in all three cases there has been a greater commitment to analyzing and looking in particular at the impact of economic globalization on women, such commitment has either remained at the level of a declared objective in work plans and project proposals or meant that women have been considered among the marginalized groups in society alongside sectors such as labour, indigenous peoples, peasants, and the urban poor. Thus, these networks have had difficulty recognizing that women's issues cut across social sectors. Except possibly for the 2003 APRN conference on women and globalization, there has not yet been a commitment to develop advocacy and policy documents rooted in feminism that would bring specific attention to women's issues and their resistance to patriarchal assumptions. Despite a social justice outlook and a commitment to social change, these networks reproduce the same type of gender-blindness with regard to economic globalization that one encounters in the dominant international relations theory. As such, they provide examples of the challenges and difficulties of stretching and extending feminist outlooks and insights beyond women's organizations and activists.

It might be productive for these three networks to turn toward feminist IR in order to enrich their critical perspective on global economic and political processes. As discussed in the Introduction to this volume, grassroots feminists and feminist IR scholars have successfully revealed how dominant IR and global economic approaches have placed a greater emphasis on masculine perspectives. D'Aoust (2007) and Tickner (1992), among others, have argued that in the dominant mainstream IR paradigm, realism in fact constituted a "malestream" approach that reflected a masculine conception and discourse, embedded in its ontology. In feminist IR perspectives, one can find a critique of how such a paradigm reifies and legitimizes the status quo by normalizing existing power relations and the dominant gender-based order as natural and as the only possible one (Battistella 2005, 245). Gillian Young (2004, 77) is quite explicit about the need to adopt a different and situated point of view: "Feminism requires an ontological revisionism: a recognition that it is necessary to go behind the appearance and examine how differentiated and gendered power constructs the social relations that form that reality."

Feminist IR scholars have also revealed how transnational coalitions are often gender-blind and end up reproducing exclusionary practices. These scholars have argued that such practices might occur within the analysis of case studies of transnational coalitions and networks, as well as at the theoretical level if one were to rely solely on mainstream and dominant IR approaches to North-South relations, including classic Marxist class-based analyses and theories of imperialism. Knowledge created by such coalitions can hide implicit, and often unconscious, assumptions wherein "types of knowledge and skills typically dominated by women are delegitimized" (Macdonald 2005, 37), particularly in the area of global economics and trade agreements (see Díaz Alba, this volume).

In moving forward and in keeping with each network's commitment to pay further attention to gender equity and women's issues, postcolonial and poststructuralist feminist perspectives might also be of use, since they have been particularly sensitive to the built-in relations of power within the international cooperation discourse (Kothari 2002; Parpart 1995). Such perspectives share a common concern with the construction of discourse and fields of knowledge, highlighting how international development has traditionally been fraught with ethnocentrism, often dating back to colonialism. Today, postcolonial feminists have found echoes within a new generation of development scholars and practitioners concerned with local knowledge and world views, as well as with dialectical methodologies in which culture and knowledge are situated and notions of class, race, and gender are problematized (Agathangelou and Ling 2004; Parpart 1995).

To integrate women's perspectives into their transnational activism, the networks could also explore what Brooke Ackerly (2000) and her collaborators (Ackerly and Okin 1999; Ackerly, Stern, and True 2006) have suggested – to use a feminist methodology of social criticism for IR as a means of respecting diversity while maintaining a critical edge. In many ways, the diversity of feminist projects associated with the WSF (as revealed in Conway's chapter in this volume), as well as autonomous organizing and knowledge production by women's organizations on global processes (see, for example, Díaz Alba's chapter in this volume), constitute positive examples for applying this methodology to transnational and cross-border advocacy. Such methodology combines "deliberative inquiry, sceptical scrutiny and guiding criteria" and may allow for social change. The first element, deliberative inquiry, "is the practice of generating knowledge through collective questioning, exchange of views, and discussion among critics and members of the society." Sceptical scrutiny refers to "an attitude toward existing and proposed values, practices and norms that requires one to examine their existing and potentially exploitable inequalities," and the guiding criteria "are a list of minimum standards, or a single standard, that critics can use to challenge existing values, practices and norms" (Ackerly and Okin 1999, 138-39). As Ackerly and Okin (1999, 156) recognize, "International activists need to develop additional strategies for supporting individual, national and local efforts without undermining the necessarily contextual character of those efforts."

Following the pioneers in feminist IR, who questioned foundational dogmas of realist and liberal approaches (Harding 1987; Peterson 2004; Young 2004), a feminist reading of globalization processes in Southeast Asia might contribute to opening unexplored avenues of knowledge creation. It could also directly address the dilemmas and challenges of applying feminist perspectives and insights to attempts at linking the local to the global. Such an endeavour would link economic globalization not only with issues of exclusion and disempowerment but also with the decision-making processes and underlying patriarchal structures that allow globalization to persist. Feminist theorizing of transnational activism might offer uncharted possibilities for imagining social transformation that can challenge patriarchy, be it from within activist networks and movements or the global and national institutions targeted.

NOTES

1 While there is relative agreement on this, its significance and its impact on political processes remain open to interpretation (Hewinson 2001).

2 Much of this research is based on unpublished documents (project proposals, annual reports, campaign plans, and so on) consulted during two field trips (May 2005 and July 2006) to Southeast Asia, at which time I visited each organization's head office or secretariat. Other primary sources come from Inter Pares archives and consulted during a short visit in March 2005.

3 It should be noted that feminist perspectives are already present in several Southeast Asian women's advocacy organizations, including Tenaganita (Protecting the Rights of Women) in Malaysia, the Asia Pacific Forum on Women, Law and Development in Thailand, and Isis International – Manila and Likhaan in the Philippines. However, these perspectives have yet to gain wide acceptance in larger and key Southeast Asian policy advocacy networks and organizations working on global economic processes affecting the region.

4 However, as the authors note, there are a number of exceptions, such as Aviel (2000), Gurowitz (2000), Lizée (2000), Piper (2001), Piper and Uhlin (2002), Price (1998), and Uhlin (2002) as well as the more recent works by Lyons (2005a, 2005b).

5 Some of the discussion on the case study analysis has been previously published (Caouette 2006, 2007).

6 Through the years, TWNF has been sent to over fifty regional and international newspapers and to fifty magazines and newsletters, with the remainder going to radio stations, press and new agencies, NGOs, journalists, and individuals. Published originally in English, several issues of TWNF are translated every year into Chinese and Bahasa Malaysia by the Penang office, into various Indian languages by the Goa and Delhi offices, into Spanish by the Montevideo office, and into Bahasa Indonesia by the Jakarta office. By 1993, TWNF issues began to be distributed by e-mail (TWN Annual Report 1996, 3).

7 One such event was the African Workshop on Women and Economic and Social Policy in Africa, held in June 1995 and organized by the African Secretariat of TWN, ENDA Third World, and the African Women's Economic Policy Network. The workshop sought to "evaluate recent and previous and current policy approaches for the advancement of women in Africa" (TWN Annual Report 1995, 88). The workshop concluded, "In spite of more than a decade of structural adjustment programme as a policy framework, the living condition of women in the continent has further deteriorated" and noted, "women experience increased violence, homelessness, social disintegration, work burden and poverty" (89).

8 Those included seven papers on a range of topics: "No. 1 Will the Beijing Conference Address the Totality of Our Oppression as Women?, No. 2 National Machinery for Women: The Centre-Piece of Post Beijing Implementation Strategies, No. 3 WTO, Women and the Environment, No. 4 Africa SAPs, Development and Gender Relations: What the Platform for Action Needs to Address, No. 5 Health for All Women, No. 6 Women as Consumers and Producers in the World Market, No. 7 Indigenous Women and the Beijing Conference" (TWN Annual Report 1996, 100).

9 See http://www.twnside.org.sg/title/gender1.htm.

10 In its 2003-05 work plan, the organization recognized such a position: "Focus has also travelled considerably from its starting point. It is today widely considered a 'key player' in the global movement for a different and better world. Its analyses of global developments are extensively consulted, as are its suggestions for structural changes" (Focus on the Global South ca. 2003, 3).

11 These included "common and/or coordinated research projects," "training in research and related technologies," and "publications" (APRN 1999, 4). Common research areas were government transparency, the impact of globalization on workers' rights and labour migration, the impact of globalization on food security, and the impact of the GATT on agriculture.

12 See the APRN website, http://www.aprnet.org/.

13 Ibid.

14 Ibid.

REFERENCES

Ackerly, Brooke A. 2000. *Political Theory and Feminist Social Criticism*. Cambridge: Cambridge University Press.

Ackerly, Brooke A., and Susan Moller Okin. 1999. Feminist Social Criticism and the International Movement for Women's Rights as Human Rights. In *Democracy's Edges*, ed. Ian Shapiro and Casiano Hacker-Cordon, 134-62. Cambridge: Cambridge University Press.

Ackerly, Brooke A., Maria Stern, and Jacquie True. 2006. *Feminist Methodologies for International Relations*. Cambridge: Cambridge University Press.

Agathangelou, Anna M., and L.H.M. Ling. 2004. Power, Borders, Security, Wealth: Lessons of Violence and Desire from September 11. *International Studies Quarterly* 48 (3): 517-38.

Asia Pacific Research Network (APRN). 1999. Narrative Report. Unpublished report (September).

–. 2000a. Project Accomplishment Report – Asia Pacific Research Network – 2nd Annual Conference (21-23 August)/Business Meeting (24 August)/Training on Information Documentation. Unpublished reports (November).

–. 2000b. Asia Pacific Research Network Conference on Poverty and Financing Development. Unpublished project proposal. Inter Pares Archives (March).

–. 2001. Corporate Power or People's Power: Transnational Corporations and TNCs Unpublished report (27-29 September).

–. 2002a. APRN Secretariat Accomplishment Report. Unpublished report (7 November).

–. 2002b. Globalization and Women Labour – Uncovering the Real Score: An APRN Coordinated Research Documentation on the Situation and Struggles of Working Women. Unpublished project. Proposal submitted to Inter Pares.

–. 2003. APRN 5th Annual Conference: War and Terror: People's Rights and Militarization of Globalization. Unpublished project proposal.

–. 2004a. Asia Pacific Convention on People's Food Sovereignty. Unpublished report (15 June).

–. 2004b. Asia Pacific Convention on People's Food Sovereignty. Unpublished project proposal. Inter Pares Archives.

Aviel, JoAnn Fagot. 2000. Placing Human Rights and Environmental Issues on ASEAN's Agenda: The Role of Non-Governmental Organizations. *Asian Journal of Political Science* 8 (2): 17-34.

Banpasirichote, Chantana, Ramesh Singh, and Dominique Van der Borght. 2002. Report of the Review: Focus on the Global South. Unpublished report (October).

Battistella, Dario. 2005. *Théories des relations internationales.* Paris: Presses de Sciences Po.

Bello, Walden. 2001. *The Future in the Balance: Essays on Globalization and Resistance.* Oakland: Food First Books.

Bello, Walden, and Kamal Malhotra. 1994. Concept Paper on the "Center for the South." Unpublished document (November).

Caouette, Dominique. 2006. Thinking and Nurturing Transnational Activism in Southeast Asia: Global Advocacy through Knowledge-Building. *Kasarinlan: A Philippine Quarterly of Third World Studies* 21 (2): 3-33.

–. 2007. Going Transnational? Dynamics and Challenges of Linking Local Claims to Global Advocacy Networks in Southeast Asia. *Pacific Focus: Inha Journal of International Studies* 22 (2): 141-66.

CI-ROAP (Consumers International – Regional Office Asia-Pacific). 1999. First Conference of the Asia Pacific Research Network (APRN). *The AP Consumer,* 18.

Commonwealth Foundation. n.d. Connecting people – Dr. Martin Khor Interview: Creating Change by Making People's Voices Heard. Commonwealth Foundation (News Archive). http://www.commonwealthfoundation.com/news/news/archive/details.cfm.

D'Aoust, Anne-Marie. 2007. Les approches féministes en relations internationales. In *Théories des relations internationales: Contestations et résistances,* ed. Alex Macleod and Dan O'Meara, 281-304. Montreal: Athéna Éditions.

Dropping Knowledge. N.d. Martin Khor. Malaysia. Activist, Scholar, Journalist. http://www.droppingknowledge.org/participants_search.php?id=557.

Eschle, Catherine. 2005. "Skeleton Women": Feminism and the Antiglobalization Movement. *Signs: Journal of Women in Culture and Society* 30 (3): 741-69.

Focus on the Global South. ca. 1994a. Appendix to Concept Paper. Unpublished document.

–. ca. 1994b. Concept Paper: Focus on the Global South – A Program of Development Policy Research and Practice. Unpublished document.

–. 1995. Draft Two-Year Work Plan, July 1995-June 1997. Unpublished document.

–. 1998. Proposed Work Plan 1998. Unpublished document.

–. ca. 2003. Work Plan 2003-2005. Unpublished document.

–. 2004. Work Plan 2004-2005. Unpublished document.

Focus on the Global South and Chulalongkorn University Social Research Institute. 2007. International Course on Globalisation and Social Transformation. Unpublished document.

Fouquin, Michel. 1999. L'industrialisation par l'exportation. In *Crise en Asie du Sud-Est,* ed. Philippe Richer, 43-63. Paris: Presses de Science Po.

Gurowitz, Amy. 2000. Migrant Rights and Activism in Malaysia: Opportunities and Constraints. *Journal of Asian Studies,* 59 (4): 863-88.

Harding, Sandra. 1987. *Feminism and Methodology: Social Science Issues.* Bloomington: Indiana University Press.

Hewinson, Kevin. 2001. Nationalism, Populism, Dependency: Southeast Asia and Responses to the Asian Crisis. *Singapore Journal of Tropical Geography* 22 (3): 219-36.

Jordan, Lisa, and Lori Udall. 1999. Focus on the Global South: Evaluation Report. Unpublished report commissioned by Novib (September).

Kaewhtep, Kanjana. 1999. A Program and Organizational Assessment of Focus on the Global South. *Focus on the Global South: An External Assessment (Final Draft).* Unpublished document (July).

Kothari, Uma. 2002. Feminist and Postcolonial Challenges to Development. In *Development Theory and Practice: Critical Perspectives,* ed. Uma Kothari and Martin Minogue, 35-51. Houndmills: Palgrave.

Lizée, Pierre P. 2000. Civil Society and Regional Security: Tensions and Potentials in Post-Crisis Southeast Asia. *Contemporary Southeast Asia* 22 (3): 550-69.

Loh, Francis K.W. 2004. Les ONG et les mouvements sociaux en Asie du Sud-Est. In *Mondialisation des résistances: l'état des luttes 2004,* ed. Laurent Delcourt, Bernard Duferme, and François Polet, 41-55. Paris: Éditions Syllepse.

–. 2005. National Security, the Police and the Rule of Law: Militarisation by Other Means. *Asian Exchange,* Special issue on Militarising State, Society and Culture in Asia: Critical Perspectives 20 (2) and 21 (1): 179-208.

Lyons, Lenore. 2005a. Embodying Transnationalism: The Making of the Maid. In *Corporeal Inscriptions: Representations of the Body in Cultural and Literary Texts and Practices,* ed. E. Lorek-Jezińska and Katarzyna Więckowska, 171-85. Torun: Nicolas Copernicus University Press.

−. 2005b. Transient Workers Count Too? The Intersection of Citizenship and Gender in Singapore's Civil Society. *Sojourn: Journal of Social Issues in Southeast Asia* 20 (2): 208-48.

Macdonald, Laura. 2005. Gendering Transnational Social Movement Analysis: Women's Groups Contest Free Trade in the Americas. In *Coalitions Across Borders*, ed. Joe Bandy and Jackie Smith, 21-41. Lanham: Rowman and Littlefield.

Malhotra, Kamal, and Walden Bello. 1999. *Background and Rationale, Focus on the Global South: An External Assessment (Final Draft).* Unpublished document (July).

Parnwell, Mike, and Jonathan Rigg. 2001. Global Dissatisfactions: Globalization, Resistance and Compliance in Southeast Asia. *Singapore Journal of Tropical Geography* 22 (3): 205-11.

Parpart, Jane L. 1995. Post-Modernism, Gender and Development. In *Power of Development*, ed. Jonathan Crush, 253-65. London: Routledge.

Peterson, V. Spike. 2004. Feminist Theories Within, Invisible to, and Beyond IR. *Brown Journal of World Affairs* 10 (2): 35-46.

Piper, Nicola. 2001. Transnational Women's Activism in Japan and Korea: The Unresolved Issue of Military Sexual Slavery. *Global Networks* 1 (2): 171-95.

Piper, Nicola, and Anders Uhlin. 2002. Transnational Advocacy Networks, Female Labour Migration and Trafficking in East and Southeast Asia: A Gendered Analysis of Opportunities and Obstacles. *Asian and Pacific Migration Journal* 11 (2): 171-95.

−. 2004. New Perspectives on Transnational Activism. In *Transnational Activism in Asia: Problems of Power and Democracy,* ed. Nicola Piper and Anders Uhlin, 1-25. London: Routledge.

−, eds. 2004. *Transnational Activism in Asia: Problems of Power and Democracy.* London: Routledge.

Price, John. 1998. Shadowing APEC: Nongovernmental Organizations Build Regional Alliances. *Asian Perspectives* 22 (2): 21-50.

Sta. Ana III, Filomeno. 1999. Executive Summary of Assessment, *Focus on the Global South (Final Draft).* Unpublished document (July).

Sundaram, Jomo K. 1998. La crise des tigres asiatiques et ses incidences mondiales: Une analyse au départ de l'Asie. In *Tigres du Sud: Crise d'un modèle ou contradictions de l'économie capitaliste,* Alternatives Sud V (3), 25-68. Louvain-la-Neuve/Paris: Centre Triconental/L'Harmattan.

Taguiwalo, Judy M., ed. 2005. *Intensifying Working Women's Burdens: The Impact of Globalization on Women Labor in Asia.* Manila: IBON Books.

Thailand Land Reform Network, Focus on the Global South, Land Research Action Network. 2004. The Struggle for Land: A Summary Discussion and Strategies at the Asia Land Meeting. Unpublished report (August).

Third World Network. 1985. *Third World Development or Crisis? (Declaration and Conclusions of the Third World Conference, Penang, 9-14 November 1984).* Penang: Third World Network.

−. 1993-2003. Annual Reports. Unpublished documents.

–. 2003. Project Proposal Submitted to Inter Pares. Unpublished document.

Tickner, J. Ann. 1992. *Gender in International Relations: Feminist Perspectives on Achieving Global Security.* New York: Columbia University Press.

Uhlin, Anders. 2002. Globalization, Democratization and Civil Society in Southeast Asia: Observations from Malaysia and Thailand. In *Globalization and Democratization in Asia,* ed. Catarina Kinnvall and Kristina Jonsson, 149-66. London: Routledge.

Verma, Vidhu. 2002. Debating Rights in Malaysia: Contradictions and Challenges. *Journal of Contemporary Asia* 32 (1): 108-29.

Weiss, Meredith. 2004. Transnational Activism by Malaysians: Foci, Tradeoffs and Implications. In *Transnational Activism in Asia: Problems of Power and Democracy,* ed. Nicola Piper and Anders Uhlin, 129-48. London: Routledge.

Young, Gillian. 2004. Feminist International Relations: A Contradiction in Terms? Or: Why Women and Gender are Essential to Understanding the World "We" Live In. *International Affairs* 80 (1): 75-88.

Building Transnational Feminist Solidarity in the Americas
The Experience of the Latin American Network of Women Transforming the Economy

CARMEN L. DÍAZ ALBA

In this chapter, I present an example of a women's movement organizing across borders that focuses on the gendered dimension of economics – specifically, structural adjustment programs and free trade agreements. The Latin American Network of Women Transforming the Economy (REMTE, or Red Latinoamericana Mujeres Transformando la Economía) is a transnational network of feminist organizations working with grassroots women. The network aims at building bridges between feminism and the economy, empowering women's movements to see free trade as a relevant issue for their agenda, and bringing a feminist perspective into coalitions of social movements opposing free trade.

As we will see in this case study, feminist critiques of mainstream transnational activism theories are relevant to a better understanding of REMTE's emergence, process of transnationalization, choice of targets, and results. These critiques suggest that there is a male bias in terms of the movements and strategies that mainstream perspectives consider, that gender dynamics inside social movements need to be addressed, and that movement impacts are viewed in an overly state-centred and short-term fashion (Beaulieu 2006; Dufour and Giraud 2007; Eschle 2005; Macdonald 2005; Marchand 2003; Staggenborg and Taylor 2005).

Following Dominique Masson's proposed scalar approach (this volume), I will argue that REMTE emerged not because of new openings in international institutions' political opportunity structures; it is instead an example of how social movements construct the transnational scale "from below." In Sonia E. Alvarez's (2000, 3) view, Latin American feminists experienced two different transnational activists' logics: "An internationalist identity-solidarity logic prevailed in the *'Encuentros*-like' intra-regional feminist activism of the 1980s and 1990s, whereas a transnational IGO-advocacy logic came to predominate in the region-wide feminist organizing around the Rio, Vienna, Cairo and Beijing Summits of the 1990s."

REMTE's case shows that the institutional-advocacy logic that is the focus of mainstream transnational social movement literature is not the only "logic of action" (Alvarez 2000) that can explain the emergence, target definition, and impacts of transnational networking. I intend to demonstrate that REMTE's targets are not only states or international institutions, but also other social movements. For this reason, we should not assess the network's contribution solely from a state- or institution-centred perspective.[1] Rather, we also need to take into consideration changes occurring in social movements at their different scales of action.

Moreover, this study highlights the gender dynamics of the broader social movement coalitions into which REMTE is inserted (for instance, the Hemispheric Social Alliance – HSA),[2] thus helping to address one of the shortcomings of mainstream transnational movement studies noted by feminist theorists (Conway 2007; Eschle 2005; Ferree and Mueller 2004; Staggenborg and Taylor 2005). REMTE's case is also interesting because the issues that it deals with – economics, structural adjustment programs, and free trade agreements – are not traditionally considered part of the feminist agenda. REMTE is thus bringing a different perspective to social movement debates, as well as new issues to the feminist agenda. The space created by this network provides grassroots women with concepts and tools from feminist economics that help them describe and analyze their daily economic experiences. REMTE has also demystified the neoliberal economy as a concern of (mostly male) experts, revealing the specific impact of economic globalization on women, and women's contribution to economic justice.

The chapter is divided into three sections. In the first section, I analyze the emergence of the network and its process of transnationalization, showing that REMTE emerged from an "identity-solidarity" logic, which is different from the logic associated with UN conferences. The second section deals with the gender dynamics within the social movement coalitions in which REMTE acts and with the challenges of bringing a feminist perspective into these spaces. In the last section, I address the impacts that the network has had on women's organizations at the domestic level and show that transnational networking reinforces feminist struggles locally by empowering grassroots women's organizations.[3]

The Building of a Transnational Network

Alvarez (1999) explains that Latin American transnational feminist activism has a history, as women have been organizing transnationally since the 1980s in feminist regional meetings (Encuentros), and in the processes of preparation for and follow-up on United Nations conferences during the 1990s (see, for example, Jelin 2003; Vargas 2003). Since 2001, feminist organizations in the region have also taken an active role in the development of the World Social Forum and of mobilizations against free trade (Alvarez, Faria, and Nobre 2004; Celiberti and Vargas 2003).

REMTE was officially created in 1997 by women's organizations anchored in grassroots and popular sectors (both rural and urban), university researchers, and NGOs from ten Latin American countries.[4] It defines itself as "a space for analysis and action that, through the generation of ideas, debates, actions, and political initiatives, seeks to contribute to women's critical appropriation of the economy, their recognition as economic actors, the promotion of their rights, and the construction of alternatives based on economic and gender justice" (REMTE 2001, my translation).

Coming from a Latin American tradition of *feminismo popular,* REMTE emphasizes popular research and education, decentralization, information sharing, and participatory methodologies. The network is critical not only of free trade, but also of social movements that may reproduce gender inequalities in their discourses and strategies against free trade agreements. REMTE has become a key participant in spaces such as the International Council of the World Social Forum and the HSA, where it strives to "advance, together with other movements and organizations, toward a global agenda that must necessarily include a feminist perspective" (M. León 2001, my translation). The following section presents the creation of REMTE, as understood by the women interviewed, and explores the logics of action at work in the emergence of this transnational network.

Emergence of a Feminist Critique of Neoliberal Economic Integration

One of the main factors in REMTE's emergence is the economic transformations that have taken place in Latin America over the past twenty years, including implementation of structural adjustment programs and free trade agreements. Economic restructuring played a significant role in the transnationalization of feminist solidarities (Brenner 2003; Desai 2002;

Moghadam 2005). Furthermore, the flexibilization of labour and privatization of public services, two characteristics of the neoliberal economic model, have had differential impacts on women and men. Because the majority of analyses on the impacts of free trade were gender-blind, feminist organizations realized the need to develop analysis and knowledge creation from a feminist perspective that could serve as a framework for collective action and would allow them to frame gender issues in the resistance to free trade.[5]

Therefore, one of REMTE's goals was to produce and disseminate feminist knowledge critical of free trade and structural adjustment programs. Sara Román, union organizer and founding member of REMTE in Mexico, explains that in the first stage of the network's creation, the idea was mainly to "bring together women's organizations working on economic issues and start looking at the economic impact that free trade was having on women specifically" (personal communication, 23 January 2007). At that time, few feminist organizations were dealing with economic issues, so the network aimed at making visible the links among macroeconomics, free trade agreements, and women's lives through popular education and the development of alternative knowledge to counter the neoliberal discourse. Thus, REMTE focused on aspects of the feminist struggle that had not yet been raised in the early 1990s: "We needed to gain a global comprehension of women's struggles and attempt to understand these struggles by engaging in a feminist critique of the economic model" (Rosa Guillén, personal communication, 3 May 2007).

Irene León, from the Latin American Information Agency, states that REMTE was "the first feminist network to enter into the debate on the liberalization of economic exchanges as well as the first feminist group to take a stand and refuse to accept free trade as a fact" (personal communication, 4 May 2007). Rosa Guillén, member from Peru and ex-coordinator of the network, explains that REMTE's founders initiated a new way of looking for women's organizations working on economic issues, that is, "seeing poverty neither through the analysis of 'gender programs' of the World Bank or the International Monetary Fund nor through their projects to alleviate poor women. Rather, we wanted to change the economic model" (personal communication, 3 May 2007).

This critical vision attracted many organizations that did not want to enter the discussion on "gender-friendly" free trade agreements. For example, Miriam Nobre, coordinator of the World March of Women (WMW) and member of REMTE in Brazil, explains, "At the moment of hegemonic neoliberalism, everything was about positive and negative impacts, only proposing minor reforms, very selective and limited issues. Having a name that affirmed the transformation of the economy – women transforming the economy – attracted a lot of people" (personal communication, 28 April 2007).

In contrast to members of other highly specialized transnational networks, most of the women participating in REMTE are not professionals in international trade or economists. Their participation in national and transnational meetings has been essential for making links between free trade agreements and women's lives.[6] For example, Miriam Martínez, coordinator of the Mesoamerican Women's space, says,

> At the beginning, we knew about trade agreements only at the theoretical level, mainly from political discussions. We didn't yet relate them to women's life experiences. The Mesoamerican Encuentros[7] have been important to furthering our understanding that the economy's impact on women's lives has to do not only with productive micro-projects ... it has to do with the corn, the water, the land, the right to a decent living ... we didn't make that link before. REMTE's contribution was crucial to improving our ability to make the connections between gender and the economy, particularly women's lives and trade agreements. (personal communication, 26 January 2007)

Participation in international meetings is seen as a very positive and enriching experience because it provides the opportunity to create transnational links and allows for exchange on national experiences to develop a feminist critical perspective of economic integration. The spaces created by social movements (counter-summits, workshops, demonstrations, coordination meetings) provide access for grassroots organizations to participate at the international scale, which is normally reserved for a small activist elite.

Constructing a Transnational Space for Grassroots Women's Organizations

In contrast to the idea that transnational social movements emerge around international institutions – such as United Nations conferences – that provide a favourable political opportunity structure, Alvarez (1998; 2000) contends that social movements also construct their own opportunities to transnationalize their struggles. She provides the example of the Latin American Encuentros to support her position.[8] This idea is shared by Dominique Masson (this volume), who asserts that transnational spaces can be created by movements and with a bottom-up approach. Masson posits that social movements play an active role in the construction of the transnational scale both materially and discursively, a process that involves organizing, constructing issues and constituencies, and mobilizing them at that particular scale.

The case of REMTE is better explained as transnationalization from below. REMTE's emergence was, indeed, a response to economic changes in the region. However, it was neither through targeting an international institution nor as a result of United Nations conferences that the network was created. Instead, the key to REMTE's creation was the transnational space already shaped by feminist activists, along with previous links among women's organizations.

The idea of a transnational network that would work on gender and economic issues was first conceived in one of the workshops at the VII Feminist Encuentro (Chile, 1996).[9] The following year, another workshop to discuss economic adjustment programs in Latin America and their impacts on women's lives was organized in Lima, Peru. REMTE was formally created at the end of this workshop (Guillén, personal communication, 3 May 2007). In reference to the role of United Nations conferences in REMTE's transnationalization process, Leonor Concha (personal communication, 20 January 2007), from REMTE in Mexico and former coordinator of the regional network, observes that Beijing "was a just a 'push,' as there was a movement building way before Beijing. What would have been the use of Beijing without prior movement construction?"

According to REMTE's participants, international institutions such as the IMF and the World Bank were permeated by a hegemonic economic discourse that considered free trade to be a positive context for women.[10] Miriam Nobre and Nalu Faria (2003, 624, my translation) argue that the strategies for gender equity proposed at UN conferences focused on the empowerment of women as individuals and on gender mainstreaming in political spaces and public policies. They find this problematic because "while women worked on the implementation of public policies and the incorporation of gender into the state's discourse, market forces were organizing women's lives at all levels."

Another motivation for the creation of REMTE was to provide a means of networking at the transnational scale with organizations that were not linked with UN conferences, at which the dominant agenda was focused more on sexual and reproductive rights than on the economy's impact on women's lives. "In my organization," says Nobre (personal communication, 28 April

2007), "the SOF [Sempreviva Feminist Organization], we were very isolated because we were not part of the United Nation's debates that addressed items on the feminist movement agenda. We were doing a lot of popular education work at the national level, we had alliances with the union and popular movements, but we didn't know where to channel the work we were doing."

Faria (personal communication, 2 May 2007), current coordinator of REMTE, states that the network was created outside the traditional space of feminism, "with groups that wanted to work with the grassroots but that were also looking for a way to enter into the debate with other social movements." Thus, although REMTE opposes the adoption of free trade agreements, its strategies are focused on the empowerment of women at the grassroots level and the creation of feminist knowledge regarding macroeconomic issues.

Bringing Feminism into Social Movement Coalitions

Since its beginnings, REMTE has worked in alliance with various social movements and has actively brought a feminist perspective into transnational spaces such as the World Social Forums, the HSA, the Hemispheric Campaign against the Free Trade Agreement of the Americas (FTAA), and the WTO (REMTE 2001). Although they believe that working inside these spaces is crucial to advancing the network's goals, the women of REMTE recognize that it is not an easy task. As feminist scholars note, the gender dynamics inside social movement coalitions are a significant variable that needs to be taken into account (Eschle 2005; Ferree and Mueller 2004; Macdonald 2005; Staggenborg and Taylor 2005). In order to study REMTE's targets and outcomes, I present some of the strategies that it uses to integrate gender into the work of social movement coalitions, and I provide an assessment of its successes and the obstacles that it faces.

Gendering the Agenda of Social Movement Coalitions

In its declaration at the 2003 World Social Forum, the WMW stated that the Forum had made partial progress toward integrating feminism. Although it was recognized, for instance, that thanks to feminists' work there were more women – and more feminists – on the panels, the WMW felt that "women's presence remains marginal and is only politely tolerated" and that there was still a long way toward "achieving genuine dialogue on the role of women and feminism in the construction of another world ... as the main struggle for many is still only capitalism" (World March of Women 2003).

The perception of how deeply feminism has permeated free trade coalitions is also equivocal. There is recognition that there have been positive changes. However, it is acknowledged that there is still much to do in terms of achieving equity between men and women beyond discourse because, as Marianne Marchand (2003) argues, women cannot simply be "added in." In the case of the HSA, Guillén's evaluation (personal communication, 3 May 2007) is rather optimistic, although she also recognizes limitations: "From the point of view of our expectations, we are still far away, but from the point of view of where we started, we have come a long way ... The HSA is a less aggressive space, less *machista* ... but nothing has been given to us; we have gained a lot but we could lose what we have gained at any moment. We have to make sure that we don't take a step back."

The people whom I interviewed observed that among representatives of the movement for global justice, the integration of a gender perspective has become part of the "political consensus." Coalitions can no longer afford to ignore gender as an important issue because this would be a violation of a political principle, according to Silke Helfrich, former director of the Boell Foundation, a financial supporter of the Women's Committee of the HSA (personal communication, 27 January 2007).

REMTE demands the presence of women who bring feminist perspectives to general debates. Such presence in panels, Guillén (personal communication, 3 May 2007) argues, does not mean that there has to be an equal number of men and women: "We recognize that we don't have feminist specialists in every subject. When we don't, instead of being there as decoration – we hate to be there as decoration – we recognize that there are fewer of us there because we haven't developed those issues. So we remind ourselves that if we want to be there, we have to develop our own arguments."

Gonzalo Berrón, coordinator of the HSA, explains that the coalition has a political commitment to gender equity and that one of its visible expressions is the existence of the Women's Committee to ensure that there are always women's organizations participating in the decision-making spheres and representative delegations (personal communication, 5 May 2007). However, Helfrich wonders whether ensuring women's participation is just a matter of being "politically correct" (personal communication, 27 January 2007). This feeling is shared among REMTE's participants, who argue that this openness remains at the level of discourse and does not necessarily translate into concrete organizational terms. For example, Sara Román explains that one problem with mixed coalitions is that "they know the discourse, but taking the initiative to push for gender equity, that is very relative ... It is also about resources. You have to have the vision that you want it to be that way. If not, it remains only a declaration" (personal communication, 23 January 2007).

Hilda Salazar (personal communication, 25 January 2007), a feminist researcher from the women's committee of the HSA, suggests that women are respected, that there is a politically correct discourse, but that "there is hardly a difference in organizational structure, in terms of women's participation ... or in the agenda. Gender is an issue that has to appear in the discussion, but it is up to women to bring it in." For example, Guillén argues, the workshops organized by feminist networks at the Encounter for Alternative Integration, held in Bolivia in 2006, "were important, but only women attended. Some men were there, but there was no acknowledgment that something was being discussed there that they couldn't miss. As a result, women's leadership was not recognized. In contrast, we had to be in all the other workshops, otherwise feminist analysis and proposals were not likely to be discussed. We still had to make a double effort to frame our agenda" (personal communication, 3 May 2007).

The coalition's documents and declarations are supposed to incorporate a gender perspective. Guillén observes that in most of the HSA's recent declarations "you can see that a more inclusive language is being used, with proposals that include those developed by us. And in the collective action plan, our action proposals are being recognized" (personal communication, 3 May 2007). She believes that REMTE has succeeded in placing new issues on the coalition's agenda: "We brought to the discussion of free trade the issue of work, women's work, paid work, but we also raised the issue of women's unpaid work; we discussed the impacts of structural adjustment programs and the reduction of the public health budget, the processes of privatization of education ... We showed that the macro-economy had a very strong impact on women and the appropriation of women's work."

Other activities that occupy much of the network's energy are popular education and involvement in the definition of methodological procedures at transnational events. Since the creation of the HSA, a Women's Committee – in which REMTE and other organizations participate – has been formed to ensure that gender remains an important issue on the coalition's agenda.[11] As such, at most of the counter-summits organized by the HSA, women's workshops are organized prior to the general meeting. At the same time, the gender dimension is supposed to be integrated throughout the event. Many workshops for women organized for the campaign against the FTAA enhanced their capacity to address the debates within social movements. For example, a few days before the WTO protests and the People's Forum in Cancun, in 2003, an international forum called Women's Rights and Free Trade Agreements was organized.[12]

Marco Antonio Velasquez, executive director of the Mexican Action Network on Free Trade, recognizes that there is still male predominance in the HSA and no equity in representation. Indeed, the importance accorded by organizations and movements in the Alliance to the demand to integrate a gender perspective is uneven. Furthermore, "it is still very partial, superficial. It always depends on feminist networks to bring issues to the table, to propose initiatives and campaigns with a gender perspective. They try to push the general organization to participate in these activities, but they don't always have the resonance required" (Velasquez, personal communication, 5 May 2007).

In Irene León's view (personal communication, 4 May 2007), men are still dominant inside mixed-gendered spaces, despite the participation of many women in the creation of new concepts and methodologies for analyzing globalization. She suggests that women have to push constantly to get mixed-gendered forums to incorporate gender beyond discourse. The "fight against patriarchy" is present in allied social movements' discourse, which is a qualitative step forward. However, she argues, "this doesn't translate into gender equity in everything else that is being discussed ... A gender perspective in the allied social movements' general demands is still not very visible."

This concrete experience reflects the argument of feminist scholars that although there is widespread participation of women in transnational activism, the recognition of their contribution remains limited, especially when the issues discussed are not seen as traditional women's issues such as violence and discrimination (Eschle 2005; Staggenborg and Taylor 2005). Access to and participation at transnational movement organizing is unequal, as resources and privilege play an important role in defining whose voices are heard when transnational spaces and discourses are constructed (Masson, this volume).

According to Mohanty (2003, 249), in most anti-globalization movements and anti-capitalist critique, gender still does not appear to be a category of analysis and a basis for organizing. Similarly, Diane Lamoureux (2004, 180, my translation) feels that feminists have to constantly insist on the need to bring a gender perspective to the overall critique of global justice movements: "The question of equity between men and women is almost always mentioned in the documents of the global justice movement, but the majority of mixed-gendered groups do not have the tools to fully integrate it into their discourse and practice."

There are still many obstacles to the substantive incorporation of gender into the agenda and discourse of global social justice movements. To make real changes in pursuing gender equity, there has to be a transformation in terms of resources, methodologies, organizational culture, procedures, materials, and evaluation criteria. Silke Helfrich (personal communication, 27 January 2007) observes, "It involves changing how you ask questions, what conceptual tools you use, what criteria you include in the evaluation, and how you systematically understand gender as a relational and internal democracy issue rather than as only a women's issue. It involves transforming the methodology and giving another quality to your work."

In spite of these limitations, Nalu Faria (personal communication, 2 May 2007) contends, women are being recognized as political subjects inside this process: "There is recognition that this actor exists, has political weight, mobilizes, and makes things happen. Although there is all this rhetoric, however, this still has to translate into concrete political action." It is precisely this type of change that REMTE aims to bring about by working hand in hand with allied social movements.

Going Beyond "Women-Friendly" Discourse

Despite the barriers described in the section above, there have been important changes in framing economic debates and coalition discussions in feminist terms. REMTE and other feminist organizations have played a key role in the development of an analysis with a gender perspective and in building consensus around the importance of integrating gender equity on a day-to-day basis.

One of the objectives pursued by REMTE within social movement coalitions is to go beyond looking at "impacts on women" or developing a "women's agenda." Miriam Martínez (personal communication, 26 January 2007) explains that REMTE wants "the women's agenda to become part of the social movements' general declaration, but we also want social movement coalitions to integrate a gender perspective on a day-to-day basis." This recognition of feminism as a particular way of analyzing free trade is not only addressing women's issues, but also aiming for change toward more egalitarian gender relations: "Our actions emphasize the feminist perspective as one of the bases of an egalitarian project, and for this reason we are in permanent dialogue with social movements. We are building these spaces together with the social movements; we don't just bring our agenda to them" (REMTE 2006, my translation).

According to the women who comprise REMTE, feminist and women's leaderships are beginning to be recognized. Miriam Nobre (personal communication, 28 April 2007) asserts that there is much more understanding and respect expressed toward women by mixed-gender organizations.[13] Rosa Guillén (personal communication, 3 May 2007) also states that REMTE is recognized as an ally, "with its own voice, its own arguments, and with political stands that have to be considered in the development of strategies alongside the *compañeros* of the HSA. We contribute not only by mobilizing women, but also with arguments and with our own agenda that renders women's oppression, discrimination, and exclusion visible."

This may be explained by REMTE's political decision to participate actively in transnational spaces in which social movements define their priorities and action strategies. REMTE has been a member of the International Council of the World Social Forum since the Forum's beginning.[14] According to Diane Matte, ex-coordinator of the WMW, feminist participation in this process is fundamental "to tighten the relations between the feminist movement and the movement for alter-globalization, and to inscribe our priorities in it and strengthen the possibilities for a real social transformation" (quoted in Alvarez, Faria, and Nobre 2004, 202). This vision is shared by Leonor Concha (personal communication, 20 January 2007), who also considers this space strategic because it allows REMTE to "build links and relationships, to have an impact. After all, the first place to have an impact is the movement itself, the social, civic, organized movement."

It has been suggested that REMTE has used transnational spaces to question gender-blind positions inside social movements. As Nobre (personal communication, 28 April 2007) explains, spaces like the World Social Forum have been very useful for opening the discussion with mixed-gender movements about feminist economics and to change the dominant vision of women as victims of free trade to one that recognizes women's contribution and feminist alternatives: "Before, they used to look at our organization as if we were a strange thing. With REMTE, we were able to go beyond the 'impacts on women' debate when discussing free trade agreements, to really question the logic of free trade from a feminist economic vision ... Now we can use the tools of feminist economics in our discourse as a result of this process." This is an important contribution because, according to Mohanty (2003, 250), "making gender and women's bodies and labour visible and theorizing this visibility as a process of articulating a more inclusive politics are crucial aspects of feminists' anti-capitalist critique."

Gonzalo Berrón (personal communication, 5 May 2007) asserts that women have always had an important role within the HSA and the continental campaign against the FTAA. Feminist activism, he recognizes, has been strong and feminists have fought for the integration of gender in the coalition's organization: "They have struggled inside the movement to transform the feminist vision into a coalition principle and they have succeeded, they have won the battle. Mistakes are still made, however, with highly political costs. Ultimately, this transformation was achieved not only because there is a constant vigilance from the *compañeras,* but also because men have really interiorized the inclusion of gender as a principle. In the HSA space, it's a first step."

According to Berrón (personal communication, 5 May 2007), women have made two other important contributions to the coalition that have made gender issues more visible. The first has to do with the development of an analysis of free trade and of the impacts of neoliberalism, particularly on women, from a gender perspective: "This was not taken into consideration in the government sector. It is very good to have a critical vision of this." The second "has to do with mobilization capacity, as women have participated in demonstrations on different occasions in the region, thus showing their political force." The change in the recognition of women is explained by Nobre (personal communication, 28 May 2007) as having to do with REMTE's presence in and alliance with the WMW as a visible movement with high mobilization capacity; the initiatives developed by REMTE in coordination with women from Vía Campesina and the WMW in the World Social Forum; and REMTE's ability to achieve agreement on key political proposals among women's organizations.

One strategy used by feminist networks has been to work together with the movements with which they have an affinity. Most of the organizations that are part of REMTE are also very active in the WMW. In fact, both representatives from the Americas for the WMW are members of REMTE.[15] This synergy can be seen at work in the World Social Forum, in which REMTE and the WMW reinforce each other by proposing seminars, workshops, declarations, and common actions, resulting in a process of issue framing that emphasizes gender at broader social movement events. For example, REMTE and the WMW co-organized a debate on poverty and feminist economic alternatives for the World Social Forum in 2002.[16] In

2003, a panel called Por outra economia: subsidiariedade, localizaçao, devoluçao e reproduçao was co-organized to discuss the market's intention to control all aspects of life (Faria 2003).

Macdonald (2005, 22) asserts that women's movements have tried to influence broader social movements, both women's and allied, inside transnational anti-free-trade coalitions. She concludes, "The ability of feminist groups to gradually encourage their social movements allies to adopt a gendered reading of processes of neoliberal restructuring, and to challenge patriarchal assumptions about the economy among their social movements allies, are clear signs of success, even if these groups have not thus far succeeded in influencing the public policy agenda of trade liberalization" (Macdonald 2005, 38).

Despite the obstacles that feminists face in attempting to get gender onto the agenda of the broader social movements in which they participate, social movement coalitions are beginning to change. REMTE's active involvement in transnational coordination spaces such as the HSA and the World Social Forum has been important for the recognition of women's participation and the incorporation of gender issues into the general agenda. Although gender is now integrated into the discourse, it remains to be translated into concrete political and organizational changes in order to achieve gender equity inside social movements critical of free trade. Only then will gender equity stop being considered a women's issue and be seen as an essential principle for a democratic, inclusive, and socially just alternative.

Impacts of Transnational Networking on Women's Organizations at the National Scale

Many studies of transnational social movements focus on their attempts to influence the state or international institutions, but Suzanne Staggenborg and Verta Taylor (2005, 46) feel that such studies are biased "toward a limited set of protest forms – mainly marches, demonstrations, rallies, public meetings, boycotts, sit-ins, petitions, strikes, and various forms of civil disobedience. Relying on methods such as newspaper event counts, these studies neglect a wide variety of tactics, including less visible protests within institutions and discursive politics." Staggenborg and Taylor see the ideological support for the struggle against women's political and social subordination as created and maintained through less visible actions in various venues. Hence, they propose to look in alternative places for social movement activity. They also offer a variety of ways of assessing movement transformation and outcomes, necessitating a "conceptualization of power and protest that is long-term and less state-centered than that of the contentious politics approach" (Staggenborg and Taylor 2005, 48).

Marianne Marchand (2003, 147) argues that "state-centrism" does not allow for an understanding and valuing of grassroots movements' different politics and articulations of power. Strategies that focus on large-scale protest against globalization, she contends, overlook or make invisible other resistance strategies used by women. She insists on the need to look at less "spectacular resistance," taking into account the wide range of possible resistance strategies. Elsa Beaulieu (this volume) concurs when she proposes to study a broad spectrum of women's movement practices instead of solely the most visible aspects of resistance (public discourse and protest) to assess movements' contribution to transforming social structures.

As we have seen, REMTE is not looking to lobby governments to include a "gender clause" or reform in free trade agreements. "Governments want to change the terms of negotiation; we want to say no to free trade" (Guillén, personal communication, 3 May 2007). Another reason for not taking the lobbying route is that it is difficult to achieve consensus at the transnational scale on when and how the network should interact with international institutions or national governments. Nalu Faria (personal communication, 2 May 2007) explains, "At the beginning, REMTE's members in some countries wanted to influence the governments and the World Bank, but this was a source of conflict between us ... Today, our action is more through mobilization, not through lobby[ing]."

Most of REMTE's impacts can be found in non-state spheres. The network's goal has been primarily to empower women, personally and collectively. According to Leonor Concha (personal communication, 20 January 2007), REMTE focuses on building up the movement because "only through a strong social movement can you have an impact. Strength has to come first, and afterward you have to be clear on what you can negotiate." Nobre (personal communication, 28 April 2007) shares this vision: "REMTE in Brazil does not organize around the state. It is more oriented toward social movements, with the World March of Women."

Another element that has to be taken into consideration when evaluating the impacts of REMTE is scale. As Masson argues in this volume, social movements and networks organize and act at multiple scales, not only the transnational one, and these scales are mutually constitutive: "We cannot assume that the internal operations of transnational feminist and women's organizations and networks are bound to the transnational scale ... [They] engage in lobbying, protest, and collaboration at a variety of scales."

According to the women whom I interviewed, a network such as REMTE is valid as long as it serves to advance and reinforce national processes. The decision to take part in a regional network, states Concha (personal communication, 20 January 2007), is intended to empower the national women's movements: "It is the building of the Mexican women's movement, not only as individuals, but as organizations ... We helped build the Latin American network with the thought that this network could serve Mexican women. It does not make sense for us to belong to a Latin American space if nothing happens with the process of Mexican women. That is why we accepted the challenge, to build the national process."

This argument is shared by Sara Román (personal communication, 23 January 2007), who recognizes that only a few groups have the potential to devote the required resources to network building: "It is not easy to build networks, and it is even more difficult to maintain them. The network is valid as long as it has its grounded organizations. It is good if you have the resources to refashion your vision, but you have to have both feet on the ground; otherwise, you have an 'outer' organization and nothing on the inside ... a big head without feet." Rebeca Salazar (personal communication, 25 January 2007) reinforces this vision, arguing that "a transnational network functions only if there is already a nationally based organization." Rosario Quispe (personal communication, 24 January 2007), a member of REMTE in Mexico and a representative from the Americas to the WMW, also states that the network has to find common axes to achieve women's participation in very different national contexts: "It is really about reinforcing organizations that already exist; otherwise, it becomes very difficult to maintain a network ... National organizations have to avoid being absorbed by the international ... it is a bidirectional process and you must remain anchored to contribute at the transnational level."

According to the members of REMTE, transnational networking has provided a framework for action and mobilization, bringing together feminist issues and economics. It has been a space to share relevant information and develop educational tools to strengthen women's movements. Nobre explains that in the past, "the economy was not even considered an issue of debate on the feminist agenda. REMTE allowed us to access the debate on the feminist economy ... We took advantage of our relationship with REMTE to get in touch with its literature and concepts ... I see that women take the opportunity to have alliances with us to start looking at economic issues; it is therefore important to have a discourse already elaborated, to know what to say as feminists in economic matters" (personal communication, 28 April 2007).

Guillén (personal communication, 3 May 2007) suggests that REMTE has been important because it has developed collective thinking – a regional strategy and position that have allowed its organizations to orient their national work and coordinate their agendas. Similarly, Faria (personal communication, 2 May 2007) states, "REMTE helped to link economic discourses and the struggle against free trade agreements with the issue of poverty. In Seattle, the slogan was 'The world is not for sale,' and we say that women are not for sale either. Then we developed the campaign 'We are women, not merchandise.'"

Being part of a continental network also enhances the level of political debate in each national organization. According to REMTE's regional coordinator, "it is another level of information, of debate and position. It changes the level of involvement and of possible alliances" (Faria, personal communication, 2 May 2007). Martínez concurs; she explains that the Latin American network allowed her organization to have a broader vision of what was happening in the region and how to resist. She suggests that REMTE is a "space that can help us make the links between different issues. It allows us to have access to many spaces and keep gender in the agenda of mixed organizations" (personal communication, 26 January 2007). At the national scale, Román argues that the mobilization of REMTE in the WMW in 2000 helped its member organizations to "link different processes and develop organizational abilities; it made local and national organizations work together again and it also brought new groups to the same space ... it allowed greater integration. It has contributed a lot in the movement's organization" (personal communication, 23 January 2007).

According to Quispe (personal communication, 24 January 2007), the WMW favoured the integration of groups that had previously been dispersed. It also gave women more experience and the confidence to participate in transnational efforts alongside members of other social movements. For example, Leonor Concha said, during the campaign against the FTAA in 2004, "We participated in the HSA's consultation campaign because we already had the experience of the national consultation on women's rights during the World March of Women" (personal communication, 20 January 2007).[17]

The WMW was also important in organizational terms, as many provincial committees were formed: "It made women participants; it raised consciousness and politicized women." This experience, Concha (personal communication, 20 January 2007) asserts, "made women visible and empowered their organizations." For some women, she says, there was a "before" and "after" the WMW, as they turned it into an educational tool for organization, mobilization, and political pressure to achieve women's rights.

Another issue mentioned in the interviews was that the WMW contributed to the development of a collective identity of feminists opposing free trade. Martínez (personal communication, 26 January 2007) explains that she "realized the diversity of women who were participating: union workers, teachers, grassroots organizations, NGOs ... very diverse. It was an opportunity to enrich my work." According to Quispe (personal communication, 24 January 2007), the WMW generated a sense of "unity, of being integrated at the world level. It expands your vision, as you see that the problem is global and that united, together, a greater force is created to struggle against this."

Finally, Guillén (personal communication, 3 May 2007) affirms that being part of an international network such as REMTE empowers the work of each national organization. She contends that regional processes such as free trade agreements have to be addressed through national organizations, with an international reference: "We are a group of organizations fighting locally, but in the continent there are many other organizations fighting. And you have the certainty that you can consult with your *compañeras* in other countries on what they are doing, what we can do together. You have the confidence that you are doing something, and that you are part of a bigger group."

As we have seen, transnational networking has empowered national organizations by reinforcing their local work and providing key information, feminist analysis, and shared strategies for actions within the region. It has also enhanced national organizations' presence and legitimacy vis-à-vis allied movements on the national scale. It should also be kept in mind that transnationalization is a bidirectional process, because, as argued by the women interviewed, transnational networks function only when there are well-grounded national organizations.

Conclusion

I have presented the experience of a transnational feminist network (REMTE) that joined other social movements, sought to organize resistance to free trade, and promoted alternatives to integrate gender equity. I have argued that REMTE is an example of a transnational network of women's organizations initiated "from below," independently of international institutions. A key reason for the creation of the network was the need to develop knowledge from a feminist perspective to generate an understanding of the gendered impact of structural adjustment programs and free trade agreements in the context of economic transformation. Transnational spaces created by social movements and the internal dynamics of feminist organizations in Latin America are also important aspects of REMTE's emergence and process of transnationalization.

REMTE's case shows that the gendered character of knowledge is an issue in feminist movement struggles. The engendering of knowledge on economic issues – part of the work that REMTE does – illustrates that the power relations around the creation of knowledge are an important issue to consider. REMTE's attempts to address the central elements of free trade in a simple and clear way – for example, by looking at the social implications of issues such as privatization of water and food sovereignty from a feminist perspective – have moved free trade from being a technical debate in the hands of specialists to an issue that is accessible to the grassroots. As Macdonald (2005, 26) observes, "The gendered character of the construction of knowledge, particularly economic knowledge at the national and international levels, is another important area that should be addressed in theories of transnational collective action."

I have suggested that we can understand REMTE better through the lens of an "identity-solidarity" logic than with an "institutional-advocacy" approach, since neither the state nor international institutions are REMTE's main target – as mainstream theories of transnational social movements too often assume. REMTE's transnationalization logic corresponds to what Alvarez refers to as transnationalization from below, because its emergence process is different from that of feminist networks formed around UN conferences and because it aims at building solidarity among social movements and empowering grassroots women's organizations.

Power dynamics within social movements should also be addressed to explain the choice of strategies and the balance of outcomes of this network. Differences – gender, class, race, North/South, NGO/social movement – within transnational coalitions are relevant for understanding social movements' evolution and impacts. Analyses that take these axes of difference into consideration will present a more adequate explanation. This case study has shown that REMTE has successfully framed gender issues in the discourse of social movement coalitions against free trade, although this sort of framing remains limited, as it still depends on activists from feminist networks to bring up these subjects. Despite limited success, it should be kept in mind that building consensus around the idea that "another world, without feminism, is impossible" is a long-term process.

Participation in mixed spaces is seen as positive, but it also presents many challenges. According to Eschle (2005, 1751), a more inclusive under-standing of the anti-globalization movement, with its different forms and in its different contexts, needs to integrate a feminist sensibility "if it is to be effective and emancipatory with the goal of transforming both feminism and the anti-globalization movement within a more equal partnership." This has been the task of both feminist scholars who challenge mainstream gender-blind theories of transnational collective action and of feminist activists across borders who agree with one of the slogans of the WMW (2003): "In order to change the lives of women, the world needs to be changed; but also, and simultaneously, that in order to change the world, the lives of women need to be changed."

Regarding the impacts on women's organizations at the national scale, I have argued that two important elements should be considered when look-ing at REMTE's contribution. First, REMTE's position on free trade agree-ments is a radical critique, and thus the network is not looking to change public policies; its goal is to contribute to causing cultural change within other social movements to make feminism a guiding principle of analysis and action. Second, the national scale continues to be an important place to look when assessing the work of a transnational social movement, as the different scales of action are interlinked and transnationalization is a bi-directional process. Most of REMTE's activities focus on the reinforcement of women's movements because building a movement requires concrete place-based work; by reinforcing local and national movements, the net-work becomes stronger at the regional and international levels. At the same time, the legitimacy of a regional network such as REMTE depends on the national work of each feminist organization. An interesting avenue for fu-ture research would be to look at the less visible work that takes place inside seminars, workshops, and meetings, as Beaulieu (this volume) suggests when she highlights the importance of meetings for day-to-day social change to women participants.

In conclusion, REMTE has provided a feminist framework for accessing economic debates that has allowed the emergence of a feminist critique of free trade agreements, giving more visibility to women and gender issues within the HSA agenda and discourse. Through solidarity and transnational networking, REMTE has advanced toward a reconceptualization of the economy from a feminist perspective that goes beyond the analysis of impacts on women.

NOTES

1 Dufour and Giraud (2007) also contend that the concept of political opportunity structure is limited in terms of explaining the trajectory of transnational networking in the case of the World March of Women.

2 The Hemispheric Social Alliance (in Spanish, Alianza Social Continental) is a network of organizations and social movements of North, Central, and South America that share information, define strategies, and work together to resist neoliberal trade integration in the Americas. In the document *Alternatives for the Americas,* HSA proposes "alternative rules to regulate the global and hemispheric economies based on a different economic logic: trade and investment should not be ends in themselves, but rather instruments for achieving just and sustainable development." See www.asc-hsa.org.

3 For this research, semi-directed in-depth interviews were conducted in Mexico City in January 2007. Interviews were conducted with seven members of REMTE in Mexico, including the former coordinator of the regional network, a member of the International Gender and Trade Network, a member of the Women's Committee of the HSA, and the director of the Boell Foundation. I also conducted interviews during the VI Hemispheric Encounter of Social Movements against Free Trade Agreements and for the Peoples' Integration of the Americas in Havana, Cuba (April-May 2007). I interviewed two members of REMTE in Brazil (the current coordinator of the regional network and the World March of Women), a member of REMTE in Peru (ex-coordinator of the network), and a member of REMTE in Colombia. I also talked to the coordinator of the Women's Area of the Latin American Information Agency, based in Ecuador, with the coordinator of the HSA, and with two members of the Mexican Action Network on Free Trade. All interviews were conducted in Spanish. English translations are mine.

4 Sara Román explains, "REMTE is constituted or integrated by women's organizations closely linked to popular sectors, inside the popular movement, not by personalities. Other networks ... are integrated by researchers who do not necessarily have an organization behind them" (personal communication, 23 January 2007). The ten countries are Bolivia, Brazil, Chile, Colombia, Costa Rica, Ecuador, El Salvador, Mexico, Peru, and Venezuela.

5 "Gender-blind economy" is a concept used by feminist economists. Norma Sanchiz, of the International Gender and Trade and Network, wrote about this in "La cegera de género en la economía" (see I. León 2005). Laura Macdonald (2005, 153) also acknowledges the gendered impacts of international trade and observes, "Trade rules are based on a gender-blind analysis that fails to take into account women's unpaid household work or unequal access to such assets as land, resources and credit, and their often marginalized status within the labour market. While women's

employment in the paid labour force often expands with trade liberalization, the jobs they gain entry into are usually poorly paid and highly vulnerable."

6 An interesting note in the case of REMTE in Mexico is the insistence on collective participation in these spaces. Leonor Aida Concha (personal communication, 20 January 2007) explains that more than fifteen women from the Mexican network have participated in international events representing REMTE. For example, in the last year, Mexican women have participated in international meetings in Colombia, Mali, Bolivia, and Brazil; most of them were not on the coordination team.

7 The Mesoamerican People's Forum is held every year to organize resistance against neoliberalism in Central America and Mexico.

8 The Encuentros were considered a resource for building regional networks and seen as "places of dialogue, negotiation, coalition-building, conflict, and contestation *among women* which foster processes of both solidarity and contention among the region's feminists and provide a supranational platform where key issues confronting Latin American feminism can be staged, debated and (re)formulated" (Alvarez, Faria, and Nobre 2004, 203).

9 The workshop was called Globalización del Neoliberalismo y Justicia Económica para las Mujeres.

10 The argument was that they had access to more job opportunities (regardless of the type of employment offered).

11 Analyzing the inclusion of gender in the struggle against the North American Free Trade Agreement, Macdonald (2005, 22) observes that despite the inclusive language of social movement coalitions, "the gendered dimensions of trade have gained relatively little exposure." However, she also notes that increased attention has been paid to the links between gender and trade since the creation of the Women's Committee: "In contrast to the transnational networks that formed around NAFTA, under the pressure of this women's caucus, the HSA has been pushed to incorporate gender issues in its analysis of the FTAA" (Macdonald 2005, 34).

12 The declaration resulting from the forum may be consulted online at http://www.ffq.qc.ca/marche2000/es/omc-2003-decl.pdf.

13 Nobre (personal communication, 28 April 2007) remembers that before the FTAA workshops with women, "Usually when feminists arrived at the meetings – to talk about gender or women's participation, men considered it was the moment to go out for coffee. But then, during the FTAA campaign meetings, these same women were talking about the core issues that were being discussed, very well informed. This had an impact on other women; they felt reinforced, recognized in their leaderships. It was such a good thing, the campaign against the FTAA."

14 According to Chandra Talpade Mohanty (2003, 248), the strategy of alliance with social movements is a key component in achieving the cultural transformations advocated by feminists: "Because social movements are crucial sites for the construction of knowledge, communities and identities, it is very important for feminists to direct themselves towards them ... These movements form an important site for examining the construction of trans-border democratic citizenship."

15 Rosa Guillén, from Peru, and Rosario Quispe, from Mexico.

16 The seminar's title was "Mujeres y trabajo: realidades y propuestas para el cambio" and the main axis was the discussion about labour, including domestic and informal work, sexual division of work, and *economia solidaria.*

17 Consultation about the FTAA, an initiative of the HSA in 2004.

REFERENCES

Alvarez, Sonia E. 1998. Latin American Feminisms "Go Global": Trends of the 1990s and Challenges for the New Millennium. In *Cultures of Politics, Politics of Culture: Re-visioning Latin American Social Movement,* ed. Sonia Alvarez, Evelina Dagnino, and Arturo Escobar, 293-324. Boulder and Oxford: Westview.

–. 1999. Advocating Feminism: The Latin American Feminist NGO "Boom." *International Feminist Journal of Politics* 1 (2): 181-209.

–. 2000. Translating the Global: Effects of Transnational Organizing on Local Feminist Discourses and Practices and Latin America. *Meridians: Feminism, Race, Transnationalism* 1 (1): 29-67.

Alvarez, Sonia E., Nalu Faria, and Miriam Nobre. 2004. Another (also Feminist) World is Possible: Constructing Transnational Spaces and Global Alternatives from the Movements. In *World Social Forum: Challenging Empires,* ed. Jai Sen, Anita Anand, Arturo Escobar, and Peter Waterman, 199-206. New Delhi: Viveka Foundation.

Beaulieu, Elsa. 2006. Social Movements, Social Change and Transnationalization: Towards a Feminist and Anthropological Framework. Paper presented at the conference *Transnationalisation des solidarités et mouvements des femmes,* 27-28 April, Université de Montréal, Montreal. http://www.cccg.umontreal.ca/pdf/Actes%20de%20l%27atelier_document.last.pdf.

Brenner, Johanna. 2003. Transnational Feminism and the Struggle for Global Justice. In *World Social Forum: Challenging Empires,* ed. Jai Sen, Anita Anand, Arturo Escobar, and Peter Waterman, 25-34. New Delhi: Viveka Foundation.

Celiberti, Lilian, and Virginia Vargas. 2003. Feministas en el Foro. *Estudos Feministas* 11 (2): 586-98. http://www.scielo.br/pdf/ref/v11n2/19140.pdf.

Conway, Janet. 2007. Transnational Feminisms and the World Social Forum: Encounters and Transformations in Anti-Globalization Spaces. *Journal of International Women's Studies* 8 (3): 49-70.

Desai, Manisha. 2002. Transnational Solidarity: Women's Agency, Structural Adjustment, and Globalization. In *Women's Activism and Globalization: Linking Local Struggles and Transnational Politics,* ed. Nancy Naples and Manisha Desai, 15-33. New York and London: Routledge.

Dufour, Pascale, and Isabelle Giraud. 2007. The Continuity of Transnational Solidarities in the World March of Women, 2000 and 2005: A Collective Identity-Building Approach. *Mobilization: An International Quarterly Review* 12 (3): 307-22.

Eschle, Catherine. 2005. Skeleton Women: Feminism and the Anti-Globalisation Movement. *Signs: Journal of Women in Culture and Society* 30 (3): 1741-60.

Faria, Nalu, ed. 2003. *Construir la igualdad: debates feministas en el Foro Social Mundial.* Cuaderno REMTE.

Ferree, Myra Marx, and Carol McClurg Mueller. 2004. Feminism and Women's Movements: A Global Perspective. In *The Blackwell Companion to Social Movements,* ed. David A. Snow, Sarah A. Soule, and Hanspeter Kriesi, 576-607. Malden: Blackwell.

Jelin, Elizabeth, ed. 2003. *Más allá de la nación: las escalas múltiples de los movimientos sociales.* Buenos Aires: Libros del Zorzal.

Lamoureux, Diane. 2004. Le féminisme et l'altermondialisation. *Recherches féministes* 17 (2): 171-94.

León, Irene. 2005. *Mujeres en resistencia: experiencias, visiones y propuestas.* Quito: ALAI, FEDAEPS, Marcha Mundial de las Mujeres, Red Latinoamericana Mujeres Transformando la Economía, Articulación de Mujeres CLOC/Vía Campesina, Dialogo Sur/Sur LGBT.

León, Magdalena. 2001. REMTE: Una organización de mujeres. REMTE. www.movimientos.org/remte.

Macdonald, Laura. 2005. Gendering Transnational Social Movement Analysis: Women's Groups Contest Free Trade in the Americas. In *Coalitions Across Borders: Transnational Protest and the Neoliberal Order,* ed. Joe Bandy and Jackie Smith, 21-42. Lanham: Rowman and Littlefield.

Marchand, Marianne. 2003. Challenging Globalisation: Toward a Feminist Understanding of Resistance. *Review of International Studies* 29 (3): 145-60.

Moghadam, Valentine M. 2005. *Globalizing Women: Transnational Feminist Networks.* Baltimore: Johns Hopkins University Press.

Mohanty, Chandra Talpade. 2003. *Feminism without Borders: Decolonizing Theory, Practicing Solidarity.* Durham: Duke University Press.

Nobre, Miriam, and Nalu Faria. 2003. Feminismo em movimento: temas e processos organizativos da Marcha Mundial das Mulheres no Fórum Social Mundial. *Estudos Feministas* 11 (2): 623-32.

REMTE. 2001. Quiénes somos? REMTE. http://www.movimientos.org/remte/show_text.php3?key=693.

–. 2006. Boletín octubre. REMTE. http://www.movimientos.org/remte/show_text.php3?key=8345.

Staggenborg, Suzanne, and Verta Taylor. 2005. Whatever Happened to the Women's Movement? *Mobilization: An International Journal* 10 (1): 37-52.

Vargas, Virginia. 2003. Los feminismos latinoamericanos y sus disputas por una globalización alternativa. In *Políticas de identidades y diferencias sociales en tiempos de globalización,* ed. Daniel Mato, 193-217. Caracas: FACES-UCV.

World March of Women. 2003. World Social Forum Perspective of the World March Women. http://www.ffq.qc.ca/marche2000/en/fsm2003.html.

Conclusion

DOMINIQUE MASSON AND PASCALE DUFOUR

As the contributions presented in this book make abundantly clear, trans-nationalization in feminist and women's movements occurs in many different settings and world regions, takes a variety of forms and spatializations, and involves a number of scales of collective action. The contributors to this book have approached this multifaceted phenomenon by drawing on the distinct feminist scholarship on transnational activism and, sometimes, on feminist international relations, as well as on less-well-known geographical and anthropological frameworks. They have also drawn, somewhat eclectically and more often than not critically, on some of the main orientations, conceptual elements, and research questions originating from mainstream perspectives on transnationalization in the social movement studies and international relations fields.

Our conclusion focuses on a number of debates emerging from both the dominant approaches and the feminist bodies of literature outlined in the Introduction to this volume, associated with the following three central questions: first, conceptualizing transnationalization as an object of analysis; second, analyzing the dynamics underlying transnationalization; and third, considering the challenges posed by the constitution of transnational solidarities. We then reflect upon the contribution, raised by many authors in this volume, of geographical approaches to a feminist research agenda. Finally, we offer some methodological orientations for studying transnationalization in feminist and women's movements.

Conceptualizing Transnationalization

Transnationalization is a notoriously elastic notion. At its core, it refers to the idea of crossing or "going beyond" (superseding) national borders. Mainstream theorizing has tended to link transnationalization in the social movement sector to the cross-border character of its actors, actions, and targets. Transnational social movements (Tarrow 1998), transnational activist networks (Keck and Sikkink 1998), transnational social movement organizations (Smith 2004), and transnational campaigns and events (della Porta and Tarrow 2005) are transnational because they feature collective actors or activists from different countries, *and* because their action takes place on the transnational stage, through either the transnational nature of the issues at stake (international or global) or that of their targets (supranational institutions or multinational corporations). These understandings have, however, been found limiting by many. Not only are they too categorical, but they fail to embrace the variety of movement actors and practices that cross borders (Siméant 2005). To the questions "What counts as transnationalization?" and "What should we be studying when turning our sights on transnational feminist and women's movement activism?" feminist scholarship has provided very different kinds of answers.

In the distinct feminist scholarship on transnational activism, the empirical reality of transnationalization has been approached in a much less formalized fashion than in mainstream research. Loose understandings of the phenomenon have allowed for an exploration that has typically encompassed a wide variety of cross-border connections and included both organizational and discursive dimensions (Basu 2000). Manisha Desai (2005, 319), for instance, defines transnationalism as "both organizing across national borders as well as framing local, national, regional, and global activism in 'transnational' discourses." Not only does this formulation feature both organizational and discursive components, but it also opens up the possibility of understanding how collective actors not organizationally involved on the transnational stage may nevertheless be transnationalizing. The chapter by Lenore Lyons in this volume is illustrative of this possibility. The Singaporean organizations that she studied have very few organizational linkages with transnational migrant workers' networks and do not participate in transnational campaigns. According to mainstream understandings, they are not engaging in transnationalization. Yet, Lyons argues, these actors are actually involved in a process of transnationalization, as they have come to frame their issue as transnational – the feminization of global migratory flux – rather than as nationally bounded, and to understand their constituency as "domestic workers" and in the terms of feminist and international discourses on women's work, labour rights, and women's rights.

The strong interest of feminist scholars in the *encounter* between domestic and transnational forms of activism, noted in the Introduction to this volume, is indicative of a quest for a more *relational* understanding of transnationalization. Such a perspective is at the core of Sonia E. Alvarez's (2000, 30) conceptualization of transnationalization as "local movement actors' deployment of discursive frames and political practices that are inspired, (re)affirmed, or reinforced – although not necessarily caused – by their engagement with other actors beyond national borders through a wide range of transnational contacts, discussions, transactions, and networks, both virtual and 'real.'" Thinking of transnationalization in such a relational way opens up the possibility of understanding it as a *process,* in which home-based, national, and local/grassroots organizations and movements are drawn to and transformed through their interaction with the actors (feminist networks, international NGOs, funders, and so on), discourses, repertoires, strategies, and resources that circulate across borders. Interesting empirical questions then become: How and to what extent are domestic organizations and movements entering "transnational feminist circuits" (Thayer 2001)? To what extent are these exchanges mono- or bidirectional? And how are power relations and situated hegemonies shaping this new field of transnational connectivity?

Transnational feminist activism has also been conceptualized through theoretical debates around divergent ways of conceptualizing the nature of potential solidarities between differently located and positioned women. These debates have produced such labels as "global feminism" and "transnational feminisms," which, in this particular context, are indexical of divergent theoretical feminist projects with strong strategic and normative components (see the Introduction to this volume; see also Conway, this volume). To the extent that feminist theorizing finds a correspondence in feminist activist practice, these labels may be useful for mapping the import of different strands of theorizing solidarity-across-difference in contemporary transnational feminist politics. A related avenue for research would certainly be to examine how and to what purposes these theoretical positionings are deployed by transnational actors in specific circumstances (Mackie 2001; see also Conway, this volume). Theoretical and strategic-normative projects, however, should not be conflated with the empirical reality of feminists' (and women's) transnational activity.

Understanding the Dynamics of Transnationalization

Among the avenues for further research and debate are the ways in which we understand the historical dynamics underlying transnationalization. At stake is the status of globalization and of political opportunity structures in the analysis of the emergence and structuring of transnational activism, as well as the existence of other logics of emergence, association, and action.

What Status for Globalization?

Inquiries about the constitution of a transnational level of social movement activity are bound up with claims about globalization. For many feminist and non-feminist scholars, globalization-from-above has engendered globalization-from-below. Globalized economic conditions, the story goes, deepen structural inequalities and give rise to resistance and opposition, while the same factors that support economic globalization – liberalized circulation of capital, goods, and people, coupled with faster communications technologies – provide the context, both constraining and facilitating, for the transnationalization of solidarities. Globalization is thus seen as the main structuring factor in contemporary transnational activism, functioning simultaneously as its impetus, its main target, and its overarching context.

There are reasons, however, for maintaining a critical distance from the more sweeping statements about globalization and transnationalism, as the timing and mechanics of this sequence are the object of serious debate. In the feminist literature, views of transnational feminist networks as being offshoots of globalization (see Moghadam 2005) are disputed, for instance by Desai (2005), Mary E. Hawkesworth (2006), and Myra Marx Ferree (2006), who argue that neither globalization nor women's transnational mobilizations are "something wholly new" (Ferree 2006, 5). Historical forays reveal that feminist and women's transnational organizing dates back to nineteenth-century internationalism and that neither supranational forms of political consciousness nor an awareness of the international nature of women's issues are a novelty of the current era (Ferree and Mueller 2004; Hawkesworth 2006; Miller 1999; Rupp and Taylor 1999). In the social movement literature, scholars such as Sidney Tarrow (2001) make similar remarks. Although there has certainly been unprecedented growth in transnational organizing since the beginning of the 1980s (Bandy and Smith 2005; Smith 1997), both feminist and non-feminist voices remark that understanding transnationalization "as an outgrowth of globalization" (Liebowitz 2001, 175) is an oversimplification that does not take into account the complex mediations of contingent causes and context-specific conditions necessary for actors to transnationalize their action. Explanations through globalization, in particular, do not help our understanding of the uneven involvement of differently located feminist and women's organizations and activists in transnational activity. More complex and contextualized approaches factoring in political processes and ideological mediations are needed (for a similar argument, see Tarrow 2005).

This being said, many feminist scholars do foreground globalization in their analysis of contemporary feminist and women's movement transnational activism. Their work has the immense merit of illuminating the gendered character of globalization processes, consequences, and resistances (see, for instance, Hawkesworth 2006; Moghadam 2005; Naples and Desai 2002), which more often than not remains invisible in mainstream/malestream scholarship. Yet, feminist and women's movements are by definition "rooted in gendered structures of oppression" (Ferree and Mueller 2004, 579) and contest gender orders and patriarchies in various ways and at various scales. Whether globalization (or gendered globalization) features as a central factor in their emergence or a central target of their transnationalizing efforts, and whether it significantly shapes their activity, should remain a matter for empirical investigation rather than an a priori determination. The extent to which references to globalization may be used by activists to resignify earlier struggles and transnational connections should also be part of the inquiry.

Contributors to the present volume have, on the whole, preferred to tread carefully on the terrain of globalization and transnational activism by choosing to privilege the actors' own understandings of their emergence and rationales for existence, targets, and contexts of operation. This methodological stance has the great merit of shifting the analytical focus away from "grand narratives" about globalization and toward the more specific global processes at play in particular instances of transnational activism. From this perspective, contributions to this volume have highlighted the role played by free trade agreements and structural adjustment programs (Díaz Alba), neoliberalism (Lopreite), and local configurations of global migratory circuits (Lyons) in shaping given cases of transnational connectivity – all the while underlining the gendered character of these processes. Moving in such a way from generality to specificity opens up possibilities for comparing how, and how much, different historicized and ideologically mediated globalized processes come to shape, or become the targets of, transnationalization efforts. "Listening" to movements rather than to the stronger claims about globalization and transnationalization also helps bring into view a more varied ensemble of stories of emergence, rationales of mobilization, objects of contestation, and targets in feminist and women's movement transnational activism.

Political Opportunity Structures and the Institutional-Advocacy Logic
Studies of transnational movement activity are similarly bound up with claims about the role of supranational political opportunity structures in fostering and shaping transnationalization. Mainstream literature in social movement studies and international relations has understood transnationalization as a shift in the institutional terrain of collective action, from the national to (or more precisely with the addition of) the international stage. This shift is seen as the direct consequence of the constitution of new political opportunity structures associated with the emergence of contemporary forms of complex internationalism and with the increased importance of existing institutions of supranational political regulation such as the EU, the UN, the World Bank, and the IMF (della Porta and Tarrow 2005; Keck and Sikkink 1998; Risse 2002; Risse-Kappen 1995). Supranational political opportunity structures, understood as the politically mediated expressions of global processes, have thus also been granted a central, if more proximate, role in the historical dynamics of contemporary transnationalization. Offering new resources, threats and alliances, balances of forces, and potential leverage on the international stage, the new supranational political opportunity structures offer movements strong incentives to transnationalize their organization, discourses, and action.

Along similar lines, feminist literature on feminist and women's transnational activism has tended to foreground the impact of the UN, highlighting its role in opening up political and discursive opportunities for the representation of women's issues, for alliance formation among differently located feminist and women's movement activists, and for providing access to resources for transnationalization. The UN's cycle of conferences on women, and especially the activities surrounding the organization of the Nairobi (1985) and Beijing (1995) conferences, is credited with spurring transnational organizing, notably in Latin America and Africa (see, for instance, Adams 2006; Alvarez 2000; Basu 2000; Snyder 2006; Tripp 2005). As exemplified in Lopreite's chapter (this volume), other UN mechanisms, such as the development of regional platforms of action on the status of women and the monitoring procedures for implementing international conventions such as the UN Convention on the Elimination of All Forms of Discrimination Against Women, have also provided invaluable opportunities for women's movement actors to transnationalize. Indeed, in recent decades UN-sponsored activities have resulted in a flurry of transnational feminist and women's organizations, networks, and events, as well as in the transnationalization and travels of feminist discourses about women's issues and women's rights.

However, recent work indicates that sections of the feminist movement sector are growing increasingly critical of UN-based advocacy politics and sceptical of its usefulness as a social change strategy (Alvarez 2000; Conway, this volume; Díaz Alba, this volume; see also Desai 2005; Druelle 2004). Some transnational actors, such as the World March of Women (WMW), have largely abandoned their original orientation toward advocacy on the international stage (Dufour and Giraud 2007). Yet, they have not abandoned the path of transnationalization altogether. This should suggest, at the very least, that the role of supranational political opportunity structures in general, and of the UN in particular, in fostering transnationalization in feminist and women's movements may be more historically contingent than initially assumed. New forms of feminist transnationalism, detached from the UN and other international institutional circuits, are currently emerging (Conway, this volume).

In addition, from an analytical point of view, too strong a focus on supranational political opportunity structures risks reducing the historical dynamics of contemporary transnationalization in feminist and women's movements to the sole operation of an "institutional-advocacy" logic, in which transnational collective actors are constituted for the primary purpose of "targeting intergovernmental organizations and international policy arenas, thereby hoping to gain global leverage in pressuring for change" (Alvarez 2000, 29). Central to the mainstream literature on transnational social movements, to feminist international relations work, and to much feminist scholarship on transnationalization, such a focus is highly relevant to analyzing many instances of transnational organizing, networks, coalitions, and campaigns. Yet, it must be kept in mind that not all forms of transnational activism are directed toward advocacy and change in or through institutions.

The "Identity-Solidarity" Logic and Movement Building

While social movement theorists tend to oppose institutional advocacy to "contentious politics" – the pursuit of oppositional politics outside the terrain of institutions and by more confrontational means – as the two main action logics underlying transnationalization, feminist scholarship tends to contrast it with what Alvarez (2000) has called an "identity-solidarity" logic. Alvarez (2000, 31) proposes that the search for transnational connectivity by feminist activists and groups may also be driven, quite distinctly from the former two propositions, by actors who "use transnational contacts as means to (re)construct or reaffirm subaltern or politically marginalised identities and to establish personal and strategic bonds of solidarity." Transnationalization thus proceeds from the desire to establish politically and ideologically significant alliances (solidarity) with like-minded activists and groups working on issues or objectives or in conditions that are similar (identity). According to Alvarez (2000, 39), "pragmatic objectives or instrumental rationales" are not central to this logic. Rather, a more expressive rationale, underlain by the need for mutual recognition, support, affinity, and complementarity, drives this quest for cross-border connections. The International Women and Health Meetings (IWHM) described by Sylvia Estrada-Claudio (this volume), REMTE (Díaz Alba, this volume), and Articulación Feminista Marcosur, the Feminist Dialogues, and the WMW (Conway, this volume) all exemplify the workings of an identity-solidarity logic in their stories of emergence and/or current operations.

Alvarez may be too quick, however, to dismiss the importance of pragmatic-instrumental rationales to the identity-solidarity logic. Various contributions to this volume, in fact, suggest the existence of a very powerful rationale underlying this logic: that of movement building. First, transnationalization may thus be understood as an answer to the imperative of building capacity in the movement sector. Exchanging place-based knowledges, information, experiences, and strategies about feminist and women's issues in order to empower and enable national or grassroots participants is often quite explicitly at the root of transnationalization efforts (for example, at IWHM meetings and in REMTE). Capacity building may also take the form of creating transnational networks oriented toward feminist or other alternative modes of knowledge production as means of guiding subsequent collective action, as in the case of REMTE and the Southeast Asian organizations studied by Dominique Caouette (this volume). Augmenting capacity through mobilization by recruiting people and organizations in various locales, expanding participation in networks and activities, and establishing and nurturing alliances with feminist and non-feminist women's organizations around the globe are central to the WMW's current work (Conway, this volume). The construction and diffusion of oppositional meanings and the mobilization of spatially distant resources, people, and organizations are very important movement processes that are intrinsic to the kind of trans-nationalization impelled by the identity-solidarity logic.

Second, the reciprocal identifications and solidarities implied in this logic are also part of a process of movement building, as they are not pre-given but need to be constituted, constructed, and maintained. As Myra Marx Ferree and Carol McClurg Mueller (2004, 598) rightly note, "Constructing solidarity based on gender" – or on any other basis, for that matter – "is a dynamic process that requires work." Transnationalization impelled by the identity-solidarity logic thus involves the – sometimes difficult – tasks of constructing intra- and inter-movement identifications and solidarities. Establishing dialogues across differences among feminists is, in this sense, the raison d'être of the Feminist Dialogues analyzed by Janet Conway (this volume). Additionally, the IWHM, REMTE, Articulación Feminista Marcosur, and the WMW all direct a significant portion of their energies toward building a more inclusive movement sector by pressing for the insertion of feminist analyses in larger cross-movement coalitions.

Movement building – the less spectacular work of constructing capacity and negotiating solidarities, far from state arenas and street protests – has so far been largely ignored by mainstream perspectives as one of the main rationales for transnationalization. Together with the expressive dimension underlined in Alvarez's conception of the identity-solidarity logic, it sheds light on some of the ways in which internal movement imperatives may play a role in bringing together activists and groups in webs of transnational connections.

To sum up, transnationalization is not propelled by a single motor, and the challenge for feminist and non-feminist scholars alike is to account for a greater diversity and interplay of deep-level structuring factors, more proximate causes and contingent conditions, and varied action logics, external and internal, in the dynamics of transnationalization.

Solidarities Beyond Borders?

Both mainstream and feminist scholars are well aware that there are difficulties with attempts at establishing solidarities across borders. Mainstream literatures consider borders and borderwork mostly in terms of the ways people and territories remain significantly bounded by nation-states – even in this era of globalization. The political, socioeconomic, and sociocultural (including linguistic) specificities of different national contexts are seen as having implications for transnational organizing and action. Feminist literature, on the other hand, tends to express a broader understanding of the borders that have to be crossed, negotiated, or left behind (transcended) in order to construct transnational solidarities. In feminist work, including feminist IR, such borders are not only national or regional (for example, North-South), but also compounded by the power relations, entwined in various and intersecting axes of difference and social inequality. The twin notions that individuals and groups are differently located in webs of criss-crossing differences and unequal power relations and that collective actors position themselves differently in relation to the multiple identifications made possible by such intersections are at the core of current feminist theorizing. These ideas inform the focus, central to feminist scholarship, on power inequalities and struggles around the issue of the representation of "women" and of difference(s) in transnational work (see the Introduction to this book). Recognizing the presence of gendered and intersectional dynamics and understanding their implications for transnational activism is both the main challenge posed by feminist analysis to mainstream literatures (for a similar viewpoint, see Ferree and Mueller 2004, 598) and its contribution to the inquiry into the possibilities and limitations of transnational solidarity-making.

The chapters by Estrada-Claudio, Conway, Díaz Alba, and Caouette in this volume illustrate some of the ways in which issues of power, differences, and inequality permeate attempts at transnationalization, not only in creating obstacles to solidarity-making – which are amply documented in feminist work – but in fostering different types of strategies to address these issues within feminist and women's movements, as well as in cross-movement coalitions. In the case of the IWHM (see the chapter by Estrada-Claudio), the practice of rotating the location of the meetings among countries and world regions appears instrumental to addressing the diversity of experiences and lives of differently located women (see also Masson, this volume). Varying the sites of the meetings is not aimed solely at ensuring broader representation; privileging Third World locations is directed explicitly at preventing the dominance of perspectives from the North. The IWHM case also shows that recognizing women's multiple identities requires the devising (and revising) of mechanisms that make it possible to represent intersectional interests in decision-making. Likewise, obstacles to participation linked to unequal access to education, language, and resources have to be countered. An array of strategies may be adopted to foster and sustain participation across difference – for instance, travel subsidies for the least advantaged, translation funds, holding pre-meetings and echo meetings, and using art and performance as pedagogical tools. This case also makes clear that coping with intersectional identities is by no means an easy task. Satisfactory mechanisms for representing intersectional identities are notoriously difficult to devise, and those of the IWHM have their pitfalls. As well, efforts at building transnational solidarities with the more marginalized may be hindered by various impediments, including limitations induced by lack of funding, national regulations on international travel, and variations in patriarchal control on women's mobility (on this last point, see in particular Beaulieu's chapter in this volume). Transnational solidarity-making practices thus appear to be embedded in the intersecting systems of difference that produce privilege and marginalization in ways that affect the nature and scope of feminist solidarity building.

Conway (this volume) makes an original contribution to the inquiry into solidarity building by highlighting how contrasting feminist analyses and political strategies affect the work of intra- and inter-movement coalition-building in major transnational feminist networks at the World Social Forum. Articulación Feminista Marcosur and the Feminist Dialogues, for instance, privilege feminist identities and reproductive/sexual body politics as bases of unity, and feminist movement building as their central (although by no means only) coalitional strategy. The WMW focuses, rather, on the place-based issues and struggles of poor and marginalized women in a context of patriarchal and capitalist globalization, with less regard for feminist self-identification. Such differences in analytical orientations would explain the WMW's stronger engagement with non-explicitly feminist women's, anti-capitalist, and social justice movements in the spaces of the World Social Forums. At the Articulación and the Feminist Dialogues, efforts at constructing solidarities are enacted mainly through practices aimed at "building discursive intelligibility" across a variety of axes of difference. According to Conway, such discourses remain, however, largely abstracted from place-based struggles and are too often academic in substance, both characteristics that may place limits on solidarity building as they tend to favour educated participants (Desai 2005). On the contrary, the WMW's focus on mobilizations around structural and material inequalities may appeal to wider grassroots and community-based constituencies. Strategies for addressing differences and constructing solidarities are thus significantly inflected by variations in understandings of feminism and preferred modes of political intervention, both of which, in turn, shape the substance of the feminist politics of coalition favoured by transnational actors.

Chapters in this volume also draw attention to the gender dynamics at play in the transnational movement sector. Transnational solidarity building is complicated by institutionalized patriarchal relations in labour, environmental, social justice, anti-globalization, and other movements. As transnational feminist activism has moved beyond feminist circles and issues traditionally identified as women's to address questions of social justice and poverty, trade, economic relations, and globalization, it has encountered resistance from its potential or existing allies. Within feminist scholarship, a number of works highlight the difficulties of making gender salient to the gender-blind analyses of non-feminist transnational movements, as well as the problems related to the continued enactment of gendered relations of power and related exclusionary practices in the day-to-day work of mixed transnational coalitions (Beauzamy 2005; Eschle 2005; Lamoureux 2004; Mohanty 2003). Caouette (this volume) shows, for instance, how women's issues and feminist perspectives have remained marginal, if not ignored, in the analyses diffused by three important knowledge-producing transnational networks in Southeast Asia on such issues as development, poverty, war, and globalization. By contrast, Díaz Alba's study of REMTE's engagement with anti-free-trade and anti-globalization coalitions demonstrates that some level of integration of feminist analyses is possible, although this integration is heavily dependent on the active and dogged pressure of feminist networks. Assessments of such struggles by participants are inconclusive, as achievements at the level of principles and discourses coexist with only partial gains in practice, especially in decision-making, organizational methodologies, processes, and strategies. Change, however, seems to be happening, and longer-term studies may shed more light on whether "inbuilt patriarchies" pose enduring obstacles to gender-inclusive solidarity building in transnational movement politics.

It is important to note that constructing more inclusive solidarities is not only about making gender salient for movements organized around other identifications. Feminist intersectional perspectives call for strategies that recognize and attempt to make relevant, in transnational movement politics, the operation of and struggles against other systems of difference, power, and inequalities. The "cross-movement dialogues" organized by Articulación Feminista Marcosur (see Conway, this volume), in which speakers from labour, women's, LGBT, and racial justice movements were invited to discuss the ways in which each movement addressed axes of difference central to the others (class, gender, race, and sexuality) are examples of such a strategy, and exemplify the kind of dialogic transversal politics theorized by Nira Yuval-Davis (2006).

Tensions along lines of power and difference appear as an inherent feature of contemporary transnational organizing, and they may play out in both disruptive and productive ways. The extent to which transnational solidarities may supersede such tensions and be truly inclusive is an empirical question. Proclamations of universalism or of transcending differences cannot be taken for granted. Such claims should, rather, be understood as performative acts that are given substance by particular agents involved in specific political projects that acquire "global" or "universal" status in the asymmetry of global cultural flows. As such, they should remain the object of scholarly inquiry (Conway, this volume; Hawkesworth 2006; Mackie 2001; Masson, this volume; Thayer 2000).

Integrating Geographically Sensitive Approaches

Inserting a concern with the spatial dimensions of transnationalization processes into scholarly analyses may be the most original contribution of this edited collection. The vast majority of the authors in this book express interest in the ways in which concepts of space, scale, and place can be used to provide better understandings of various facets of transnationalization in feminist and women's movements. This interest reflects the genuine heuristic potential of geographically sensitive approaches. On the whole, the authors in this volume suggest that a closer look at the geography – or, more exactly, geographies – of transnationalization in feminist and women's movements is warranted.

Adopting a geographically sensitive approach complicates understandings of transnationalization in interesting ways. First, it challenges dominant views of "the transnational" as a mere "level" of movement activity, a simple step up on a ladder of pre-given planes or platforms for political action. Because it involves the deployment of collective action processes in and through space, and more precisely the stretching of such processes beyond state boundaries, the transnational, it is argued, is a constructed scale of movement activity. Attending to such construction reveals a diversity of spatialities, the significance of which has been insufficiently assessed. Masson (this volume) suggests that these variations may provide entry points into different histories, trajectories, and logics of association in ways that may illuminate the extent to which we need to alter, specify, or go beyond dominant references to "globalization" and "political opportunity structures" to account for current expressions of transnational feminist organizing. Variations in the spatial reach of transnational networks and organizations (the expanses of space that they span and the kinds of places that they bring together) and in their geographical grounding (places of origin, density and dispersion of their participants) also have potential analytical import for understanding the constitution of feminist solidarities, as well as the representation of place-based differences in transnational feminist politics.

Second, integrating geographically sensitive approaches challenges single-level analyses of transnationalization by offering feminists a three-dimensional perspective encompassing relationships between and across different scales of movement activity. To the extent that they involve member groups and activists primarily embedded in other scales and places, transnational organizing and action should be analyzed as multiscalar phenomena, and the relationships between the different scales – organizational dynamics, division of labour, power relations, and the like – should be elucidated (Masson, this volume). Such a perspective inspires Elsa Beaulieu's portrayal (this volume) of the variety of organizational scales involved in the organization of the WMW in Brazil, and of the participation of local member groups, such as the Centro Feminista 8 de Março, in the March's transnational processes and action. Carmen L. Díaz Alba (this volume) also draws on multiscalar understandings to show how REMTE and its national member groups reinforce each other through information sharing, exchange of strategies, and mutually enhanced legitimacy. Analyzing transnationalization in multiscalar terms is fully compatible with feminists' search for more relational and processual conceptualizations of transnationalization. A multiscalar and relational perspective would also be useful to furthering the exploration of the travels of transnational framings, as these get appropriated and adapted at other scales and in specific place-based contexts (Lyons, this volume; see also Thayer 2000, 2001).

Third, adopting more geographically sensitive approaches also encourages feminists to delve deeper into the relationship of "place," or geographical location, to transnational organizing, framing, and politics. As Masson (this volume) notes, feminists do claim to be attentive to geographical location. However, in feminist theorizing the significance of place is often lost to that of other positionalities or subsumed in broad references to Western, North/South, or First World/Third World locations. While such references do capture fundamental asymmetries in global power relations, they are far from fully grasping the importance of place for the analysis of transnationalization. Much transnational organizing, for example, is in fact world regional (Tarrow 2005). The comparison by Melinda Adams (2006) of transnational organizing in two world regions helps to illustrate the differences that place makes. For instance, democratic transition and political liberalization have occurred, on the whole, later in Africa than in Latin America, with consequences for the timing and extent of African women's transnational organizing. Latin America and Africa are also places where certain issues have been more central than others. Peace building, conflict resolution, and the gender dimension of HIV/AIDS, Adams notes, have found particular salience in African networks. Moving meeting locations from continent to continent, and from country to country, is also indicative of activists' recognition that places, with their different histories, circumstances, and political traditions, are linked to the representation of differences and of differently located women.

In these and other ways, place matters for analyzing transnational movement activity. Yet, one of the challenges of working with the concept of place is also to acknowledge that places are neither homogeneous nor closed upon themselves: they are permeable to outside influences, for instance, in terms of discourses, priorities, and strategies. How and to what extent transnational networks, organizations, and activists are embedded in place-specific ways is an empirical question for future research. Furthermore, collective actors and activists may position themselves differently regarding their own and others' place-based specificity. Transnational feminist networks "may be embedded in place-specific ways," Conway writes in this volume, but they may "eschew place-based specificities" in the conduct of their meetings and in their discourses. The Feminist Dialogues, for instance, has constructed itself as largely "place-less" on both counts. The WMW, by contrast, sees itself as a coordination of place-based groups and activists, negotiating place-based differences and autonomy in day-to-day organizing and political discourse (Conway, this volume; see also Conway 2008). Eschewing or recognizing place-based specificity makes for very different transnational feminist politics and has participatory, representational, and strategic implications that need further attention.

Finally, the integration of geographical concerns can direct feminist inquiries into an overly neglected aspect of transnationalization: that of its consequences, in terms of social change, in the everyday lives of women. In this perspective, Beaulieu (this volume) chooses to draw on Massey's understanding of the ways in which differential access to public space and mobility are involved in the spatial deployment of patriarchal relations. She then shows how, for rural women in western Rio Grande do Norte (RN), Brazil, participating in meetings held under the banner of the WMW challenges the local regime of patriarchy. As transnationalization processes unfold across scales and touch ground in western RN, they are seen to trigger rural women's mobilization and, in turn, to foster private struggles around their rights to travel, away from domestic chores and unaccompanied by a male relative, as well as around the gendered division of labour and patriarchal controls in the household. New feminist *habitus,* subjectivities, and visions of the world are produced, she argues, via the WMW's spatial practices, through women's struggles over mobility, political organizing, and solidarity building across proximate and remote geographical spaces (see also Beaulieu 2007). As the potential of feminist transnationalism to transform the daily lives of most women is currently under dispute (see Desai 2005), it is clear that more research is needed on the ways different forms and modes of trans-nationalization can effectively foster social transformation.

Furthering Feminist Research – Methodological Orientations

Transnationalization in feminist and women's movements is still an emergent field of study, and much work remains to be done in order to gain a better understanding of transnationalization processes. Foregrounding gendered and intersectional power relations as they articulate in transnational organizing, framing, and solidarity building are the distinct contributions of feminist scholarship and should remain central to research design. Casting a broad net and keeping open the definition of what counts as transnationalization open has proven to be productive for feminist research, as has bringing to light the multifaceted ways in which transnationalization operates in contemporary feminist and women's movements. Bringing further conceptual order into such diverse expressions of transnationalization and guiding future research through more formalized theoretical frameworks and research agendas are, it seems to us, what the field needs at present.

In terms of data-collection methodologies, feminist research has so far relied mostly on case studies. Qualitative methodologies featuring interviews, documentary or archival analysis, institutional ethnography, and observation (direct or participant) have yielded rich data, documenting specific experiences in a detailed manner and enabling insights into the finer workings of transnational processes and encounters. There has been, however, very little use of quantitative methodologies in feminist work. Yet, in social movement studies, large surveys administered in transnational gatherings, such as anti-globalization events or World Social Forums, have generated valuable knowledge regarding the characteristics of activists and participating organizations. Although quantitative methods cannot provide in-depth portrayals of transnationalization processes, they can "help to answer fundamental questions about the extent of transnationalism, including its intensity, breadth and spread" (Wong and Satzewich 2006, 7). Feminist scholarship on transnationalization, it seems to us, could greatly benefit from larger-scale research (in the sense of methodologies embracing more than one case) as well as from comparative research. As Beaulieu (this volume) points out, knowledge produced about the WMW in western RN is located knowledge. It does not foretell how the WMW's processes take shape elsewhere in the world, or even in other regions of Brazil. Similar transnationalization processes may be at work in different places, but they may be expressed or may unfold quite differently. Comparative strategies, in this perspective, could greatly contribute to furthering feminist understandings. This would require the development of theoretical frameworks and research methodologies specifically designed to ensure meaningful correspondence between the cases studied.

Finally, adopting relational and multiscalar approaches to transnationalization implies moving toward multi-sited and multiscalar research (see Beaulieu, this volume). Following the crossing of borders and the travels of transnational actors, events, and discourses in multiple sites and at multiple scales, however, raises for scholars the daunting obstacles of distance (social and physical) – that is, of languages, of cultures, and of access to the means of time-space compression. Transnationalizing the research process itself seems an appropriate solution. Transnational collaboration in multi-sited and multiscalar feminist research could effectively address issues of mobility, as well as differences in languages and knowledge of context, while offering the possibility of combining insider and outsider perspectives in research design. Can transnational collaboration be extended to feminist research projects involving multiple sites and multiple scales? While acknowledging the difficulties inherent to such an enterprise, we certainly think that it is a highly desirable and exciting prospect for future feminist research.

REFERENCES

Adams, Melinda. 2006. Regional Women's Activism: African Women's Networks and the African Union. In *Global Feminism: Transnational Women's Activism, Organizing, and Human Rights,* ed. Myra Marx Ferree and Aili Mari Tripp, 187-218. New York: New York University Press.

Alvarez, Sonia E. 2000. Translating the Global: Effects of Transnational Organizing on Local Feminist Discourses and Practices and Latin America. *Meridians: Feminism, Race, Transnationalism* 1 (1): 29-67.

Bandy, Joe, and Jackie Smith, eds. 2005. *Coalitions across Borders: Transnational Protest and the Neoliberal Order.* Lanham: Rowman and Littlefield.

Basu, Amrita. 2000. Globalization of the Local/Localization of the Global: Mapping Transnational Women's Movements. *Meridians: Feminism, Race, Transnationalism* 1 (1): 68-84.

Beaulieu, Elsa. 2007. Échelles et lieux de l'action collective dans la Marche mondiale des femmes au Brésil. *Lien social et politiques* 58: 119-32.

Beauzamy, Brigitte. 2005. Quel est le coût de l'intégration des mouvements féministes à la sphère altermondialiste? *Anthropologie et sociétés* 29 (3): 59-76.

Conway, Janet. 2008. Geographies of Transnational Feminism: The Politics of Place and Scale in the World March of Women. *Social Politics* 15 (2): 207-31.

Della Porta, Donatella, and Sidney Tarrow, eds. 2005. *Transnational Protest and Global Activism.* Lanham: Rowman and Littlefield.

Desai, Manisha. 2005. Transnationalism: The Face of Feminist Politics Post-Beijing. *International Social Science Journal* 57 (184): 319-30.

Druelle, Anick. 2004. Que célébrer 30 ans après l'Année internationale de la femme: une autre crise au sein des mouvements internationaux de femmes? *Recherches féministes* 17 (2): 115-69.

Dufour, Pascale, and Isabelle Giraud. 2007. Globalization and Political Change in the Women's Movement: The Politics of Scale and Political Empowerment in the World March of Women. *Social Science Quarterly* 88 (5): 1152-73.

Eschle, Catherine. 2005. Skeleton Women: Feminism and the Anti-Globalisation Movement. *Signs: Journal of Women in Culture and Society* 30 (3): 1741-60.

Ferree, Myra Marx. 2006. Gobalization and Feminism: Opportunities and Obstacles for Activism in the Global Arena. In *Global Feminism: Transnational Women's Activism, Organizing, and Human Rights,* ed. Myra Marx Ferree and Aili Mari Tripp, 3-23. New York: New York University Press.

Ferree, Myra Marx, and Carol McClurg Mueller. 2004. Feminism and Women's Movements: A Global Perspective. In *The Blackwell Companion to Social Movements,* ed. David A. Snow, Sarah A. Soule, and Hanspeter Kriesi, 576-607. Malden: Blackwell.

Hawkesworth, Mary E. 2006. *Globalization and Feminist Activism.* Lanham: Rowman and Littlefield.

Keck, Margaret E., and Kathryn Sikkink. 1998. *Activists Beyond Borders: Advocacy Networks in International Politics.* Ithaca: Cornell University Press.

Lamoureux, Diane. 2004. Le féminisme et l'altermondialisation. *Recherches féministes* 17 (2): 171-94.

Liebowitz, Debra J. 2001. Constructing Cooperation: Feminist Activism and NAFTA. In *Feminist Locations: Global and Local, Theory and Practice,* ed. Marianne DeKoven, 168-90. New Brunswick, NJ: Rutgers University Press.

Mackie, Vera. 2001. The Language of Globalization, Transnationality and Feminism. *International Feminist Journal of Politics* 3 (2): 180-206.

Miller, Francesca. 1999. Feminisms and Transnationalism. In *Feminisms and Internationalism,* ed. Mrinalini Sinha, Donna Guy, and Angela Woolacott, 225-36. Oxford: Blackwell.

Moghadam, Valentine M. 2005. *Globalizing Women: Transnational Feminist Networks.* Baltimore: Johns Hopkins University Press.

Mohanty, Chandra Talpade. 2003. *Feminism without Borders: Decolonizing Theory, Practicing Solidarity.* Durham: Duke University Press.

Naples, Nancy A., and Manisha Desai, eds. 2002. *Women's Activism and Globalization: Linking Local Struggles and Transnational Politics.* New York: Routledge.

Risse, Thomas. 2002. Transnational Actors and World Politics. In *Handbook of International Relations,* ed. Walter Carlsnaes, Thomas Risse, and Beth Simmons, 255-74. London: Sage.

Risse-Kappen, Thomas, ed. 1995. *Bringing Transnational Relations Back In: Non-State Actors, Domestic Structures and International Institutions.* Cambridge: Cambridge University Press.

Rupp, Leila J., and Verta Taylor. 1999. Forging Feminist Identity in an International Movement: A Collective Identity Approach to Twentieth-Century Feminism. *Signs: Journal of Women in Culture and Society* 24 (21): 363-86.

Siméant, Johanna. 2005. Des mouvements nouveaux et globaux? Sur les mouvements sociaux "transnationaux" dans quelques ouvrages récents. Paper presented at the Congrès de l'Association Française de Science Politique (AFSP), "Où en est la sociologie des mouvements sociaux," 15-18 September, Institut d'Études Politiques de Lyon, Lyon. http://scpo.univ-paris1.fr/fichiers2/SIMEANT%20-%20papier%20colloque%20AFSP.pdf.

Smith, Jackie. 1997. Characteristics of the Modern Transnational Social Movement Sector. In *Transnational Social Movements and Global Politics: Solidarity Beyond the State,* ed. Jackie Smith, Charles Chatfield, and Ron Pagnucco, 19-42. Syracuse: Syracuse University Press.

–. 2004. Transnational Processes and Movements. In *The Blackwell Companion to Social Movements,* ed. David A. Snow, Sarah A. Soule, and Hanspeter Kriesi, 311-35. Malden: Blackwell.

Snyder, Margaret. 2006. Unlikely Godmother: The U.N. and the Global Women's Movement. In *Global Feminism: Transnational Women's Activism, Organizing, and Human Rights,* ed. Myra Marx Ferree and Aili Mari Tripp, 24-50. New York: New York University Press.

Tarrow, Sidney. 1998. *Power in Movement: Social Movements and Contentious Politics.* New York: Cambridge University Press.

–. 2001. Transnational Politics: Contention and Institutions in International Politics. *Annual Review of Political Science* 4: 1-20.

–. 2005. *The New Transnational Activism.* Cambridge: Cambridge University Press.

Thayer, Millie. 2000. Traveling Feminisms: From Embodied Women to Gendered Citizenship. In *Global Ethnography: Forces, Connections and Imaginations in a Postmodern World,* ed. Michael Burawoy, Joseph A. Blum, Sheba George, Zsuzsa Gille, Teresa Gowan, Lynne Haney, Maren Klawiter, Steven H. Lopez, Seán Ó Riain, and Millie Thayer, 203-33. Berkeley: University of California Press.

–. 2001. Transnational Feminism: Reading Joan Scott in the Brazilian Sertao. *Ethnography* 2 (2): 243-71.

Tripp, Aili Mari. 2005. Regional Networking as Transnational Feminism: African Experiences. *Feminist Africa,* April. http://www.feministafrica.org/.

Wong, Lloyd, and Vic Satzewich. 2006. Introduction: The Meaning and Significance of Transnationalism. In *Transnational Identities and Practices in Canada,* ed. Lloyd Wong and Vic Satzewich, 1-15. Vancouver: UBC Press.

Yuval-Davis, Nira. 2006. Human/Women's Rights and Feminist Transversal Politics. In *Global Feminism: Transnational Women's Activism, Organizing, and Human Rights,* ed. Myra Marx Ferree and Aili Mari Tripp, 187-218. New York: New York University Press.

Contributors

Elsa Beaulieu is a PhD candidate in anthropology at Université Laval. Her doctoral dissertation is focused on the World March of Women in Brazil. She holds a master's degree in regional studies from the Université du Québec à Chicoutimi, and a graduate diploma in community economic development from Concordia University. She is a feminist activist and organizer and has been involved in the World March of Women and various other feminist groups and struggles since 1999. Her current research focuses on feminist theories of globalization and on the spatial, political, and alternative local and regional development practices in transnational and multiscalar social movements such as the World March of Women. Her work has been published in *Lien social et politiques* and in *Altermondialisation, économie et coopération internationale* (book chapter).

Dominique Caouette, assistant professor in the Department of Political Science at the Université de Montréal since 2004, teaches international relations, development studies, and Southeast Asian politics. Prior to this, he was a lecturer at the University of Ottawa and worked for over five years with a non-governmental organization, Inter Pares. His current research interests include transnational advocacy networks, global social movements, and armed resistance in Southeast Asia and Latin America. His work has been published in *Kasarinlan (A Philippine Quarterly of Third*

World Studies), Pacific Focus, and *Relations.* A revised version of his PhD dissertation completed at Cornell University, "Persevering Revolutionaries: Armed Struggle in the 21st Century, Exploring the Revolution of the Communist Party of the Philippines," is forthcoming with Ateneo de Manila University Press.

Janet Conway is Canada Research Chair in Social Justice and an associate professor in the Department of Sociology at Brock University in St. Catharines, Ontario. She is the author of *Identity, Place, Knowledge: Social Movements Contesting Globalization,* published in 2004 by Fernwood, and *Praxis and Politics: Knowledge Production in Social Movements,* published in 2006 by Routledge. Her publications on anti-globalization movements and the World Social Forum have appeared in politics, sociology, law, geography, and women's studies journals. Her emerging research focuses on pan-indigenous movements in the Americas, indigenous social and political thought, and strategies for decolonizing the emancipatory movements of modernity.

Carmen L. Díaz Alba holds a master's degree in political science from the Université de Montréal. She currently works with a non-governmental organization, Instituto Mexicano para el Desarrollo Comunitario, in Guadalajara, Mexico. Her areas of research and action are social movements, gender equity, popular education, and the politics of water. She is also a research assistant in the socio-political studies department at the Instituto Tecnológico y de Estudios Superiores de Occidente. Her work has been published in *Lien social et politiques* (this article was later translated into Spanish for the *Journal Contexto Latinoamericano*) and *La Ventana, Revista de Estudios de Género.*

Pascale Dufour is an associate professor in the Department of Political Science at the Université de Montréal. She focuses on collective action and social movements in comparative perspective, especially in the context of globalization. Her work has been published in *French Politics, Canadian Journal of Political Science, Canadian Journal of Sociology, Mobilization,* and *Social Science Quarterly.* She has also co-edited thematic issues on transnationalization in *Lien social et politiques* (2007) and *Politique et société* (2009). Her emerging research examines practices of local social forums in Quebec and France.

Sylvia Estrada-Claudio is a doctor of medicine who also holds a PhD in psychology. She is director of the Center for Women's Studies and a professor in the Department of Women and Development Studies, College of Social Work and Community Development, at the University of the Philippines. She is the author of *Rape, Love and Sexuality: The Construction of Women in Discourse* (University of the Philippines Press, 2002). Estrada-Claudio considers herself more of an activist than an academic because she has spent most of her life working in the Philippine social movement. She is co-founder and now chair of the board of directors of Likhaan, a non-governmental organization providing policy analysis and advocacy, health education and training, community organizing, and reproductive and sexual health services to poor women and their families in five urban and four rural communities. She is also chair of the board of the Women's Global Network for Reproductive Rights, which has offices in Manila and Amsterdam. For the past twenty years, she has been providing free psychological services to women victims of violence and other women with special needs.

Débora Lopreite is an instructor in the Department of Political Science at Carleton University. Her research interests include global and comparative social policy, gender, politics and public policy, and international development. A native of Argentina, she has a PhD in public policy from Carleton University (2009). Her doctoral dissertation, *Challenging the Argentine Gender Regime: The Multiscalar Politics of Biological Reproduction after Democratization,* places Argentina's reproductive policies in a global and comparative perspective. She has published in the field of Latin American politics with EUDEBA (Universidad de Buenos Aires) and the Consejo Latinoamericano de Ciencias Sociales, and in the field of science and innovation with McGill-Queen's University Press and University of Toronto Press. Her postdoctoral research focuses on reproductive policies in conservative gender regimes of Latin America and Southern Europe.

Lenore Lyons is Research Professor in Asian Studies at the University of Western Australia. She has conducted research on gender and the state in Singapore, and has published widely on the women's movement in Singapore, migrant worker activism in Singapore and Malaysia, and citizenship and sovereignty in the Singapore-Indonesia borderlands. Her book *A State of Ambivalence: The Feminist Movement in Singapore,* was published by Brill Academic Publishers, Leiden, in 2004. Her work has appeared in a number of edited collections and in journals, including *Women's Studies Quarterly,*

International Feminist Journal of Politics, Critical Asian Studies, Asian Studies Review, Asia Pacific Viewpoint, and *Citizenship Studies.*

Dominique Masson is an associate professor at the Institute of Women's Studies and the Department of Sociology and Anthropology at the University of Ottawa. Her current research interests include social movements' and women's movements' engagement with the politics of rescaling at both the regional (subnational) and transnational scales, as well as issues of state restructuring and relationships between states and women's movements in the Canadian context. In 2005, she published an edited collection on women and the restructuring of public policy in Canada (*Femmes et politiques. L'état en mutation,* Presses de l'Université d'Ottawa). Her more recent work has appeared in *Social Politics, Geojournal, Politique et sociétés, Caderno do CRH,* and *Canadian Journal of Regional Science.*

Diane Matte has been a member of Concertation des luttes contre l'exploitation sexuelle (http://www.lacles.org) since its inception in 2004. She is a long-time feminist activist and worker in the anti–male-violence-against-women movement and the feminist movement as a whole. She was the coordinator of the Bread and Roses Women's March Against Poverty in 1995 and one of the women behind the World March of Women, which has become a worldwide movement against poverty and violence against women. She coordinated the International Secretariat of the WMW from 1997 to 2006 before continuing in anti-violence work.

Index

Printed and bound in Canada by Friesens

Set in Futura condensed and Warnock Pro by Artegraphica Design Co. Ltd.

Copy editor: Käthe Roth

Proofreader: Stephanie VanderMeulen

Indexer: Noeline Bridge